# SUFI MINDFULNESS YOGA

*A New Approach
to Mindful Living*

W. BRIAN MCPHERSON, PH.D.

Year of the Book
135 Glen Avenue
Glen Rock, PA 17327

Print ISBN:    978-1-64649-152-0

Ebook ISBN:    978-1-64649-153-7

## DEDICATION

To the memory of Pir Vilayat Inayat Khan, may peace and blessing b upon him, and to Dr. Vijayendra Pratap.

Pir Vilayat, the founder of the Sufi Order International, now the Inayat Order, brought light and inspiration to me in my search for how sounds and mantras influence our emotions. His teachings came to me at a time when I was unmoored and gave my life purpose. For his direction I will forever be grateful.

The leadership and deep knowledge of yoga philosophy that Dr. Pratap, the director of the Yoga Research Society, has always demonstrated, have served as a role model for me. In each of his classes it is a joy to soak up the warmth and human understanding that he exudes.

# CONTENTS

# INTRODUCTION

I dropped out of college in my senior year upon hearing Ram Dass read from his seminal work *Be Here Now*.[1] During the subsequent two decades, I shuttled between yoga ashrams and Sufi centers where various chanting sessions uplifted and transported me. Throughout this period as a spiritual vagabond, a desire to understand how mantras worked, in a western scientific sense, swelled to a point that I felt an urgency propelling me to finish my undergraduate degree and go on to earn my Ph.D. in psychology.

My psycholinguistic studies have focused on the connection between the physiology of speech and the physiology of emotions. The results of this work unveil a detailed understanding of the physiological effects of speech sounds on emotions. Regrettably much of the academic world has little interest in this work or even in the premise that individual phonemes (a phoneme is a technical term for an indivisible unit of speech sound) have an emotional value. When I approached leading scholars of linguistics, they showed no interest in my efforts to demonstrate that a phoneme conveyed a particular meaning, in spite of the obvious connection between the content purring of "mmmmm" to indicate pleasure, and the luxuriating "aaaaah" to express relaxation. My research has supported these and other less obvious sound-emotion relationships which I indicate and explain in this work.

Armed with the knowledge of the emotional impact of phonemes I reviewed various mantras I had practiced through the years. In doing so, I discovered some astonishing new associations between what Sufis call the Names of Allah and the *Yoga Sutras*—an ancient text underlying the philosophy of many modern schools of yoga. The *Sutras* list explicit stages and blockages to achieving yoga—an ecstatic state often described as union with God or universal consciousness; however, they offer no unambiguous blueprint for overcoming obstacles and advancing toward the goal. Incredibly, many of the Names of Allah can, with proper understanding and guidance, serve as explicit practices that help you conquer specific pitfalls that keep you from realizing this desirable objective of yoga.

Once I explain the scientific understanding of how individual speech sounds can affect emotions in the first part of this work, I will reveal in the second part dozens of individual practices, based on an enhanced, mindfulness interpretation of the Names of Allah. Furthermore, it will be shown how these exercises fit into the framework of the *Yoga Sutras* in a way that facilitates your efforts for spiritual growth.

Although the Names of Allah come directly from the heart of Islamic worship practices, this work does not take an Islamic perspective. Instead I write this from the perspective of a psychologist trained in western science. My work will demonstrate how one can benefit from practices using the Names of Allah in a logical and rational approach to achieve the spiritual goals extolled by yogis. One does not need to have a devotional or religious bias to take advantage of this work. In a non-devotional setting, practices with the Names in the manner described in this book can enhance mindfulness and help achieve emotional balance, as well as deepen spiritual endeavors.

For those who already know and use the Names of Allah I do believe that learning from my work can intensify an existing devotional use of the Names. I must add that I am not saying that my interpretations and methods of using the Names imply that other understandings cannot be valid. Many Islamic scholars have written about the Names and have motivated many people to use the Names meaningfully. I hope that those reading this who already have a personal, significant relationship with the Names will find this work compatible and complementary to how they already find inspiration from the Names.

Please realize that I must use language to describe emotions and circumstances that one must experience in order to develop a personal understanding of such concepts. My choice of words might not, at times, convey my experience and my own understanding in a way that best facilitates the reader's understanding. For this and any other shortcomings in this work I apologize.

# PART ONE

## The Historical and Scientific Foundation

# CHAPTER 1
## SUFISM, MINDFULNESS, AND THE YOGA SUTRAS

### *Sufism*

Scholars do not agree on the origin of Sufism. Many believe this belief system arose contemporary with Zoroastrianism, circa 600 BCE.[2] Others point to an Islamic origin occurring after the 8th century CE.[3] Still others claim Sufism originated in India from men who studied with yoga masters and then returned to their middle eastern homes and adopted the Islamic faith.[4] Many today refer to the Sufis as a mystical branch of Islam, and most Sufis do live in Islamic majority countries,[5] but some argue that this confluence of Sufism with Islam only reflects the Sufi proclivity to inclusiveness.[6] Indeed many contemporary Sufis promote the idea that all religions share deep similarities that far outweigh their differences, perhaps most elegantly stated in Pir Vilayat Khan's book *Toward the One.*[7]

The spiritual practices of Sufis vary, but the majority of those which exist in publicly available written form involve something called the Names of Allah. These Names consist of ninety-nine individual Arabic words, or in two instances phrases, that Sufis and other Muslims believe describe attributes of God, or Allah. A more liberal interpretation assigns the Names to different aspects of universal consciousness, or a panpsychic force that pervades all matter. Taking this approach allows one to use the Names, such as those described in this work, without subscribing to a theistic viewpoint.

Seeing the Names as denoting characteristics of universal consciousness bears similarities to Plato's idea of forms or Jungian archetypes. Each Name describes, through its inherent sounds, an archetypical human emotional response to a common situation. Think of each Name as proscribing an ideal way to act and feel emotionally. This reflects not just the traditional Sufi idea that the Names represent divine attributes, but also the philosophy that one should behave in a particular way when faced with certain conditions. Accordingly, the use of the Names as prescribed in this work provides guidance for dealing with everyday situations, some problematic, some not. One might consider these situations the archetypical emotional challenges or opportunities a human faces. Each Name addresses a particular universal scenario and provides valuable instructions via the sounds in the Name. These sounds generate a psychological approach to the challenge that allows you to stay in a mindful state of awareness and keep you from getting caught up in distracting drama.

Those who utilize the Names to deepen their spiritual experience believe that the specific combinations of sounds found in each Name generate a specific psychological impact. Although mainstream western linguists have long held the point of view that the sounds of language arbitrarily ascribe meaning to a word, Sufis claim that the sounds themselves carry the meaning. According to the Sufis the ninety-nine Names "mean what they say."[8] Even some western religious scholars have remarked on how sounds play an important and significant role in passages in the Qur'an, the Islamic holy book which contains many of the Names.[9] Moreover, current research in linguistics has begun to appreciate that individual sounds do have a psychological valence, uprooting the traditional view of a lack of relationship between sounds and meanings and giving some strength to the position held by the Sufis.[10] This book takes this viewpoint and expands on it. It shows from a scientific, non-religious perspective, how the Names of Allah have psychological significance due to the nature of the Names, i.e., due to the inherent psychological valence of the sounds in the Names and the order in which those sounds appear.

## *Mindfulness*

Mindfulness practices have left their cozy enclaves of yoga ashrams and Buddhist temples and have arrived on the main stage of American culture. A search online for books on Amazon.com using the word "mindfulness" returns a multitude of hits. Consider that the ever-expanding catalog of popular books focused on the topic includes *Buddha's Brain*[11], by prominent neurologist Rick Hanson, *Waking Up,*[12] by ardent atheist and philosopher-neuroscientist Sam Harris, and the many titles by Jon Kabat-Zinn,[13] the renowned clinical psychologist and developer of Mindfulness-Based Stress Reduction.

The strategies advocated for mindfulness meditation found in today's canon come primarily from Buddhist sources. They instruct the practitioner not to try to adjust or change or reject thoughts, but to just watch them and let them proceed without trying to analyze anything. The student should not question whether she or he is doing things right, but simply maintain awareness of the present moment. If the student recognizes that the mind has wandered, virtually all of today's authors offer the counsel of watching the breath. "Always bring yourself back to the breath," stands as the universal guidance given to prospective mindfulness practitioners.[14] Just noticing each inhalation followed by each exhalation serves as a valuable tool in the process of bringing a person into awareness of the present, at least for some people.

Evidence for the benefits of mindfulness meditation abounds, with stress reduction and emotion regulation often cited in scientific literature.[15] The Sufis have a practice called Remembrance which they claim induces these same benefits. Remembrance involves the repetition of the word "Allah," which means "The One" in Arabic, and which most simply translates as "God." Remembrance can also involve the repetition of one or more of the ninety-nine names (or attributes) of Allah.

Not only are the benefits of Sufi Remembrance said to match those of mindfulness meditation, the directions for engaging in Remembrance also mimic, to a degree, the directions for Buddhist mindfulness. The directions for both state that one should just let thoughts and emotions simply pass without dwelling on them while engaging in the practice. If thoughts wander, simply come back to the practice, watching one's breath for traditional Buddhist mindfulness, and awareness of the name you repeat for Sufi Remembrance.

The exercises presented in this work can be considered a form of Remembrance, since they use the Names of Allah; however, they differ from traditional Remembrance practices in the rules that dictate when and how to use them. The main difference between this work and traditional Remembrance and traditional mindfulness meditation lies in how one treats thoughts and emotions during the practice. The techniques described in the second half of this tome require you to monitor thoughts and emotions and make them part of the practice instead of ignoring them. This attention to the immediate psychological outlook gives them a holistic approach to mindfulness because it fully subscribes to the main tenet of mindfulness—be aware of the present. If you ignore thoughts and feelings, how can you say that you are staying aware of the moment?

Although at first blush you might think that paying attention to thoughts and feelings defeats the underlying principle of mindfulness by getting lost in thought, but when engaged with the practices in this program, you do not analyze thoughts and feelings. Instead you simply recognize them and then react in the appropriate manner—typically with a subtle type of intentional breathing. This response almost parallels the typical mindfulness meditation instructions of just "watch the breath"; however, the catch phrase becomes "regulate your awareness through breathing." This directive will become clear once we broach the individual practices. However, before we advance toward that goal we need to investigate how the tenets of yoga fits into the system.

## The Yoga Sutras

The practices presented in this work share some attributes of Buddhist-inspired mindfulness meditation, Sufi Remembrance, and yoga. For this reason I give the exercises described herein the name Sufi Mindfulness Yoga (SMY). The *Yoga Sutras*[16] consist of a set of 196 short verses, or sutras, separated into four sections, or chapters. Hindus consider this work, recorded by Patanjali over 1600 years ago, to be a sacred text; it forms the basis of many current schools of yoga. The Yoga Sutras provide a theoretical framework for practicing meditation and achieving yoga, a Sanskrit word that means union, and in this context union with the divine. Patanjali states the goal of yoga as the cessation of the modifications of the mind, which he later equates to a mental state called samadhi.

The Sufis have a goal of controlling *nafs*, psyche or mental energy.[17] Sufis consider the nafs the main obstacle from attaining an enduring meaningful relationship, sometimes indicated as a merger, with divine consciousness. They hold this belief without regard to the *Yoga Sutras*. However, we do know that Sufis have known about Patanjali's work for hundreds of years. Al-Biruni gets credit for the first known Arabic translation of the *Yoga Sutras* dating to around 1000 CE.[18] His interpretation of Patanjali's second sutra translates as "Yoga is control over psychical energies (nafs)," which perhaps better defines yoga than the traditional English translation of "cessation of the modifications of the mind."

Patanjali's fourth sutra specifies five distinct types of mind modifications that take us away from clarity of mind and our pure nature. A rough translation from the original Sanskrit lists the modifications as: Right Thinking, Wrong Thinking, Imagination, Memory, and Sleep. Subsequent verses give terse descriptions of each mental issue. However, to the question of how you should eliminate your mental ponderings the work gives only the vague guidelines of "persistent practice and non-attachment." The detailed practices of SMY fit into the framework of the Yoga Sutras in a way that affords the practitioner means to address the five mental disturbances expounded by Patanjali. For each of these issues SMY has a specific practice, which appears in the second half of this work.

In addition to working for the cessation of mental intrusions as a means to attain yoga, in his 23rd sutra of the first chapter Patanjali claims that one can attain samadhi by surrender to *Isvarah*—a Sanskrit word that often gets translated as *Divine Consciousness.* Patanjali's work doesn't elaborate on how one might achieve such surrender or what psychological processes it entails. However, SMY presents specific practices meant for those who take this path toward the goal of samadhi.

The first chapter of the *Yoga Sutras* Patanjali calls Samadhi Preparation, and as mentioned above SMY provides the practical resources necessary for the stated goals. In the objectives outlined in Chapter 2—Seeker Preparation—we also find many useful ways to employ SMY. This second section of the ancient text lists the eight steps one must progress through as a student of yoga: self-restraints or yamas, observances or niyamas, posture, regulation of breath, sense withdrawal, concentration, contemplation, samadhi. The last six stages in this array focus on a unified issue denoted by the level's name. In contrast, the first two stages each consist of five separate rules. Together these ten decrees amount to something akin to the Ten Commandments of the Bible.

Yoga's stated self-restraints include refraining from violence, lying, theft, sexual promiscuousness, and possessiveness of material goods. SMY does not have specific exercises to engage in if you would breach one of these instructions, as it does when addressing mind alterations. However, many of the practices of SMY can be seen as ways to defuse situations which might otherwise lead to a violation of one of these proscriptions.

The five observances demanded by the second step of yoga exhort a seeker to purity, contentment, austerity, self-study, and self-surrender to divine consciousness. Again SMY does not have corresponding practices for these niyamas, however, it does provide exercises that have the same goals, but not in a one-to-one correspondence. This follows from the practical reality that one can reach a particular goal in more than one manner.

The three sutras on posture—rung three of the yoga seeker's ladder— offer only the vague recommendation that steady and comfortable posture should be obtained through relaxation of effort and meditation on the endless. Achieving proper posture, according to Patanjali, will prevent the attack of opposites. While his instructions may prove useful to some, it lacks clarity on the nature of such attacks. SMY has specifics that bring these sutras into focus and provides ways to address problems of posture.

With the remaining five stages SMY also comes into play in some fashion, although it varies from Patanjali most in stage four, breath regulation. For SMY breath regulation goes along with each practice in various subtle ways. In contrast Patanjali calls for the practice of stopping the breath as a way to enter trance states. With each of the final four steps of yoga, SMY does have a specific practice, and the higher the level, the more refined and in some ways the simpler—and at the same time more difficult to achieve—solution offered by SMY.

The principles underlying SMY—applying mindfulness to the psychological significance of the Names of Allah—fit into the framework of the Yoga Sutras and apply in various settings and manners. Like traditional mindfulness practices you can use SMY in meditation that you engage in for an extended period of time in a quiet, restful location. You can also utilize SMY in an impromptu fashion by simply watching the emotions and thoughts as you go about everyday living. If you detect specific, perhaps troublesome, thoughts or emotions during daily endeavors, you can work through such situations by remembering a Name that applies to that type of circumstance and allows you to stay focused on the present in an even keeled fashion.

Another manner for utilizing SMY entails devotional practices—that is, a practice akin to Bhakti yoga, in which a person feels an emotional pull toward an outside force. This outside force usually gets referred to as God, but the force doesn't have to be considered a deity in the traditional sense, but may also be something characterized as a form of universal consciousness that seems to pervade all matter, a panpsychic force.

Finally, you can also take advantage of SMY during times of reflection in a quiet setting like meditation, but with a focus on daily happenings. The purpose of such reflections in the context of SMY consists of pondering situations where one might have used an SMY response in order to have kept a better emotional and mindful outlook. By reflecting on an incident you can re-experience the feelings at that moment and use an SMY practice, that is, a specific Name, to work through the emotions that pervaded at that time. This can help you process the experience and resolve any lingering emotional effects. This kind of reflecting can also help establish a positive way to respond whenever a similar situation occurs in the future.

Before exploring any of the SMY exercises that apply to specific problems or stages expounded in the Yoga Sutras, we must develop an understanding of the physiology of emotions, the physiology of speech, and integrate these two disciplines. This scientific background will distinguish SMY from traditional meditation and typical Sufi Remembrance practices, and pave the way for establishing SMY as a viable path for achieving not just the goals laid out by Patanjali, but also becoming a new enlightened program for a mindful existence.

# Chapter 2
# The Psychology and Physiology of Emotions

In the first half of the twentieth century the study of psychology coalesced around its first post-Freudian major movement, behaviorism. Behavioral psychologists had little interest in what people thought or the emotions they felt. Instead they believed that the study of human psychology should focus on behavior, which, they argued, could be attributed to a combination of genetic makeup and environmental exposure. Behaviorists considered consciousness, emotions, and mental introspection collateral products that resulted from an individual's observation of his or her own behavior. They believed these concepts had nothing to do with instigating behavior, and therefore had little scientific interest in them.

Behavioral psychology slowly became supplanted by cognitive psychology beginning in the 1960s. Concepts ignored by behaviorists such as mental representation, language, and memory, play the central role to cognitive psychologists. By the 1980s cognitive psychology had taken over the discipline, coming into its own at the same time as the rise of the computer in society. Largely due to the influence of the computer, many cognitive psychologists saw the mind as an information processor. Many more searched for a way to create artificial intelligence, adopting a parallel distributed processing approach that they saw in humans. Emotions almost seemed like irrelevant epiphenomena to those riding the crest of the cognitive psychology wave. That is not to say nobody studied emotions in the 1980s. Many did, to be sure, but they did not share the spotlight with cognitive psychologists as they do today.

Since the turn of the century two major new scientific journals devoted to publishing research on emotions have appeared. The establishment of the journals *Emotions* in 2001 and *Emotion Review* in 2009 reflect science's growing interest in the study of emotions and mark a significant turning point in the evolution of the still relatively young science of psychology. Indeed, this treatise on Sufi Mindfulness Yoga, which focuses on emotional states, reflects this change in the psychology zeitgeist. Mindfulness practices can no longer ignore the fact that we constantly experience emotions and moods, even during meditation. The goal of mindfulness meditation has not changed. We still want to clear the mind and exist in the present, but we can achieve that goal much more quickly if we learn how to control our distracting thoughts and their accompanying emotions and alter them in a manner that allows them to work for our mental and emotional clarity.

One of the most popular and successful ways to examine human emotion expression and emotion recognition in others involves the cataloging of facial expressions. Psychologists have learned that people of all cultures convey emotions using facial expressions in the same manner. This important discovery lets us know that humans have innate emotions not linked to cultural norms. Thus when examining the physiology of emotions, we do not just look at a particular culture's physiological parameters. The emotions of Patanjali's Hindustan of two thousand years ago, the emotions of the Middle Eastern Sufis, and the emotions of Buddhists, whether ancient or of the current day, all share a common human physiology.

Scientists interested in the physiology of emotions have tried to establish the basic physiological processes underlying emotions. Many different physiological measures have been used in this effort, including heart rate or electrocardiogram (EKG)      , respiration, blood pressure, skin conductance or galvanized skin response, electroencephalogram (EEG), and neurohormone and neurotransmitter levels.[19] Although studies have produced lists of physiological components of various emotions, there is no universal agreement on how to characterize a single emotion with a specific list of physiological responses. Knowing the exact nature of every physiological process underlying every emotion presents a huge challenge. It is extremely difficult to get reliable measurements of the physiological process underlying emotions, since laboratory conditions make obtaining genuine emotions problematic.

In spite of the inherent difficulties in attempts to catalogue the physiology of specific emotions, looking at physiological processes has led to a useful system based upon physiological principles, but with a practical taxonomy that takes a holistic rather than reductionist approach. This scheme categorizes the physiological processes associated with emotions along three continuums, usually referred to as dimensions of emotions. The broadest names for the three dimensions of emotion are arousal, pleasure, and control.[20]

Using this concept you can characterize each emotion as belonging somewhere on each of these continuums from a low or empty value to a high or full value. For example, you might describe the emotion of joy that you experience from receiving an unexpected, but highly desirable gift as high on arousal, full of pleasure, and low on or empty of control, that is, you played no part in the events that precipitated the emotion. Describing an emotion in this manner implies certain physiological characteristics. The high arousal indicates increased blood pressure and increased heart rate. A high level of pleasure would suppose an increase in neurotransmitters and endorphins associated with the experience of pleasure. Finally, low control might reflect reduced brain activity in the area of executive functioning.

Two things about this way to depict emotions need further explanation. First, not every emotion has to fall on the low or high end of the spectrum of each scale. Some emotions may remain neutral on a dimension. Second, the ratings for what gets referred to as the same emotion may vary from one situation to another. For example, the joy that you feel when you receive an unexpected gift might rate high on arousal, high on pleasure, and neutral on control, but the joy that you feel when you give someone a gift could get rated as neutral on arousal, high on pleasure, and high on control. This can and does occur because we often use the same word to describe feelings that have nuanced differences. In this example, in both instances we call the emotion joy, but in the second case less arousal takes place and you feel in control.

The idea of dividing our understanding of human psychology into three divisions goes back at least to Plato, who saw humans as composed of reason, spirit, and appetite. More recently Freud used the terms id, ego, and superego. These classifications had no specific physiological basis. The first division based on physiology came in the 1960s from neuroscientist Paul MacLean, who published detailed evidence that the brain has three distinct parts, each tied to a particular type of human behavior. MacLean identified the basal ganglia as the reptilian brain because of its presence in our evolutionary past going back to reptiles. This part of our brain, located primarily in the brain stem, controls arousal levels, aggression, and other instinctual behavior by regulating the neurotransmitters that modulate these behaviors.

MacLean dubbed the second brain division the paleomammalian brain, citing its first appearance in early mammals. This portion of the brain, also known as the limbic system, consists of the amygdala, hypothalamus, hippocampus, and cingulate cortex. One of this structure's primary functions consists of controlling behavior in regards to things that give pleasure and displeasure, such as feeding and social interactions.

The third part of MacLean's triune brain, the neomammalian brain, consists of the neocortex. Only in later mammals does this structure appear highly developed. The ability to control the environment through cognitive processing and complicated behaviors derives primarily from the neocortex. Language, executive decision making, and mental processing that makes humans unique, takes place in the neocortex.

I should note that many criticize MacLean's model of the brain as too simplistic. They argue that his evolutionary claims don't hold up, and they see the divisions as somewhat arbitrary, noting the overlapping of functionality between different parts of the brain. However, others argue that the simplicity of the model gives it its power. These psychologists state that these simple divisions allow an understanding of human behavior that would not be feasible if one tried to understand the behavioral impact of each of the thousands of individual parts of the brain, as reductionists endeavor to do. MacLean's holistic approach has wisdom, which becomes clear when we reconsider the division of the physiology of emotions into three dimensions stated above.

Each of the three dimensions of emotion connects directly to one of the three components of the triune brain. The physiological substrate for the arousal dimension of emotion resides primarily in the basal ganglia, the reptilian brain. The physiology responsible for experience along the pleasure continuum lies mainly in the paleomammalian brain, or limbic system. The neocortex, or as MacLean calls it the neomammalian brain, contains the physiological structures responsible for determining our feelings concerning control of emotion. This does not mean that the limbic system and neocortex play no role in emotional arousal or the limbic system and basal ganglia play no part in our experience of control of emotions. The three parts of the brain contain many connections between them. However, when considering the physiology behind emotions, the majority and controlling physiological determinants for a particular emotion dimension correspond to one particular part of the triune brain. This tripartite way of looking at emotions plays an important role in Sufi Mindfulness Yoga and will make sense once all the pieces of the puzzle get arranged into place.

So far we have succeeded in condensing the complicated science of the physiology of emotion down to six terms, two for each emotion dimension. We can use these three pairs of terms: relaxed/aroused for the arousal dimension, unpleasant/pleasant for the pleasure dimension, and internal/external control for the control dimension. Next we will see that we can reduce these six terms down to phonemes, i.e., individual speech sounds.

# CHAPTER 3
# PHYSIOLOGY AND THE
# PSYCHOLOGICAL IMPACT OF SPEECH

The thesis of SMY rests on the association between specific speech sounds and their corresponding emotional valences. I will present evidence that each speech sound has a unique emotional quality generated via the physiology involved in producing the sound. We generate each speech sound by shaping the mouth in a particular manner, and the processes of shaping the vocal tract tie the sound to a particular emotional feeling. As mentioned previously psychologists have shown a connection between facial expression and emotion that holds true across cultures. The connection between the physiology of speech and the emotion generated should not come as a surprise. Emotions are tied to facial expressions. Speech is tied to mouth shape, which is a subtle form of facial expression. Thus speech sounds have a physiological connection to emotions, and like facial expressions and emotions, these ties between individual speech sounds and specific emotions are also universal, i.e., not culture or language specific.

Although I will show each individual phoneme has a specific and unique emotional quality, the strength of these connections between phonemes and emotion does not have the magnitude as the robust connections found between facial expression and emotion. Speech sounds connect to emotions in a subtle fashion because our species has developed a much richer use of phonemes, i.e., language. By associating groups of phonemes (words) to particular meanings (things, actions, etc.) we use language to communicate complex ideas. This practical application of phonemes overshadows the inherent emotional nature of the sounds, but does not eliminate it, as I will demonstrate.

I realize that the general consensus of the academic linguistic community in the United States holds that individual speech sounds do not convey any meaning or specific emotional content. I have a friend who was a graduate student in the linguistic department of the Massachusetts Institute of Technology, considered by many as the premier school for linguistics in the United States. She wanted to write her Ph.D. dissertation on the idea that speech sounds had a specific underlying meaning, but the department would not let her. Undeterred, she did her Ph.D. work on this topic in a European University, where a strong bias against the idea does not prevail. She has written about sound symbolism, the name given to this area of study, in a work published by the Oxford University Press.[21] Her work demonstrates a rich history of philosophers and linguists who have approached the idea that phonemes carry an inherent meaning. Many of these scholars point to the manner of articulation as one way to explain the underlying reason for phoneme semantic value. My work focuses on this premise with a slight twist—instead of semantic significance I look at emotional relationship. This strategy stems from my work as a psychologist and from my goal of understanding how to use speech sounds to modulate emotions.

I have approached various noted scholars about the emotional valence of phonemes and got push back or just plain ignored. I can't help but feel that the reason for such denials stems from a territorial imperative on the part of these academics. That is, they recognize a viewpoint foreign and contradictory to their own ideas jeopardizes their own standing. I am not deterred by this stonewalling, because I know that there is ample evidence that points to the connection between emotions and individual sounds, as I will show in this chapter. First, we need to review a bit of speech physiology, starting with vowels.

## *Vowels*

Linguists have recorded and observed the speech sound production of hundreds of different human languages. They have discovered that every known language shares three fundamental vowel sounds or phonemes.[22] Every language has an /â/ (as in father), an /û/ (as in moon), and an /î/ (as in s<u>ee</u>).[23] These vowels earn the moniker "primary" in the sense that other vowels can be thought of as composed of components of these three fundamental sounds.

The shape in which you hold your mouth determines the vowel sounds you produce. You can demonstrate this on yourself very easily. Hold your mouth open with your jaw dropped down and begin to vibrate your vocal cords. Now while continuing to vibrate the vocal cords at the same rate, slowly raise your jaw and purse your lips into a rounded shape. What did you hear? With your jaw wide open when you vibrate your vocal chords you emit an /â/, as in father. As you changed the shape of the mouth by raising the jaw and pursing the lips the sound will gradually switch until an /û/, as in moon, comes forth.

Besides the /â/, /û/, and /î/ being universal, you can understand another reason why these vowels get characterized as primary by studying the relative height of the jaw, and the position of the lips. If you plot these vowels using the height of the jaw as one axis and the position of the lips in relationship to the rest of the mouth as the other axis you will get a graph that looks like Figure 1. The jaw is lowest for the /â/. For the /û/ the lips purse out, but for the /î/ the lips are pulled back. We see that the position of the jaw and lips articulate which vowel sound gets produced.

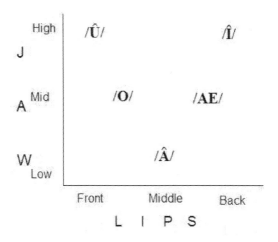

*Figure 1. Vowel space, defined as jaw position and position of the lips.*

Now add the vowels /o/ as in "show," and /ae/ as in "say," to this picture. For the /o/ and the /ae/ the jaw is halfway between where it is for the /â/ and both the /û/ and the /î/. The lips are slightly pursed for the /o/ keeping them somewhat away from the tongue, but for the /ae/ the lips are closer to the tongue. Figure 1 also shows these additional vowel sounds. The vowels /â/, /û/, and /î/ occupy the corners of this "vowel space," the primary positions. Any other vowels that you might add will also lie within the triangular space defined by the "primary" /â/, /û/, and /î/.

Of course, the vocal cords play a prominent role in creating speech, but they do not articulate which sound gets produced. They simply vibrate in an identical manner for all vowel sounds. The physiological components of speech which allow humans to create an impressive array of different speech sounds, both vowels and consonants, consist of three primary articulators—the jaw and lips, which we have already discussed, and the tongue. Some consonants have additional articulators, including the teeth, glottis, and pharynx, but the jaw, lips, and tongue form the three primary speech articulators for consonants. The tongue plays the biggest role in consonant production. It engages in the articulation of more than half of the consonants in English and most languages, as we will see in a later section.

## *Vowels and Emotions*

Vowels differ from consonants in one basic fashion. Vowels result from an unconstricted vocal tract, while consonants all constrict the vocal tract in some manner. In a sense the vowels function in an empty vocal tract. If you look at these "empty" speech sounds and juxtapose them with the empty poles of emotion dimensions you will find something quite remarkable. Research has shown that each of the empty poles of the emotion dimensions has an association with one of the primary vowels.

One of the most intuitive relationships between sound and mood is the connection between /â/ and relaxation, i.e., empty arousal. What sound do you make when you slip into a hot tub or when someone gives you a back rub? "Aaaah," of course. In physiological terms your jaw drops into a relaxed pose and the sound just oozes out. "Aaaah," emphatically announces that you are beginning to relax or moving into a relaxed state. It would almost seem that studies supporting this sound-mood relationship almost don't need to be done, although such work has supported such a connection. For example, in one study when experimenters asked people to rate a number of different phonemes on the arousal scale, 1=very relaxed sounding and 5=very excited sounding, the /â/ rated as most relaxed. In another study, when people heard an /â/ they could more easily recognize words with a connection to relaxation than if they had heard a different sound. Psychologists interpret this effect as evidence that the /â/ has a semantic value connected to relaxation and hearing the sound activates neural circuits in the brain associated with relaxation. The neural activity lingers briefly and if a person sees or hears a word pertaining to relaxation during this brief period, it takes less mental effort to recognize the word. This effect is called a priming effect and such effects provide some of the best evidence for a semantic connection between two stimuli.[24]

Some studies have shown a relationship between a primary vowel /û/ and the empty end of the pleasure dimension of emotion. One such study had people listen to one of two stories that varied primarily on the frequency of the /û/ sound. Those who listened to the story with the greater frequency of /û/ rated their experience as more unpleasant than the other group of listeners. Another study demonstrated that people could recognize words that had associations with unpleasantness better if the words were preceded by an /û/ sound than if the unpleasant words were preceded by another sound. In other words the /û/ has a priming effect for the semantic category of unpleasantness. These findings make intuitive sense when you consider the natural reaction of an exclaimed "ooo" (rhymes with "moo") to something disgusting, perhaps a squished bug. An "oooh" seems to express an unpleasant reaction better than any other sound.[25]

Two lines of evidence link the /î/ sound to feelings of being externally controlled, the empty extreme of the control dimension. In one study an /î/ sound facilitated, or primed, the recognition of words associated with lack of control, for example fright, and danger. In this case the external control loomed as threatening.[26] This fact should come as no surprise if you think about the sounds most often associated with situations in which you feel that you have no control. Consider an amusement park ride where your body is placed in uncomfortable positions that give you feelings that you are about to fall precipitously without any control possible on your part. What is the sound that you are most likely to hear people emit during those rides? Without a doubt you hear screams of fright and excitement, the high-pitched squeal of /î/. My wife makes the same sound when a mouse or bat finds its way into our house unexpectedly.

The other evidence connecting the /î/ to external control involves external control that lies beyond materiality, a sought after and highly desirable external control. Individuals with religious belief often desire to have an external force guide or control them in important decisions they have to make. Do religious devotees go around screaming /î/ to invoke the will of an external being? Well, no, not exactly. Certainly they don't scream, but some religious traditions, including the Sufis, use a high-pitched soft-spoken /î/ sound in ceremonious ways to evoke a benevolent type of external power. Pir Vilayat Khan, former leader of the Sufi Order International, discussed the use of the sound /î/ to invoke a feeling of external control in his book *Toward the One*. He wrote, "You go out into it, EEEE. Don't think about producing a beautiful sound. Don't sing it. It's supersonic, it's like the hissing of a serpent, when you catch yourself doing it right you suddenly feel as though you were hearing the sound of the planet Mercury." [27] This is an interesting contrast to the screaming of /î/ in situations where you lack control, definitely more of a gentle surrender to external control, rather than a terrified scream.

## *The Connection Between Primary Vowels and Consonants*

Consonants present a more complex picture than vowels. For one thing, no universal consonants exist and consequently arguments for primary consonants do not make sense. The reason for the lack of universal consonants probably stems from the multiple ways to generate them. You produce consonants by constricting the vocal tract in some way. Vowels on the other hand require unrestricted airflow. You can constrict air to produce consonants in many more ways than you can vary the shape of the mouth and still keep it open enough to produce a vowel. The nature and number of vocal constrictions varies from language to language. Some languages have numerous guttural consonants produced through constrictions in the throat, others have several nasal consonants made by forcing air through the nasal passage. Many languages have sounds produced by stopping the flow of air completely before releasing it. Some consonant-rich Eastern European languages have over three dozen consonants, while relatively consonant-poor Polynesian languages have as few as eight.

Although no primary consonants exist, we can place consonants into categories based on their physiological connection to primary vowels. We do this by starting with the mouth position of the three primary vowels and then constricting the vocal tract. Obviously numerous ways exist to constrict the mouth from any given starting point, but we shall base the constriction on the physiological component that most distinguishes each vowel. If we keep the constriction of each vowel to a single physiological component, we arrive at some rather interesting results.

## Constriction of the Jaw and the Arousing "rrr"

First, consider the constriction of the vocal tract from the position of the primary vowel /â/. The jaw plays a unique role in producing the /â/ sound. To pronounce an /â/ the jaw must be lower than it is for any other sound. This makes the jaw the logical choice of which physiological component to use for constricting the vocal tract to form a consonant associated with /â/. To constrict the vocal tract starting from the /â/ position, you must simply raise the jaw while keeping the position of the tongue and lips relaxed and unchanged. Since the tongue may rest at slightly different positions for an /â/ sound, creating a consonant by this constriction does not necessarily produce a unique consonant. If the tongue lies slightly forward while producing the /â/ sound and then kept forward while raising the jaw, the /l/ (as in like) sound results. However, if the tongue seats comfortably back instead of forward while an /â/ is produced, then a constriction by raising the jaw will yield an /r/ consonant sound (as in roar).[28]

The /l/ and /r/ have very similar acoustic parameters that make perception difficult for people whose native language does not contain these sounds, such as Japanese. The language of native Hawaiians has an /l/ but no /r/. A native Hawaiian speaker with no exposure to other languages will usually speak an /l/ instead of an /r/ when trying to pronounce foreign words that contain an /r/. For example, the English word "merry" turns into "melly." Almost all languages have either an /r/ or an /l/ sound. Since the /r/ sound does not involve the use of the tongue, but the /l/ needs the tongue to be slightly extended from its normal position, the /r/ sound is the closest "relative" to the /â/.

You can understand what makes the formation of an /r/ via constricting the jaw from an initial position of /â/ remarkable when you look at its emotional valence. Remember that the emotional quality of the /â/ falls at the empty end of the arousal scale of emotions. Well, the emotional resonance of the /r/, the constricted /â/, falls at the other end of the relaxation spectrum. That is, people perceive an /r/ as more arousing than any other sound.

The work connecting high arousal to /r/ comes from more than one source. In one simple study people rated the /r/ as more arousing than any other sound. In a priming study people could identify arousing words more easily if they heard an /r/ just before seeing the word.[29] Some studies have shown a connection between lowered speech pitch and dominance.[30] This conclusion is intuitive. Think about your impression of a man who speaks in a high-pitched voice. His authority is likely to be challenged. Someone trying to make an impression that he, or she for that matter, is a qualified leader, will use a speaking voice in front of others that will be lower in frequency than the voice that same person uses for more personal interactions with friends.

To achieve the lower speaking voice the speaker can simply lower the fundamental frequency of the voice. However, a listener perceives a series of overtones along with the fundamental frequency. It is the overtones that determine which speech sounds you perceive and not the fundamental frequency used by the speaker. The mouth acts like a filter on the vibrations produced by the vocal cords. When you produce an /r/ sound you only let pass through the vocal track overtones on the lower end of the spectrum. The higher overtones get attenuated by the filtered effect of the mouth. So even if another phoneme has the same fundamental frequency as an /r/, listeners will perceive the /r/ as lower in frequency. This makes the /r/ sound the best choice if you want to choose a single sound to intimidate someone. The /r/ sound is what is left of the human's ancestral growl—the sound emitted to ward off any would-be foe seeking to move in on a territory or mate.

## Constriction of the Lips and the Pleasant "mmm"

Next consider the primary vowel /û/. Since from a physiological viewpoint the lips play the most significant role in the production of the /û/ sound, the constriction for this primary vowel takes place with the lips. You can produce four different English consonants simply by closing the lips. Two consonants, the /b/ and /p/, involve closing the lips momentarily before opening them. These consonants are labeled "stop" consonants because of the momentary stoppage of the airflow. They differ on the timing of the vibration of the vocal cords. For the /b/, the vocal cords begin to vibrate just before the lips release the air. For the /p/, air escapes the lips prior to any movement of the vocal cords.

The other sounds created through lip constriction are the continuously sounding /m/ and /w/. To produce a /w/ the lips do not close completely, but only come close to closing. The /w/ also requires the tongue to pull back somewhat and curl slightly. With the /m/ the lips close completely and stay closed as you force air through the nose. The /m/ is one of the most universal consonants, found in practically every language. Because you form this through the complete constriction of lips it lies at the opposite extreme to the /û/ on the physiological component of the lips. And, it should come as no surprise by now, the /m/ lies on the opposite end of the pleasure continuum from the /û/. In other words the /m/ registers as the most pleasant of all sounds.

In an amazing number of languages the word for mother starts with an /m/ or contains at least one /m/ sound.[31] Linguists have suggested that the finding of /m/ in words for mother is not a coincidence. The only vocal sound an infant can make when breastfeeding is an /m/. Thus, the /m/ sound appears to be associated with mother, nourishment, and from a child's perspective, all things pleasant. In fact, this connection between /m/ and pleasantness appears to follow us into adulthood. Adults asked to rate various speech sounds gave the /m/ the highest rating on the pleasantness scale.[32]

Another piece of evidence that connects the /m/ sound with pleasantness is a bit less scientific and more anecdotal but certainly interesting in its own right. Think about how you might indicate to someone that something is good. Can you express goodness without words but still using speech sounds? If so, what sound or sounds would you use? These questions or some very similar ones must have been on the minds of Madison Avenue advertising agents whenever they were commissioned to do TV commercials for the Campbell's Soup Company in the 1960s. Anyone who watched commercial television during that era will probably remember the Campbell slogan of "mmm, mmm, good." The expression "mmm" did not need any translation. Everyone who heard the advertisement knew implicitly that it was an expression of enjoyment. How many times have you yourself used the expression to indicate to your favorite cook your appreciation for a dish or meal or some other thing that you found pleasant? Quite a few, I'd wager.

The same people citing the connection to the /m/ sound and pleasantness based on a nursing baby's perspective point out that the /û/ may be associated with unpleasantness for a related reason. If a child is suckling at the mother's breast then the lips are closed and all is well. A contented /m/ may be all that the child would express. However, when the child cannot find mother's breast she feels for it with an open mouth. With the mouth open trying to find a source of nourishment the lips will be in the approximate position for making a

/û/ sound. The experience of the child, one would surmise, would be the absence of pleasure.

## Constriction of the Tongue and the Controlling "nnn"

The primary physiological component of the /î/ is the tongue. This comes through process of elimination. Physiologically speaking there are three primary speech articulators—the jaw, lips, and tongue. Since the jaw and lips have associations with the other two primary vowels, it makes sense to pair the tongue with the /î/. Looking at the physiology of producing the /î/ sound it isn't easy to see how the tongue plays a role, however, there is a subtle projection of the tongue when saying an /î/ sound. Furthermore, evidence does support the connection between the tongue and the control dimension of emotion, as we shall see.

We use our tongues to create many different consonants via distinct vocal tract constrictions. Some of the consonants formed in this manner flow continuously as you pronounce them, that is, the same sound persists for a brief period of several milliseconds. The English language has ten of these, including /th/ as in think, /th/ as in they, /sh/ as in she, /zh/ as in measure, /ng/ as in ring, /n/, /z/, /s/, /y/, and /l/. English also has six consonants articulated with the tongue that are not expressed as a continuous sound, but instead involve a stoppage of airflow, and thus get referred to as stop consonants. They include /t/, /d/, /j/, /ch/, /k/, and /g/.[33] From this large number of consonants articulated by the tongue we need to identify which sound or sounds expresses the feeling of internal control, the opposite of the /î/ sound which expresses the sentiment of external control.

We do not have to pick a sound at random to fill this position on the continuum of emotional control. The most efficient and complete way to use the tongue to constrict the vocal tract is to push the tongue against the top of the mouth. To make the /n/ we must use forceful, physical control and push the tongue hard up against the roof of the mouth. Other sounds do not require as much force from the tongue. Although the /ng/ does require more force overall, because that sound uses the back of the tongue some of the force used to make the sound comes from the action of muscles in the jaw. When we look at the other evidence, we find that many languages employ an /n/ sound to express a concept that strongly suggests control. In English this word is "no." The /n/ promotes the feeling of being in control without debating or talking about it. This makes sense if you think about how a parent typically uses "no" to control a child. There is no questioning or debate necessary.

| | Emotion Dimension | | | | | |
|---|---|---|---|---|---|---|
| **Details of Dimension** | Enjoyment level | | Excitement level | | Locus of Control | |
| **Active physiological component** | Lips | | Jaw | | Tongue | |
| **Pole of emotion dimension** | Unpleasant | Pleasant | Relaxed | Aroused | External | Internal |
| **Primary Vowel** | /û/ | | /â/ | | /î/ | |
| **Corresponding Consonant** | | /m/ | | /r/ | | /n/ |

*Table 1. Relationships between primary sounds and dimensions of emotion.*

Table 1 shows all of the sound-emotion relationships discussed so far. These primary sound-emotion relationships form the foundation for building further sound-emotion relationships.

## Other Consonants

For other consonants we also look at the physiological characteristics in order to determine their emotional valence. Dividing the remaining 20+ sounds that will be used in SMY into groups that share common articulatory mechanisms makes the task of exploring the emotional significance of them easier. That division yields five distinct consonant types, including stops, fricatives, nasals, liquids, and glides (also called approximants). Most of the consonants that SMY uses exist in English; however, several native Arabic guttural consonant sounds used do not occur in English—more on these in the next sections.

## Stop Consonants

One of the largest groups of speech sounds that linguists put into the same category based on the manner in which they are produced is called "stop" consonants. In order to pronounce a stop consonant you must momentarily stop the flow of air before releasing it in an explosive fashion. Linguists classify stop consonants of all languages based on two different factors referred to as voicing and point of articulation. Voicing can be either voiced or unvoiced.[34] With voiced stop consonants the vocal cords vibrate before the air is released. For the unvoiced group the air gets expelled before the vocal cords vibrate. For example, when pronouncing a /p/, you release air before the vocal cords begin vibrating, but whenever a /b/ is uttered the vocal cords vibrate before the air is released. Try pronouncing these two consonants while placing a finger on your throat over where your vocal cords are located. When saying the /p/ you will not feel any vibration, but repeat the /b/ and the vibration is easily felt.

The second factor identifying stop consonants is the physical point in the mouth where the airflow is constricted, labeled the point of articulation (POA). For the /b/ and /p/ sounds the lips provide the POA; for the /d/ and /t/ sounds the constriction takes place by putting the tip of the tongue at the alveolar ridge just behind the teeth. Table 2 shows both voicing and points of articulation for all stop consonants used by SMY.

| | | Point of Articulation | | | | |
|---|---|---|---|---|---|---|
| | | Tongue part and location | | | | |
| | Lips | Tongue tip behind teeth | Mid tongue on palate | Back of tongue on velum | Pharynx | Glottis |
| **Voiced** | /b/ | /d/ | /j/ | /g/ | /gh/ | |
| **Unvoiced** | /p/ | /t/, /t̪/ | /ch/ | /k/, /q/ | /kh/ | /'/ |

*Table 2. Stop consonants classified by Voicing and
Point of Articulation characteristics.*

Table 2 includes four stop consonants not found in English, including two sounding similar to someone pronouncing an English /g/ and /k/ with a scratchy throat that get represented by /gh/ and /kh/ respectively. For these guttural sounds the airflow is stopped by pushing the base of the tongue against the back of the throat. The two other Arabic stops include a sound very similar to the English /t/ indicated by /t̪/ and one called ayin and designated by /'/. The /t̪/ differs from /t/ only by a rounding of the shape of the lips; the ayin, or /'/, gets articulated via the epiglottis, that is the flap of skin just above the vocal cords constricts to stop airflow.

The voicing classification and point of articulation determine what emotional valence a sound generates. The POA establishes which emotion dimension gets activated. For example, the lips stimulate the pleasure dimension. The voicing influences how the triggered emotional quality gets treated. With a voiced sound the vocal cords start to vibrate before the air is released. This creates a feeling in the speaker of holding on to the feeling associated with the POA. An unvoiced consonant generates an attitude of wanting to release the emotional quality involved. Thus /b/ holds on to a pleasurable or full feeling; /p/ releases that feeling.

Several stop consonants require the use of the tongue to stop the flow of air. This means that the mental or control dimension of emotions is involved. The part of the tongue which stops the airflow determines the type of subtle emotion control. The base of the tongue connects to the jaw, the physiological axis for arousal, but the tip of the tongue has no such relationship. Stop consonant sounds articulated by the tip of the tongue (/d/, /t/) get associated with control that plays out strictly on a mental level—emotions concerned with abstract ideas and concepts. Stop consonants articulated with the back of the tongue (/k/, /q/, /g/) correspond to control that includes a physical element. When the mid-portion of the tongue forms the POA the control shares both physical and mental aspects—ideas about physical entities.

If you use the back of the tongue to close the air passage in the throat and create a guttural /gh/ or /kh/, physical control also gets expressed, either as an effort to hold on to it with the /gh/ or letting it go with the /kh/. The difference between the /g/ and /gh/ as well as the difference between the /k/ and /kh/ seem to be a matter of emphasis. The greater stress needed for the guttural sounds creates a feeling of urgency not found in the non-guttural pair.

The constriction for the /'/ takes place closer to the vocal cords than any other constriction. This point of articulation does not have an association with any emotion dimension, but because this occurs at the vocal cords it has an overall effect on the emotion of speaking. With a constriction at the glottis vibrating the vocal cords cannot take place. Thus the constriction creates an emotional swelling; it can feel as if you have a lump in your throat. This buildup before the actual articulation of the sound can be characterized as a feeling of emotional confusion, or as an emotional quandary. The confusion gets resolved in a feeling of emotional catharsis as one releases air and speaks the sound. I realize the enigmatic nature of this description. Defining the emotional nature of the ayin seems destined to such mystery. The ayin has the reputation of carrying a mystical quality.

Table 3 depicts the stop consonants and their emotional qualities. To "look up" the emotional quality of one of these sounds, use the row and column labels associated with the sound. For example, the value of /d/ equates to "Holding on to Mental Control." A /k/ generates "Release of Physical Control."

| | | Control | | | | Emotional Buildup |
|---|---|---|---|---|---|---|
| | Pleasure | Mental | Global | Physical | | |
| **Holding on to** | /b/ | /d/ | /j/ | /g/ | /gh/ | |
| **Release of** | /p/ | /t/, /t̲/ | /ch̲/ | /k/, /q/ | /kh̲/ | /'/ |

Table 3. Emotional valence of stop consonants.

Remember, we are talking about the emotional meaning of a sound. Do not expect a single word or phrase to adequately address this meaning. The meaning has a very real experiential component to it and no scientific nomenclature, no matter how good, can do this emotional meaning justice. Only on an individual basis can you realize what the /k/ or /d/, or any other sound for that matter, means emotionally, and even then how you see or interpret this meaning may vary depending upon other factors affecting your mood. This limitation does not keep the above interpretations from being useful, as we will see.

## Fricative Consonants

Fricatives, formed by forcing air across a narrow constriction of the vocal tract, compose the largest group of English consonants, including /f/, /v/, /th/ (as in thing), /t̲h̲/ (as in they), /s/, /z/, /sh/ (as in shoe), /zh/ (as in vision), and /h/. SMY includes two fricatives that do not occur in English, /h̲/—another Arabic guttural sound similar to English /h/, and /dh/, a sound similar to English /t̲h̲/. I will provide more details on these sounds shortly. As with stop consonants, you can categorize fricatives using both voicing quality and POA. However, the voicing qualities of fricatives differ slightly from those of stop consonants. Since fricatives do not stop the airflow, determining the voicing characteristic based upon the air release in relation to when the vocal cords vibrate does not make sense. Instead unvoiced fricatives remain unvoiced for the duration of the sound, just as voiced fricatives remain voiced.

Since unvoiced fricatives create a sound simply through the friction of the airflow through a narrow passage and voiced fricatives create sound both through this constriction and through the vibration of the vocal cords, unvoiced fricatives require a stronger force of air to generate an equivalent volume level of sound. This plays a role in determining the emotion impact of the fricatives. Unvoiced fricatives convey a stronger or more urgent emotion compared to the voiced fricatives, but voiced fricatives connote an earthier or grounded emotion because the vocal cords vibrate at a lower frequency than the sound created by unvoiced fricatives, which consists of rather high frequencies.

Table 4 shows English fricatives categorized by their voicing characteristic and their point of articulation.

| Point of Articulation | | | | | | |
|---|---|---|---|---|---|---|
| | Upper teeth on lower lip | Tongue position | | | Pharynx | Glottal |
| | | Upper teeth | Behind teeth | Mid-front palate | | |
| **Voiced** | /v/ | /th/, /dh/ | /z/ | /zh/ | | |
| **Unvoiced** | /f/ | /th/ | /s/ | /sh/ | /h/ | /h/ |

Table 4. Fricative consonants classified by
Voicing and Point of Articulation.

The teeth play a role in two pairs of fricative sounds, and as with the stop consonants the point of articulation determines the nuance of meaning these sound convey. The teeth's location in the jaw gives them an association with the arousal dimension. This makes sense if you think about the aggressive potential of biting inherent with the teeth, but since with these sounds the upper teeth are kept from the lower teeth, with the lips (in the /f/ and /v/) or the tongue (in the /th/, /th/, and /dh/), the arousal is non-aggressive or dampened and fused with pleasure for the /f/ and /v/ and mediated with mental control for the other three sounds. One might characterize this kind of controlled arousal as careful, as in taking care not to bite. As noted above the /dh/ has nearly the same sound quality as the English /th/ as in they. The tongue position for the /dh/ is held somewhat looser and back from the teeth compared to the English /th/, but not quite as far back as with the /z/.

The /s/ sound corresponds to the exercise of a degree of mental control, but not control of a necessarily focused nature. It signifies the stream of consciousness experienced in daily life. As we navigate our world we characteristically have a steady barrage of mental chatter, typically a smattering of verbal checks and reassurances tied to our awareness of how we negotiate our physical, social, and mental environment. This ostensibly verbal attentiveness seems to give us a sense of identity, stability, and the ability to function. (Although I would argue—and do so in this work—that self-identification through one's stream of consciousness leads to a false identity, and that only through mindfulness free from mental chatter can one realize a true identity.) The emotional valence of /s/ fits what many call the ordinary conscious state.

So what does voicing do to the inherent emotional value of the /z/ compared to the /s/? The unvoiced /s/ has greater stress compared to the voiced /z/. The /s/ has more energy and higher frequencies than the /z/. This additional energy allows the /s/ to carry a stronger feeling and awareness of stream of consciousness than the /z/, while the lower frequencies and less energy of the /z/ give it a more measured, grounded, laid back feeling without the focus or pressing nature of the /s/.

The sustained /sh/ (as in shoe) and /zh/ (as in vision) also fall into the same category as the /s/ and /z/. All of these sounds correspond to a type of stream of consciousness. With the /sh/ and /zh/ the awareness in the stream focuses on some physical element of the environment, because the tongue constricts the airflow further back than for the /s/ and /z/. Reacting to or processing stimuli corresponds to a /sh/ or /zh/ feeling.

The point of articulation of the /h/, the glottis, has no direct interaction with the tongue, jaw, or lips. Thus by itself the /h/ has no direct impact on any of the dimensions of emotion. However, constricting the glottis reduces the energy available for producing sound. This reduction of energy determines the /h/'s emotional significance. If the /h/ follows a sound it functions as an emotional broom to sweep away the emotional valence of the previous sound. Speaking the /h/ reduces the energy available for the feeling of the companion sound, often a vowel. Thus, an /h/ preceded by an /â/ results in relaxation getting reduced, in other words a development of tension, stress, or some level of arousal. When the /h/ begins a sequence or phrase it indicates a beginning with low energy and thus corresponds to some form of fatigue, either physical, emotional, or mental.

We can point to a difference between the emotional qualities of the /h/ and /ḥ/, due to their slight difference in point of articulation. The /ḥ/ gets articulated at the pharynx. The constriction entails pushing the base of the tongue slightly back to block the airflow. This does not occur with the /h/. This involvement of the tongue with the /ḥ/ contributes to its emotional valence. Like the /h/, the /ḥ/ allows less air for sounds before and/or after it, and thus provides less energy for those sounds. The use of the back of the tongue means that the reduction of energy occurs with some physical control. Like the /h/ when the /ḥ/ follows a sound, the emotional valence gets swept away, and when the /ḥ/ begins a word it indicates fatigue. The /h/ has similar emotional qualities as the /ḥ/ but the /h/ lacks the strength or depth of feeling of the more emphatic /ḥ/ because of the smaller scale of the constriction.

Table 5 shows the emotional qualities of the various fricatives that have been introduced.

| Emotional Quality | | | | | | |
|---|---|---|---|---|---|---|
| | Tenderness/ Contentedness | Relaxed Control | Stream of Consciousness | Processing Stimuli | Exhausting | Tiring |
| **Grounded** | /v/ | /th/, /dh/ | /z/ | /sh/ | | |
| **Stressed** | /f/ | /th/ | /s/ | /sh/ | /h/ | /h/ |

*Table 5. Emotional valence of fricatives.*

## Nasal Consonants

In addition to stop consonants and fricatives, most languages, including English, contain a third group of consonants—nasal sounds—produced by forcing air through the nasal passage. The English language has three nasal sounds, including /m/, /n/, and /ng/ (as in sing). We have already discussed the feelings associated with the /m/ and /n/ sounds. We won't use the /ng/ in SMY. This sound adds a physical component to the emotional value compared to the /n/ because to make the /ng/ the back of the tongue gets engaged.

## Liquid and Glide Consonants

English has three sounds categorized as liquids or glides—the /l/, /y/, and the /w/. The /l/, called a "liquid" consonant by some linguists, has two positions, one for when the /l/ begins a syllable and one for when the /l/ comes at the middle or end of a syllable. To say the /l/ in lake you must touch your tongue to the roof of the mouth, but for the /l/ in kale the tongue makes no connection to the rest of the mouth. These physiological attributes result in a sound with two slightly different emotional meanings. When the /l/ comes at the beginning of the syllable it expresses control. The strength of the control associated with the /l/ does not approach the strict control expressed by the /n/, or even the /s/ or /z/, both of which have tighter constriction due to their fricative nature. Compared to the /n/, /s/, and /z/ the /l/ is laid back. The initial /l/ lets air flow more freely than any of the fricative sounds, and involves only the tip of the tongue. The control the initial /l/ expresses might best be described as that which one normally exhibits to navigate through daily living when you are on autopilot. The /l/ at the end of a syllable expresses even less control. In these instances the tongue does not rise, indicating a control that lets things flow. In fact, the tongue flattens out and opens the airway in a manner that suggests giving up of control.

The /y/ and /w/ are both called approximants as well as glides. An approximant consonant constricts the airflow more than a vowel, but less than a fricative. These are also called semi-vowels. You articulate the /y/ by raising the back of the tongue. This creates a mood characterized by a sustained effort to control the physical. In order to pronounce a /w/, you put the lips in the almost the same position as you do to pronounce a /û/. When a vowel other than /û/ or /u/ follows the /w/, as in the case for all of the uses of the /w/ in SMY, the emotional valence takes on a feeling of releasing unpleasantness, since the lips move away from the /û/ position.

## Hamza, the non-letter

One final "letter" needs introduced, the hamza, signified by /'/ (ending single quote, as contrasted the ayin, /'/, which uses a beginning single quote). I put the word *letter* in quotes because although Arabic uses the hamza in spoken and written language, many do not consider it a letter, but rather put into the category of punctuation mark, since it is written with another letter. The /'/ gets articulated as a short break in the breath or speaking of a word. It often gets characterized as an unvoiced glottal stop, since the glottis cuts off the air as the vocal cords stop vibrating. The psychological effect is an abrupt break from the previous sound.

That brings us to the end of the discussion of the individual sounds and their corresponding emotional valences. We now shift to combinations of sounds and how you can modulate moods selecting the appropriate words.

# CHAPTER 4
# COMBINING SOUNDS

With these relationships between sounds and emotion one can begin to understand the emotional impact of words, and how words can prove useful in mood regulation and/or enhancing spirituality. For our purposes all of the words considered in the work of SMY are taken from the ninety-names of Allah, or simply the names of Allah. For brevity's sake I will refer to them as Names, with a capital "N." Many authors have written about the Names, and although there appears a great deal of convergence on a majority of the Names cited, not all lists of ninety-nine Names agree. My choice of which Names to include comes from what I have seen as the most popular, or at least the ones I have seen most frequently in the various books and websites on the Names that I have come across.[35]

## SMY Words

The exercises that form the core of SMY use words with two or more phonemes that elicit or correspond to specific emotions or moods. I chose the ninety-nine Names of Allah as the SMY words for this book for several reasons: traditional Sufi practices utilize these Names, many of them fit into a framework established by the *Yoga Sutras*, and most importantly the Names provide a rich choice of meaningful sound combinations that, when used propitiously, help the seeker develop a beneficial meditation practice and also cope with the most common psychological, emotional, and mental challenges that individuals face in today's, or any, society. The principles of SMY do not exclude the use of words other than the names of Allah.

Which SMY word that you choose at any given time depends upon the emotional state you wish (or need) to work with and the goal emotional state you want to attain. The emotional state you work with will always determine the first letter, or sometimes first two-letter combination, in the SMY word. This will often consist of a problematic situation or feeling, for example anxiety, troublesome thoughts, physical discomfort, or other negative circumstances. However, SMY can also enhance mindfulness of positive sentiments like thankfulness or awe. The emotional goal will always establish the final letter or sometimes the final two-letter combination of the SMY word. The intervening letters work to move the practitioner from the initial state to the final in a logical, efficient, and effective manner.

To understand how an SMY word works take the word RÂM, not a name of Allah but rather the name of a Hindu god spoken by Gandhi immediately after he was shot and before he expired. When used following SMY rules, RÂM takes you from an aroused /r/ state to a pleasant /m/ state. It does this with the help of an intervening /â/. You can think of this in an SMY context as first noticing, "Oh, I'm emotionally unsettled (high arousal). I need to relax (/â/) so that I can feel pleasant (/m/)." SMY always requires that first step, the noticing of the current state. Other schools of thought on mindfulness recommend that you just ignore thoughts or feelings, but in SMY you use thoughts and feelings as a starting point.[36]

Although from ample anecdotal evidence I find that certain words used in an SMY context work by taking the speaker from an initial state to a final state, I don't believe this same concept works for all mantras. Many mantras in various religions, especially Buddhism and Hinduism, seem to work in a different manner because of their length. The sounds in a long mantra meander through a number of emotional valences which makes it difficult for emotional attention to latch on to the long twisting stream. These long mantras more likely work by repetition of key sound combinations with the intermediate sounds acting more or less as fillers. However, with short sequences, such as the single words that comprise 98% of SMY words presented in this work, the emotional attention can be focused. *And* provided that you follow the SMY guidelines, i.e., your current or problematic emotional state corresponds to the initial sound and your target mood matches the final sound(s), then the SMY word can work with your emotional attention and modulate your mood.

## *Applying SMY Words*

Emotional attention plays a key role in SMY practice. Many who practice chanting a mantra do so without paying attention to the emotional qualities of the sounds that they emit. True, they will necessarily feel the emotional impact due to the inherent nature of speech sounds, but the power of SMY depends upon developing the ability to use emotional attention. Although when practicing SMY you can always say the word, the word does not need to be spoken. SMY adheres to the Sufis' belief that one can experience a name of Allah in three different modes: a physical mode of simply saying the Name out loud; saying the Name silently; and feeling the Name in the mind or an emotional fashion only.

Rosina-Fawzia Al-Rawi, a highly regarded Sufi from the Shaduliyya tradition, states in her book *Divine Names* that: "The silent repetition of the Names is recommended once the seeker ... clearly wants to put all his energies, aspirations, and will into the path."[37] Certainly, one can simply say or hear an SMY word sub-vocally, and whether speaking out loud or silently hearing the word, if one focuses awareness—emotional attention, on the feelings associated with the emotional valence of the phonemes that comprise the Name—maximum benefit will be achieved. In fact, just focusing emotional attention on the feeling alone will suffice to gain benefit from the SMY word.

The second part of this book contains individual practices. Before learning and using the practices that follow you need to appreciate that a restrained approach will likely serve you best. When Sufis teach similar practices, they typically do not assign more than one particular Name at any given time. A student then adopts the new task and works with it until the teacher feels that the learner has mastered it in a satisfactory manner and can thus advance to working with another new Name. The reader must decide when to add another word on which to focus. If you push on too fast you run the risk of overload and the very real possibility that you will forsake any further learning. Someone taking on too many new exercises at once will often find themselves overwhelmed with new facts to remember and as a result feel that the program of SMY involves too many mental gyrations. Instead of reaching a calm meditative state such a person may feel that this mental agitation defeats the purpose of mindfulness. You need to have sufficiently automatized each exercise before moving to another. How long this takes will vary from person to person and from one SMY practice to another.

One can begin reading the practices with the first Name that appears in the text and read straight through to the end. If you take this approach, it makes sense to read for understanding but not for remembering. That is, don't try to study all ninety-nine Names in succession in an attempt to learn them all in a way that would allow you to use them in practice. Rather, if you read straight through you should try to understand how each word works in a theoretical manner. Take notes, perhaps, about those Names that strike an initial chord and beckon you to come back for a deeper infusion, but don't try to retain the information on the first read.

The structure of the second part of this book lends itself to approaches other than straight through reading. One such method would be to focus on a single chapter, or possibly a single Name. You should determine the choice of an individual Name or group of Names based on your self-identified emotional parameters. That is, try to identify the particular psychological dimensions of your daily habits or meditation practices that you find somewhat bothersome. Pay attention to your arousal level, pleasure valence, and whether you feel in control of physical, emotional, and/or mental process. Your psychological mood based upon such an analysis will determine the first sound or first sound-combination. Table 6 shows a list of the first sounds and the corresponding mood, along with which chapter you will find Names that address each mood.

| Sound | Chapter | Associated Psychological State |
|:---:|:---:|:---|
| /s/ | 5 | Awareness of stream of consciousness |
| /z/ | 5 | Awareness of grounded mental processing |
| /ma/, /mâ/ | 6 | Awareness of a pleasant situation |
| /sh/ | 7 | Pondering physical surroundings |
| /n/ | 8 | Feeling in control |
| /d/ | 8 | Holding on to a feeling of mental control |
| /t/ | 8 | Letting go of mental control |
| /l/ | 8 | Letting things flow |
| /r/ | 9 | Agitated, stressed, or vigilant state |
| /q/ | 10 | Reluctant or austere relinquishing physical control |
| /k/ | 10 | Surrendering control of physical realm |
| /kh/ | 10 | Stressed surrender of physical control |
| /gh/ | 11 | Feeling stressed and needing to keep physical control |
| /b/ | 12 | Feeling drawn to or wanting to retain a pleasurable experience |
| /ḥ/, /h/ | 13 | Physical, emotional, or mental tired feeling |
| /mu/ | 14-17 | Falling short of a desirable goal |
| /w/ | 18 | Letting go of emptiness |
| /'/ | 19 | Feeling as though you will burst with emotion |
| /j/ | 20 | Holding on to a feeling of global control |
| /a/, /â/ | 21 | Feeling relaxed or withdrawn |
| /dh/ | 21 | Considering control of physical elements |
| /f/ | 21 | Contentment |

*Table 6. Moods and their corresponding sounds and chapter locations.*

# PART TWO

## The Practices

# Chapter 5
## Dealing with Stream of Consciousness

SMY works not by ignoring thoughts and feelings, but by focusing your awareness on them and dealing with them. After all, these thoughts comprise your present state and the oft-stated goal of mindfulness is to be aware of the present. Perhaps the most ubiquitous part of a person's psychological existence consists of the seemingly endless mental chatter that gets referred to as "stream of consciousness." The phonemes /s/ and /z/ correspond to the kind of stream of consciousness that pervades most persons' daily living and indeed spills over into a beginner's mindfulness practices. The SMY Names beginning with /s/ and /z/ deal with the different variations of mental processing that comprise stream of consciousness. They work by modulating your psychological makeup from this existing mentally active /s/ state to one more conducive to mindfulness, that is, a clear mind uncluttered by the mental gyrations of the typical stream of consciousness.

The use of the Names beginning with /s/ and /z/ presupposes that your emotional state involves a rather neutral level of arousal and pleasure. Thus Names beginning with these sounds can prove useful during meditation when you are neither excited nor lethargic, neither ecstatic nor depressed. Don't use a Name beginning with either /s/ or /z/ to address aroused or lethargic feelings, or a very happy or a very dark mood. Names that deal with the non-neutral levels of arousal and pleasure appear in later chapters.

Each of the five Names in this chapter applies to a separate type of stream of consciousness, which correspond to a separate types of mind modification. When trying to understand the distinction between these general types of thought it helps to refer to the goal of yoga as stated by Patanjali in the *Yoga Sutras*—cessation of the modifications of the mind, which include Right Thinking, Wrong Thinking, Imagination, Memory, and Sleep. From a psychologist's point of view four of these conscious mental gyrations, i.e., Right Thinking, Wrong Thinking, Imagination, or Memory, are not mutually exclusive. That is, at any particular time the entire contents of the mind cannot be identified as one of these types of thinking. Instead our complex conscious state often contains more than one mental variation going on simultaneously. Sleep stands by itself. Sleep indicates a lack of active processing in the mind, while for each of the other types of mental variations some form of cognitive processing exists. Knowing that, let's first examine the nature of each of Patanjali's variations in isolation.

For the purposes of SMY we will consider Right Thinking as referring to thinking about or holding in your mind a concept or idea that you believe to be correct, something that you do not need any further information to evaluate. This would include a belief, a truism, or even an opinion. The standard interpretation of Right Thinking does not include opinion because you can form opinions based on incorrect information. This interpretation argues that only opinions based on reliable sources qualify as Right Thinking. With SMY you must rely upon your own subjective evaluation. If you consider something correct, then that assessment determines why you would classify the thought as Right Thinking.

In contrast, for use in SMY Wrong Thinking refers to thinking about a problem or situation for which you do not know the proper solution or road forward, where something appears wrong to you, incomplete or awry. Again, the interpretation of Patanjali's Wrong Thinking differs from this one. That understanding of Wrong Thinking considers it any thought based on a false concept. Since ignorance cannot recognize itself, you will never identify any current, active thought as Wrong Thinking. These types of thoughts will always go undetected and thus the term has no use in a self-evaluation system such as SMY. Furthermore, the categorization of Wrong Thinking as thought based on incorrect knowledge leaves no clear category for thoughts associated with seeing problems. Since we spend much cognitive energy pondering problems, SMY finds regarding Wrong

Thinking as pondering about a problem a useful categorization for which a valuable SMY Name applies.

Thought involving problem solving can also involve the type of mind modification called Imagination, whenever you are imagining solutions to a problem. Wrong Thinking, thinking about a problem, and Imagination, imagining a solution to the problem, can coexist. For SMY you need to identify the most salient of these two when they occur together. If your focus dwells on the problem without a solution, then Wrong Thinking prevails. If you have a solution in mind, then Imagination has taken over.

Imagination, the third mental modification identified by Patanjali, has many flavors. In addition to working on solutions to problems, Imagination includes pondering plans for the future, something that could happen but has not yet occurred or taken shape. You can also use Imagination to replay the past with a twist added as a "should have" or "what if." Many folks apply Imagination to the present, for example imagining what someone else might be thinking or feeling. And of course Imagination can also refer to pure fantasy, something with no connection to any phase of reality. During meditation you can easily drift into such daydreams, the realm of Imagination.

Memory needs little explanation. Simply put, anything you recall from a previous experience falls into this category. A psychologist would refer to this as long-term memory, or perhaps episodic memory. I will not use Patanjali's term Memory to refer to what psychologists call *working memory*, the part of the mind where current thought takes place. Right Thinking, Wrong Thinking, and Imagination all take place in this arena.

Even if you distinguish Memory (of events and facts) from working memory used by Right Thinking, Wrong Thinking, and Imagination you still can't necessarily disentangle mental events into one particular category. Both Right and Wrong Thinking often get triggered from traces of (long-term) Memory. For example, Wrong Thinking can happen when you think about an incident that occurred at work that has left something unresolved. Right Thinking might result from remembering something that went well. Imagination often accompanies these thoughts, too. You can use Imagination to consider how something you remember as wrong could have been changed for the better, and when you remember something that went well, you might use Imagination to plot a glorious future that this success will lead toward.

Patanjali's final mind modification, Sleep, presents a curious case. How does your mind make modifications during sleep? Most would surmise that it refers to dreaming. A common translation of Patanjali calls Sleep the absence of thought. For SMY, think of Sleep as an almost zombie-like state in which active cognition ceases and you function on autopilot—a situation resembling daydreaming, but without active participation, as opposed to Imagination. The expression "veg out" captures this mental condition. Imagination differs from Sleep in that your mind actively pursues an idea with Imagination, but with Sleep things fade in and out of awareness without direction or purpose.

Although you often cannot put the entire content of your thoughts at any given moment into a specific one of these five cognitive buckets, these mental modifications form the starting point for using SMY to address mental chatter. You start by identifying the most salient or most pressing type of mental disturbance. For example, beginning mindfulness practitioners often report thoughts such as "Am I doing this wrong?" and other doubts typical of Wrong Thinking. They may use Memory to try to recall specific instructions about how to meditate and they may also use Imagination to think about what they might modify. When thinking about these thoughts you can identify both Memory and Imagination, but it's the Wrong Thinking that needs to be addressed.

But why do this? Patanjali states that the suppression of all modifications can be achieved through persistent practice and non-attachment, but he doesn't specify the practice. That leaves followers of Patanjali with the nebulous practice of non-attachment, a vague sounding idea, but very much like advice given in popular mindfulness practices today. They tackle the question of how to cope with mental distractions during meditation by advising you to ignore them. Just let them alone. According to the prevailing wisdom of those who teach and write about mindfulness, making an effort to analyze thoughts that occur during meditation should be off limits. You are told to recognize thoughts simply as "events arising, lingering, and passing."[38] Or to tell yourself, "Hush, now, it's time to relax and be quiet. There's nothing important to talk about right now...."[39] Or when you recognize a thought processes "acknowledge it by just calling it 'thinking.'"[40]

I challenge this conventional wisdom. These instructions contradict the notion of "not rejecting your experience" and being "fully engaged with yourself, with the world" that also permeates the mindfulness literature.[41] To stay fully engaged with the world you shouldn't ignore your thoughts and the emotional baggage that always accompanies the jumbled notions of Right Thinking, Wrong Thinking, Imagination, and Memory (and many other psychological states addressed in subsequent chapters). You should work through them to attain your goal—a lucid mind and self-aware state. You can help clear each of these different types of mental modifications with the use of one of the Names, which you will see not only facilitates the curtailment of the mental modification, but does it in a mindful but non-attached manner.

## *Finding Peace with SALÂM*

When a person first sits down to meditate using any approach, including SMY, one implied question, "Am I doing this right?" often dominates the mental landscape. Your mind tends to swirl with self-doubt when you engage in a new challenging endeavor. Of course in this mix of analytical insecurity you use Memory to bring to mind the steps the practices dictate you should follow to overcome uncertainly. You may employ Imagination to bring test scenarios to mind and consider what alternatives you could use. Flashes of Right Thinking might make brief appearances as you think that you have understood at least some aspect of the problem. However, from a functional standpoint Wrong Thinking holds the upper hand. The issue at hand, wondering how to meditate correctly, constitutes a problem. This Wrong Thinking precipitates the other mental activity. In virtually all situations when your mind dwells on a reality-based quandary, you need to address Wrong Thinking before considering any of the other types of mind modifications.

In situations where our mental meanderings coalesce around a problem that leads to Wrong Thinking, you can use SMY principles to feel the emotions expressed by the phonemes in the word SALÂM to help rescue your mind from the intruding predicament and transport yourself back toward mindful awareness. The initial sound /s/ corresponds to the existing psychological internal chatter, the verbal stream of consciousness flowing in your awareness as you mull over your predicament. The /l/ assumes the next role. You can ignore the short /a/ vowel. Its insertion into this word keeps the acoustics correct, but it plays an insignificant part in the progression of feelings.

The emotional valence of /l/ can vary based on its context. You articulate /l/ with the tongue, the physiological component that plays a role in the feeling of internal control. However, when you pronounce /l/ you have minimum tension in the tongue, compared to other sounds made with the tongue. Air actually flows around the tongue rather freely during articulation of the /l/. This contrasts to the role of the tongue in virtually all other consonants and distinguishes the emotional quality provided by /l/. The /l/ lets feelings flow around it. When /l/ begins a syllable, it lets feelings flow into the following emotional quality. For example, if the sequence consists of /lî/, the feelings flow gently into the external control expressed by /î/.

When saying SALÂM the /l/ lets the focus on the problem, expressed by /s/, flow into relaxation provided with /â/. Thus /salâ/ portion of SALÂM results in a relaxing of control, and letting things flow as if on autopilot. This provides an exit from the effort to analyze the problem you face. This step follows the advice of those who counsel to ignore thoughts, but in a more proactive manner. As soon as you recognize your mind's engagement in problem-solving Wrong Thinking, let go of any effort for control—any attempt to solve the issue—and relax. The final feeling, the /m/, should come naturally at this point. Letting go of your mental struggle and relaxing will feel good.

Using SALÂM in response to Wrong Thinking makes sense on simply an intellectual level, but the power of SALÂM goes far beyond the intellectual level into a very real physical and emotional dimension. The SMY pattern for SALÂM allows you to let go of whatever problem you face, relax, and enjoy yourself—a true recipe for peace.

You could sum up this SMY exercise that combats Wrong Thinking as "let go of thoughts associated with your problem(s) and relax, perhaps with a deep breath, and bring yourself back to a pleasant state of awareness." This recipe looks very similar to the most common advice given in treatises of mindfulness meditation: "Let go of your thoughts and watch your breath." I find it no coincidence that these similarities exist. Also don't think that SALÂM's appearance as the first SMY exercise as coincidental. Because doubt and Wrong Thinking pervade most beginner attempts at mindfulness meditation, SALÂM should hold a key position in your SMY repertoire, at least for beginning meditators.

The usage of SALÂM can prove beneficial outside of a meditation setting. If while you drive, or sit waiting for something, or other situations where you catch yourself mentally stewing over a problem, you can step back from the issue and find solace through the use of SALÂM. Once you recognize the /s/ of Wrong Thinking, exhale and let the flowing /l/ take over before a strong inhalation into a relaxing /â/ and allow the pleasant /m/ to melt away the mental effort.

## Traditional Use of SALÂM

The Arabic word *salâm* translates into English as *peace*. Muslims use *salâm* to help to bring peace to an individual or situation. The SMY interpretation of *salâm* fits snugly with this traditional understanding. Not all of the traditional Arabic meanings and Sufi uses of the Arabic words will show a direct correspondence to the purpose of the SMY employment of the word. I find it interesting to compare SMY usage to the traditional one, and will provide such commentary for each Name.[42]

## *The Certainty of Right Thinking and SAMÎ'*

How often do you engage in something called Right Thinking when not in a meditative state? If your job requires decision making, then you would likely utilize it on a regular basis. If you get into an argument, do you stake out your position with this mode? I would guess that most of us do, at least to some extent. People with a religious bent know this way of thinking. Opinions, beliefs, reasons, contentions, claims all fall under the Right Thinking category. For most people some kind of Right Thinking occurs on a regular basis. We live in a multifaceted world and need to know how to negotiate complex situations that require confidence for optimal results. If you believe in yourself and in what you are doing, then you engage in Right Thinking.

What about Right Thinking during meditation? You may occasionally think of a solution to a problem or part of a job that has been haunting you or dwell on a recent opinion you have held about a current topic. With SMY one type of Right Thinking will likely arise. You will begin to recognize that you have just done something in accordance with the practices. A feeling of "I got it right" or "this is how it needs to be done" often arises when tasked with a new challenge. One should expect this, at least at first. After you gain more competence, and reciting and feeling the emotional impact of the Names takes place with less mental effort, such self-reassurance will fade. In any case when you do experience a flash of Right Thinking during meditation you can use SAMÎ' to move your meditation into a more desirable state.

Don't limit the use of SAMÎ' to a meditation setting. Often we let our opinions, beliefs, and other forms of Right Thinking take over our being. A strong opinion can lead to an abrasive personality if left unchecked. If you flaunt your viewpoint or let a strong belief grip you, your level of mindfulness suffers, along with your status in the eyes of those whose beliefs do not coincide with yours. Mellowing your Right Thinking of everyday living with SAMÎ' can prove advantageous and increase your appreciation of views other than your own.

SAMÎ' serves as a formula to remedy Right Thinking by getting you to forgo your hold on the belief that you have a grip on some truth. When you recognize your righteous Right Thinking moment, characterized by the /s/ feeling, a pleasant /m/ feeling should happen easily, practically automatically. Thinking that you have a corner on the truth feels good to most everyone. Once you have recognized the /sam/ of

Right Thinking you need to cede control to an outside force via /î/. Feeling that you are willfully yielding control to an outside force should not prove difficult to a religious person, especially in the circumstance of Right Thinking. A Sufi would acknowledge that only via the force "the One," that is Allah, do you have access to Right Thinking. When letting go in this manner, you should not think of this force by the name "Allah," or by any name, but just let yourself feel the submission to the power that you recognize in the force. This acknowledgment will in most instances generate a strong emotional reaction, one that needs cleared with an ayin, /'/. This final sound clears out the attachment to the Right Thinking and puts you back on an even keel emotionally.

For non-believers the feeling of surrender to an outside force may prove difficult. However, one can still take advantage of the Name SAMÎ' by engendering a feeling that some force other than what you self-identify as has generated the Right Thinking. This attribution needs to take place in order to get past the mode of Right Thinking. You may achieve this by realizing that the mental representations of the thoughts are not you—separate yourself from them. As you attempt to sidestep the Right Thinking and be in the present moment, it should generate an emotional buildup—giving up the feeling of being right doesn't come easy. As the emotion arises just let it evaporate with the help of the ayin. This process takes place like they teach in many mindfulness classes where they tell you to call such thoughts "thinking." The catharsis afforded by the ayin lets you acknowledge that Right Thinking simply consists of a particular kind of mental activity.

To summarize, applying SMY principles to the SAMÎ' pattern allows you to let go of your thoughts about being correct on some matter. It accomplishes this with a pleasant, cathartic discharge of your controlling feelings and acceptance of your lack of control and recognition that the truth of your Right Thinking is only an illusion generated by your mind's existence in a physical body. SAMÎ' acknowledges that you can only experience the real truth that you seek and not just think it.

Use SAMÎ' to let go of the feeling that you know something. The "truth" varies from person to person, from one moment to the next. Whatever truth that has seized you, SAMÎ' allows you to simply hear it in your mind and recognize it as a mental modification and let it pass.

## Traditional Use of SAMÎ'

*Samî'* translates into English as *all-hearing*. Muslims use *samî'* to promote the ability to hear everything clearly, even divine ethereal sounds. The SMY interpretation of SAMÎ' roughly equates to all-hearing in the sense that what one can consider as Right depends on an individual's viewpoint and belief system. You should strive to keep an open mind and hear all beliefs without prejudice.[43]

## *Returning to Reality from Imagination with SABÛR*

A common form of mind modification present during meditation is Imagination. Your mind engages in Imagination as a form of escape. During meditation, especially for beginners, imaginative daydreaming occurs frequently. You do not consciously look for an escape to the boredom of meditation, but without knowing how it happened you will find yourself off somewhere in proverbial la-la land fantasizing about something much more interesting than just sitting still. If these imaginative thoughts don't engage the problem solving of Wrong Thinking, or simply use Memory to recall specifics of an event, then the mind modification falls under the Imagination category. A fine line exists between Imagination, Wrong Thinking, and Memory, and it is up to the practitioner to decide to which bucket the thoughts belong. If the thoughts carry a tension, it indicates a problem and Wrong Thinking and you need to relax with SALÂM. However, if the thoughts act as a diversion with no particular driving force to solve an issue then you need to bring yourself back to the present reality. SABÛR accomplishes this.

After the initial /s/ in SABÛR, comes the next significant sound, a /b/. You form a /b/ with the lips. Thus the /b/ connects to the pleasure dimension of emotion. In the context of SABÛR the /b/ represents our holding on to a mind full of pleasant daydreams. (If unpleasant feelings dominate your daydreams, then you will need to see a later chapter that deals with such issues.) When you identify your daydreaming, when you have that "aha" moment that recognizes daydreams at work, then you need to release these imaginative thoughts. The /û/ provides the means to empty the pleasant ruminations from the mind. The /û/ doesn't indicate an unpleasant feeling, but rather an empty or austere answer to the holding on to pleasure, indicated by the /b/, generated by the wandering Imagination. The /û/ drains away any good feeling that the imaginative thoughts afforded. The final /r/ brings you back to physical reality with a little arousal—just enough to awaken you from the daydream. It helps to feel the arousing through tightening the muscles in the abdomen as you exhale.

With Wrong Thinking you use SALÂM to relax and let go of the tension associated with problems. In contrast, with Imagination you use SABÛR to end your relaxed, dreamy state. In the former the arousal level needs to taper off, but in the latter mindfulness of the present has slipped, indicating that the arousal level has fallen too low and needs to be raised. However, the /r/ at the end of SABÛR should raise the arousal level to neutral, not to a point of agitation. As with SALÂM you may have to repeat feeling the SABÛR pattern more than once to bring your attention back to normal.

You can also utilize SABÛR during normal daily processes whenever your mind drifts into daydreaming or plotting and planning about something distant from your current situation. SABÛR can bring your awareness back to a more mindful state and let you focus on the present.

## Traditional Use of SABÛR

*Sabûr* translates from the Arabic to English as *patience*. Muslims use *sabûr* to promote patience in waiting for a desired result and to keep from acting in haste. No obvious connection between patience and squelching the thoughts of an imaginative mind exist and none needs to exist to validate the SMY use of the pattern based on this word. However, in my experience of Imagination during meditation my mind typically wanders in a manner that has me planning what to do in the near future, or how something I recently experienced fits into what I might do, or how I could change something that I have done so that next time I might have a better outcome. All of these Imaginative thoughts focus on accomplishing something in the future. SABÛR helps me put these thoughts aside and refocus on meditation. In that way SABÛR does help me achieve patience.

## *Remembering and SAMAD*

Memories play a role in Wrong Thinking, Right Thinking, and Imagination. In fact most memories serve one of the more prominent forms of mind modifications. However, on occasions you can experience Memory outside of the context of remembering problems or chores, opinions or facts, and reveries or daydreams. Sometimes a Memory just grabs you and sits in your awareness. Sometimes lyrics to a song keep replaying in your mind. If such Memories do not engender unpleasant feelings then use the Name SAMAD to encourage the Memory to fade away and continue your mindfulness practice. However, if unpleasant memories plague you, then you would do better with an SMY word beginning with another letter, as detailed in a later section of the book.

With the Name SAMAD you only use the /s/, /m/, and /d/, as the vowels in the word do not carry a valence in this context. Once you notice a Memory modification let the recognition bring on a pleasant feeling, perhaps easiest done by focusing your awareness on your chest area as you breathe in. This registering of the pleasant /m/ amounts to smiling at yourself and acknowledging the imprint of memory as part of your existence. At this point you need to accept the memory and let it pass, and just acknowledge your whimsical mind's ability to forage through the past. Once you have relinquished the memory you should have a refreshing feeling of having grabbed control of your meandering mind. You can facilitate this by feeling the control offered by /d/ as you exhale. It helps to let your awareness focus on the point in your mouth where the tongue touches to articulate the /d/ sound. If you can hold on to that feeling of control, that /d/ feeling, you will have cleared your mind of the particular thoughts about the memory.

SAMAD can also work in everyday scenarios. If you catch yourself in a distracted mood dwelling on a past event you can reestablish a mindful awareness of the present using SAMAD. This does not imply that you should avoid all memories of events, especially precious ones. However, if memories interfere with paying attention to your present reality, then SAMAD provides a means for you to acknowledge the memory and gently relish the goodness of it, with the /m/, before allowing it to fade away as you exert control over your thoughts.

## Traditional Use of SAMAD

*Samad* translates into English as *eternal* or *never changing*. Muslims use *samad* to promote the experience of the everlasting, unchanging quality of something. One uses the SMY sequence of SAMAD to turn and first embrace and then let go of the past and see it as an aspect of something of yours, something you control, the gift of experience from the universe.

## *Bringing Awareness Back to Focus with ZÂHIR*

At times your mind may wander in a manner that tends toward losing focus. You may notice your consciousness stream meandering among thoughts of nothing in particular. Your thoughts have no specific problem in sight, no particular memory grabbing you, and nothing seemingly standing out as right or wrong—you just seem to be witnessing ideas and images willy-nilly. This state of mind resembles the fifth modification of mind stated by Patanjali in the *Yoga Sutras*, Sleep. If your mind drifts in this manner, then you can utilize the Name ZÂHIR to bring your awareness back to focusing on the present.

The state of mind this word deals with gets identified by the first two letters /zâ/, which indicates a relaxed, unfocused stream of consciousness. The aroused /r/ forms the target for this relaxed unfocused state. You want to generate just enough of the arousal from /r/ to bring back the focus of awareness to the present and out of the depths of the mental doldrums. The intermediate sound of /h/ provides the bridge from the initial state to the target one. The /h/ exhausts or drains out your comfortable mental state so that the arousal dimension of awareness can rise. When you attempt to feel the

/h/ taking away the relaxed consciousness stream /zâ/ state, it can help to feel air getting pushed out through the tightening of the abdominal muscles. A continued focus on those muscles can facilitate the onset of the arousing /r/.

Situations where ZÂHIR applies have similarities to those suitable for SABÛR. Both circumstances qualify as daydreaming. Whenever a daydream focuses intently on an idea or image, SABÛR works best. If your daydream has no particular focus, that is, seems less intense and meanders aimlessly, then ZÂHIR will apply.

## Traditional Use of ZÂHIR

The Arabic translation for *zâhir* is *the manifest*. Muslims use the Name *zâhir* to produce a feeling of being present, letting one's existence be known. At times you need to get away from your drifting mind and back to a more present state. Using *Zâhir* in the context of SMY can facilitate this transition.

## *Chapter Summary*

The Names in this chapter begin with sounds corresponding to a psychological state called stream of consciousness. If you find that you can't get certain thoughts out of your mind, or that you want to address that constant nagging "monkey mind" that keeps disturbing your attempts at quietude or meditation, then the Names in this chapter can provide some relief. These Names do not apply if your thoughts agitate you emotionally or make you anxious or depressed. The Names just work on quieting mental gymnastics.

The Names in this chapter afford an excellent starting point for developing a meditation practice provided you don't have troubling emotions and/or physical issues plaguing you. If you can just sit down with the goal of paying attention to the present and quieting the mind, then the five Names in this section can prove beneficial. When your mind keeps trying to figure out what it should be doing, use SALÂM to calm it. If your thoughts keep turning to planning for what to do after meditation, use SABÛR to bring it back to your current reality. If your mind goes off in haphazard daydreaming, ZÂHIR can bring you back.

Use SAMAD to address persistent memories that won't seem to go away. Finally, you can clear out self-righteous thoughts or feelings of strong beliefs with SAMÎ'.

# CHAPTER 6
## ENHANCING MINDFULNESS OF PLEASANT MOODS

Although turning to the Names of the previous chapter to begin a meditation practice makes sense, these Names alone do not produce a profound state. They can only help quiet your mind and prepare for such an experience. The group of three Names that begin with /ma/ found in this chapter can help take you into a deeper meditative state. Once you have begun to have some success with controlling your mental gymnastics, perhaps by using the first set of Names, you can turn to the Names in this chapter to establish a more rewarding practice.

It is possible to experience periods of happiness not generated by words or mental chatter. Seasoned practitioners of meditation often report spontaneous bouts of joy. One way to facilitate such moments has to do with breath awareness. If you "watch" your breath, that is pay attention to the breathing process, it can also help calm the chatter of the mind—thus, the common advice given by many meditation programs. As you inhale you can often generate a noticeable pleasant /ma/ feeling. You can use SMY principles to deal with these. One might ask: "Why bother addressing a pleasant experience with SMY?" Although such times do not necessarily present emotional problems, they do present an opening for self-indulgence and can lead to states lacking mindfulness. However, by using SMY principles in time of pleasant experiences you can attain something even better. Some might call that better thing "yoga" or union with God. A non-believer might want to rename it "mental clarity." That is the reward for the use of the Names beginning with /ma/.

SMY breaks down what triggers a pleasant /ma/ feeling into three categories: 1) external conditions and surroundings, something perceived outside our being, 2) internal reactions to thoughts not directly related to anything existing in the immediate external surroundings, and 3) external physical reality that feels strongly emotionally connected to an internal notion of self. For each of these instances a single Name applies that can generate a satisfying mindful state.

Along with the three Names beginning with /ma/, this chapter also presents three Names beginning with /mâ/. One can distinguish pleasant feelings by noting whether or not they induce relaxation, an /â/ feeling. Typically the moods associated with the relaxing /mâ/ take on a flavor of indulgence and need an SMY Name that corrects this by expelling the momentary lapse from mindfulness. Thus, these Names don't have the potential for generating the deep mystical states that the Names beginning with /ma/ do.

The use of these six Names should occur if the pleasant feeling occupies the central focus of your attention. This focus can occur in a spontaneous fashion or it may happen when you consciously choose to dwell on something pleasant (as noted with your breath). Either way the pleasant aspect of the awareness must play the central role for these Names to apply. For someone who has learned how to quiet the typical stream of consciousness during meditation and has no physical or emotional distractions, these /ma/ and /mâ/ states can often occur.

### *Reacting to Pleasant Surroundings with MALIK*

During meditation, or for that matter at any time, your attention can dwell on a fortuitous physical situation, for example, a comfortable new home, a new or upgraded vehicle, a satisfactory job. You have many options for how to react to such recognition of good fortune. You can be thankful, maybe joyful, perhaps even a bit prideful, if you see yourself as responsible for the goodness that you perceive. The Name MALIK offers a contemplative and meditative option for such pleasantness. Using MALIK in these situations can honor the pleasant feeling while maintaining a mindful meditative state.

When you feel a pleasant, not relaxing, /ma/ due to some aspect of the surroundings, avoid any subtle draw of the pleasant situation. In SMY, as in any mindfulness meditation, you don't want to feel any attachment, as good as that may feel. Certainly Buddhists would advise non-attachment as key to meditation. This makes sense in SMY, too. Although the pleasant feeling is not bad in itself, you should not let it control you, or rather control your attention. Thus, the target feeling in this situation is to let go of the feeling that you are in physical control. The /k/ best represents this feeling. However, you don't want to move directly from the /ma/ to the /k/, as that transition is too abrupt. Instead, first move from the /ma/ to an /l/, a sound that corresponds to loose control. After recognizing the pleasant /ma/, you should first feel the flowing, loose mental control of the /l/ before giving way to a /k/ feeling.

You may wonder how you can recognize a pleasant state of your mind without generating a modification, an /s/ feeling. This can happen through simple awareness of the moment, especially during a meditation session in which you have been quieting the mind. You can know something without sub-vocally telling yourself that you know it. If you tell yourself, then you will experience the /s/ state. However, you can simply recognize a physical pleasant /m/ feeling, switch to letting things flow with /l/, and then end with /k/, let go of any feeling of physical control. This can progress most easily when feeling the /lik/ while you exhale. When you become aware of the /ma/ feeling, inhale. Then exhale, feeling the letting go expressed by the /l/ before completing the exhalation feeling the physical release of the /k/. It's as simple as "watching the breath." Practice MALIK often during meditation.

## Traditional Use of MALIK

*Malik* translates into English as *sovereign ruler* or *king*. Muslims traditionally use this word to create a sense of power or authority. SMY usage of MALIK allows you to feel a sense of goodness in the world without having mental attachment to that condition, that you have been blessed, that the universe is treating you kindly. Use MALIK in response to feeling power or greatness, not to attain it.

## *Reacting to a Pleasant Idea with MATÎN*

Pleasant moments often come to us for unknown reasons, like a general feeling of "just happy to be here." This can often happen when pursuing knowledge, being intellectually curious, or just during meditation. Although internal pleasant reveries share characteristics with Right Thinking, they do have distinct markers. The pleasure in Right Thinking comes when the mental chatter of your stream of consciousness generates and holds on to a thought in which you believe. Other pleasantness has a more spontaneous origin such that you cannot directly associate it with an idea specifically generated through mental chatter, for example: feeling good because you know something without reviewing it with internal language to reinforce the idea. In these instances the use of MATÎN can help nudge those pleasant feelings toward a higher-level awareness.

The target feeling in this situation consists of a rather paradoxical /în/ combination. The paradox stems from the juxtaposition of the external control feeling of /î/ and the strong internal control feeling of /n/. This combination of external control followed by internal control appears at the end of several Names of Allah. The pairing generates a profound emotional effect. You feel that you relinquish control to an outside force. The Sufis recognize this force as Allah. Immediately after feeling the presence of this force you feel in control. How can one feel under control of an outside force and in control at the same time? How do you express the ineffable? You have likely heard the saying "you have to let go of it in order to have it" or something similar. You have that same kind of situation with MATÎN.

The /în/ combination lets you feel that by letting go you have everything under control. Yoga philosophers might argue that the explanation for this paradox involves the nature of the self that feels the control. This argument centers on the goal of meditation, or the goal of yoga, which they point to as the union of personal awareness with a higher consciousness. Some call this consciousness God. Others call the higher power universal consciousness, Atman, or universal self which you have started to internalize. The external and internal are becoming one. The Sufis put it this way: "There is nothing, only He.

Where are you? You are from Him and you have returned to Him."[44] A more modern explanation might characterize /în/ as: if you clear away mental effort with /î/, the empty pole of mental control, then clarity itself will appear via the /n/, a sound of pure mental focus or control with no stream of consciousness.

As with most of the Names you don't proceed directly from the initial feeling to the target feeling, but first pass through an intermediate state. In this case, because an internal (non-verbal) inspiration has initiated the pleasant feeling, you should let go of any notion of mental control via the /t/ sound. You want to disown any claim to internal control of the thought that precipitated this feeling. This letting go of control facilitates the movement into external control and the /în/ combination. The process of experiencing MATÎN consists of a rather subtle emotional twist, and it takes time to gain proficiency in applying the Name, but the reward makes the journey worthwhile. Deep meditation facilitates its mastery.

Again as with MALIK, "watching the breath" for MATÎN can provide the key. Inhale into the /m/ feeling and then exhale a /t/ letting go of mental control to feel the /în/ paradox. One can progress from MALIK to MATÎN. As you gradually experience MALIK, the physical aspect that triggers the initial /ma/ glides into mental awareness. This transition facilitates the switch from MALIK to MATÎN. The generic feeling of letting things go generated by the /l/ gets supplanted whenever you realize that what you release consists of an idea, which needs a /t/ instead of an /l/. Once you have left the physical realm you don't need the /k/ anymore. Instead you enter into the depths of a meditative mind with the /în/.

## Traditional Use of MATÎN

*Matîn* translates into English as *steadfast* or *firm*. Muslims traditionally use this word to build a sense of resolve concerning some issue or situation. The SMY understanding does not correspond to the traditional one in any obvious sense. However, when you consider that under SMY reasoning *matîn* applies to times when you want to transform a pleasant feeling, gained from an idea you hold, into a feeling of being part of a universal mind, then you might begin to see *matîn* as establishing a firm foundation of being.

## Reaching an Ecstatic Level of Awareness with MAJÎD

For pleasant moments triggered by physical surroundings, MALIK works to improve mindful awareness. For pleasantness brought on by internal circumstances or insight, MATÎN works in a similar manner. Sometimes a surge of pleasant emotion arises that has neither strictly a physical source nor solely a mental one. That is, the pleasure somehow seems to occur as a positive emotional response to something physical that triggers an internal sense of belonging. The Name MAJÎD can help you realize those moments in a way that enhances the experience and brings you to a deeper state of mindfulness.

The formula for MAJÎD includes a target similar in some respects to that of MATÎN. Both of these Names have external control followed by some form of internal control as the target. In the case of MATÎN the internal control consists of /n/, a strong feeling of being in control. The /d/ in MAJÎD clings to the feeling of being in mental control. However, since it follows the /î/, the strong feeling of control blends the internal with the external. The difference in intermediate sounds/feelings in these two Names further distinguishes the effect of their usage. The /t/ in MATÎN releases mental attachment to the pleasant feeling, while the /j/ in MAJÎD holds on to the feeling of self-control generated by the pleasantness. You articulate the voiced, stop /j/ with the middle portion of the tongue. The middle part of the tongue corresponds to internal control of both physical and mental facets of emotion. This combination reflects our nature in the way that consciousness gets embedded in matter, where consciousness represents the mental and matter the physical. Thus the voiced /j/ sound/feeling conveys a desire to keep control over a unified self, neither mental nor physical alone.

Carrying the pleasant sensation, /m/, into the feeling of control of both physical and mental, /j/, and then sensing a merging of internal with external control, /îd/, causes the awareness associated with MAJÎD to have characteristics akin to descriptions of the state of samadhi mentioned in the *Yoga Sutras*. Much has been written about samadhi in the yoga literature. Most of these sources preface their words with some caveat like, "No words can adequately describe this state," but then go on with words... quite a few in many cases. Two of the most common short descriptions include "the knower and the known become one" and "an intense ecstatic feeling of being connected to everything." The first of these descriptions gives an intellectual viewpoint of the experience, while the second points to the emotional quality and the reason why words fall short.

If you do not have personal experience of such a state, when you hear it described with "ecstasy" and "connected to everything," you can only scratch your head and wonder what that must feel like, or perhaps shake your head in disbelief. However, before you dismiss the other-worldly nature as self-delusions of religious fanatics of some sort, consider what noted neuroscientist and ardent atheist, Sam Harris, has written on the topic. In his book, *Waking Up: A Guide to Spirituality without Religion,* Harris writes: "There were periods [during his years of meditation] during which all thought subsided, and any sense of having a body disappeared. What remained was a blissful expanse of conscious peace that had no reference point in any of the usual sensory channels."[45]

Mastery of MAJÎD can take a lifetime.

## Traditional Use of MAJÎD

*Majîd* translates into English as *majestic* or *glorious*. Muslims traditionally use this word to promote a feeling of majesty or appreciation of the glory of God, aka Allah. The blissful state associated with the SMY understanding of *majîd* easily fits into the class of glorious and majestic experiences.

## *Responding to Feelings of Good Fortune and Beauty with MÂLIK-UL-MULK*

Sometimes, due to the physical circumstances surrounding us, you may experience an overwhelming feeling of happiness or pleasure that puts you in a peaceful, relaxed state, a /mâ/ feeling. When good fortune affords such moments you can use MÂLIK-UL-MULK to maintain mindful awareness and avoid indulging in the feeling and getting lost in a daydream about your supposed specialness. You should seek the target of letting go of physical control. Because of the propitious situation that engendered the /mâ/ feeling you don't need control, and at the same time don't want to be controlled by the circumstances.

The first /k/ in MÂLIK-UL-MULK releases the physical control, but the Name does not stop there. The MÂLIK portion moves into /ul/, a somewhat reluctant feeling of letting things flow. This follow-up to the MÂLIK suggests that the initial letting go of physical control may not have finished without ramifications. The /ul/ captures the nature of the impact that MÂLIK has—that this particular kind of letting go does not come without discomfort, nor without regret. And certainly that makes sense. Its seems a natural instinct to keep holding on to control of something that powerful that it yields a captivating /mâ/ feeling. However, you need the /ul/ to gently move away from the treasured /mâ/ before moving into a /mu/ feeling, a bittersweet combination of pleasantness and displeasure. Bittersweet in the sense that you realize that, yes, it was a beautiful moment, but it cannot be retained. You need to let it go. This /mu/ sets up the final /lk/ that is a last effort to let things flow along without physical control, and this time it can take effect.

Using MÂLIK-UL-MULK in response to a fortunate experience of a /mâ/ moment could prove helpful, but one need not wait for such prosperous times to employ this Name. In fact the use of MÂLIK-UL-MULK during times of reflection and remembrance can help engender such /mâ/ moments for which you would then have the beneficial response of MÂLIK-UL-MULK ready in the wings, so to speak. Can the repetition of MÂLIK-UL-MULK really create such moments? This boils down to the question of whether the repetition of any Name can create the emotional state for which the Name theoretically resonates. Sufis believe, without a shred of doubt, that the Names do exactly that. As to the question of whether MÂLIK-UL-MULK can get you to see something in the world as mind-blowingly pleasant, consider that some think that such a feeling can occur from "every grain of sand," to quote a Nobel Laureate.[46] In other words it's all in the mind, anyway.

## Traditional Use of MÂLIK-UL-MULK

*Mâlik-ul-mulk* translates into English as *the eternal owner of sovereignty* or *the ultimate owner*. Muslims traditionally use *mâlik-ul-mulk* in order to develop a feeling of dignity and of being in control of one's own destiny. The SMY usage of *mâlik-ul-mulk* does fit this traditional interpretation in the sense that SMY usage applies to a physical situation that generates a relaxed pleasant feeling, a feeling that an owner might have when surveying their realm.

## *Reining in Hyper Thoughts with MÂNI'*

Sometimes a thought or idea triggers an overwhelming satisfying reaction, a wow kind of sensation that feels not just pleasant but also engenders a wave of emotion that washes over the body with a comforting "ah" feeling. This kind of scenario constitutes a /mâ/ combination. These types of occasions often strike as an "aha" moment and seem as though you have discovered some universal truth or great secret that you want to shout about. However, these /mâ/ flashes of insight can just as often act as the tip of something that takes hold of your imagination and flails it around as long as you hold on to the illusion of having discovered something of great depth and importance, when in reality it is only a delusion.

Whenever one of these /mâ/ moments occurs, you need to exercise restraint and control and not go rattling away indiscriminately and acting foolish. MÂNI' can help you abide with these great swells of thought in a mindful, alert manner, such that when the emotional surge dissipates you can properly evaluate the merit of the thoughts. These /mâ/ moments require a /n/ response that enables internal control to rise and keep the situation grounded. Tapping down the beautiful /mâ/ idea and bringing it under control with the /n/ can create an emotional reaction—a gotcha moment. The /'/ follows the /ni/ (the /i/ carries no valence but simply separates the two consonants) creating a cathartic ending to the captivating /mâ/ generating idea which releases you from your reverie.

## Traditional Use of MÂNI'

*Mâni'* translates into English as *the preventer*. Muslims traditionally use *mâni'* in an effort to keep something from occurring. The SMY usage of *mâni'* has the flavor of prevention in the sense that it applies the mental brakes and keeps you from going off half-cocked when a seemingly great idea appears.

## *Experiencing delightful times with MÂJID*

MÂJID and MAJÎD share many of the same sounds/feelings, the opening /m/ indicating the Names work with pleasant scenarios, and the final /d/ giving them both the target feeling of holding on to mental control. They also both share the /j/ sound/feeling which expresses a longing to keep control over an integrated self, which has both mental and physical aspects. Although these similarities do keep the effect of these Names related, the differences between the Names keep them distinct in their effect and when they best apply. The key difference between these two Names, /â/ versus /î/, points to their different effect and usage. In MAJÎD the pleasant feeling, for which you feel in control of—the /maj/—leads into the /îd/ combination, the exquisite feeling of external control that merges with internal control. In MÂJID the pleasant feeling itself has the central role as it brings on an awestruck relaxing feeling, which, again as with MAJÎD, this yields a feeling of total control of the self. However, the power of the /mâj/ takes on a special captivating flavor and removes the possibility of feeling outside control, and instead you feel only internal control, represented by the /d/. While both MÂJID and MAJÎD develop powerful emotional reactions to pleasant feelings, MAJÎD transcends the initial pleasant feeling into one of a more divine nature, but MÂJID focuses on the sentiment of awe generated by the /mâ/ before holding firmly on to a mental state of control.

## Traditional Use of MÂJID

*Mâjid* translates into English as *the noble*. Muslims traditionally use *mâjid* to promote a dignified feeling. The SMY interpretation of *mâjid* fits well with this understanding.

## *Chapter Summary*

The three Names beginning with /ma/ correspond in an interesting manner to three states of mind mentioned in Patanjali's *Yoga Sutras*. Patanjali describes three stages of meditation as: Contemplation, Concentration, and Samadhi. You can use MALIK when you contemplate your pleasant surroundings. If you get more deeply involved in meditation you evolve into a mental concentration that ignores the physical aspects and focuses on mental awareness, at which point MATÎN resonates. Finally, as you reach the deepest possible realm of awareness, akin to the samadhi of the *Yoga Sutras*, you enter the domain of MAJÎD.

You should not confuse states characterized by /ma/ with those of a /mâ/ nature. The former can lead to deeper and deeper meditative states, while the latter expose forms of indulgence. Of the three Names beginning with the awestruck /mâ/ MÂJID alone lets you reap a reward, so to speak, from the occasion. That is, MÂJID lets you hold on to the beauty of the moment. This follows from the type of situation for which MÂJID applies compared to the other two. MÂNI' applies to ideas or thoughts that floor you with their grandeur, and once acknowledged you must not grasp hold of them and lose yourself but return to mental control. MÂLIK-UL-MULK functions as a way to react to overwhelming beauty in your environment, and this too you must let go of to avoid attachment and mindlessness. However, because MÂJID addresses beauty that incorporates both mental and physical aspects, you get to feel in control and hold on to this moment. The Names beginning with /ma/ don't have this issue of indulgence. All three of those Names blend the feelings into a progressively better mindfulness without the need to steer away from the circumstances that precipitated them.

# CHAPTER 7
## ANOTHER STATE SIMILAR TO
## STREAM OF CONSCIOUSNESS

Two SMY Names begin with /sh/, another sound generated in a similar manner to /s/ and /z/ which characterizes stream of consciousness. All three of these sounds are sibilants, however the point of articulation for /sh/ occurs with the middle of the tongue as opposed to the tip which you utilize to form an /s/ or /z/. Because the tip of tongue generates /s/ and /z/, these sounds spawn mental gyrations associated with internal processes. Pressing the middle portion of the tongue upwards to produce the /sh/ gives the deliberations connected to this sound an association to something in the physical environment, since the further back you move on the tongue the greater the connection to mental interaction with physical aspects of control. The two Names in this chapter take different approaches to these types of mental modifications.

### *Witnessing the World Around You with SHAHÎD*
When attention gets diverted or distracted by something in the environment the mind will automatically process the stimulus. You cannot avoid this innate characteristic that has real survival benefits. However, you do have choices in how to deal with petty and/or annoying distractions that pose no particular threat and do not need any response, neither physical, nor emotional, nor mental. Simply ignoring the interruption as if it never happened would be ideal. However, often these interruptions can trigger some kind of mental chatter. You can avoid such ensnarement of distracting stimuli by practicing the Name SHAHÎD.

The /sh/ represents the automatically generated mental processing of a new stimulus, often a sound from something on the street outside or from an appliance or machine nearby. The target of /d/ puts us in the state of holding on to control. You want to get past the intrusion and reach a state of control by going through two intermediate states. First, drain out the /sh/ feeling using an /ḥ/. This stops the automatic mental processing of the distraction. Then recognize the outside control, represented by the /î/, coming from the interrupting stimulus. Once you have done these preliminary steps you can gain control with the /d/.

SHAḤÎD can work in both a meditation setting and in everyday situations. In both scenarios the use of the Name keeps your attention from being hijacked by some irrelevant outside stimulus and brings you back to a mindful present. This Name corresponds to the fifth step in yoga—sense withdrawal. By practicing SHAḤÎD you can better retreat into your inner world and facilitate success in the highest three rungs of yoga.

## Traditional Use of SHAḤÎD

The English translation of *shaḥîd* is *the witness*. Muslims use this name to enhance a feeling of awareness, usually of a particular phenomenon or occasion. The SMY interpretation of *shaḥîd* fits this theme comfortably.

## *Expressing Thankfulness with SHAKÛR*

The Name SHAḤÎD applies to situations where you don't want to let something in the environment distract you. In contrast, the other Name of Allah beginning with the /sh/ sound/feeling, SHAKÛR, helps in letting you show appreciation for something in your surroundings, for example the smell or sight of food that provides you sustenance. Showing appreciation, or thankfulness, does not usually fit into the framework of traditional mindfulness meditation. However, you can enhance mindfulness with SMY in a variety of contexts. It only requires a minimum of a few moments to put the practices to work. Certainly, you can use SHAKÛR during a typical meditation session. If you recognize a smell or sound which you appreciate, then by all means use SHAKÛR instead of SHAḤÎD. For example, if the sound of the furnace firing up intrudes on my awareness, I can recognize a feeling of appreciation with SHAKÛR for the heat that will soon result from the source of that sound. But don't limit the use of this SMY word, or any SMY word, to a traditional meditation setting. Any time you feel appreciation for something you directly perceive and have the opportunity for a few moments of reflection you can embrace that sentiment with an SMY rendition of SHAKÛR.

The target in this instance consists of the /ûr/ combination. The presence of the /û/ feeling might give one pause. Why feel unpleasant about something that you appreciate? Shouldn't that generate a feeling of pleasure? The answer to these queries has two parts. First, think of the /û/ as an empty, austere feeling devoid of pleasure, but not necessarily unpleasant. Reverence requires one to adopt such a countenance. Show your thankfulness not by indulgence but by expressing how the gift fulfills a need, some emptiness within. This brings us to the second component of the /ûr/ combination. The entity for which you express gratitude, for which you acknowledge need, brings something to your physical self. The /r/ part of the /ûr/ represents the energy, or sustaining force which the object provides.

The intermediate sound/feeling of SHAKÛR, the /k/, allows the release of any thought of being in control of the physical item which has aroused your attention. This release facilitates the feeling of emptiness of the /û/ and lets you back away from the possible pleasure derived from the stimulus. The release afforded by the /k/ also allows you to attribute the energy coming via the /r/ to something outside of you instead of being under your control.

## Traditional Use of SHAKÛR

The English translation of *shakûr* is *the appreciative.* Many use *shakûr* to express appreciation for something beneficial. The SMY use of *shakûr* follows this understanding.

## *Chapter Summary*

The mental processes represented by /sh/ have a connection to the physical environment. You get a constant barrage of stimuli from your environment and require successful filtering out of unimportant sensory data in order to function at an optimal level. Sometimes an unwanted noise or noxious smell or arresting sight can divert our attention. If you have trouble ignoring thoughts about the physical surroundings, especially during a meditation session, you should use SHAHÎD to address distractions and withdraw from the sensory input. On the other hand if you find something in your surroundings attractive and useful you can apply SHAKÛR to let you appreciate such physical amenities in a mindful, non-indulgent manner.

# CHAPTER 8
## OTHER MENTAL CONTROL ISSUES

The states of mind associated with stream of consciousness discussed in previous chapters, corresponding to /s/, /sh/, and /z/, cover many of the mental issues associated with stream of consciousness that can interfere with mindfulness. This chapter looks at four additional mental states that often impede one's effort to stay in the present. The issues that the Names in this chapter address quite often can be tied to the vows and observances of the *Yoga Sutras*; however, direct references will not always be made to these associations because it would tend to cloud the real issue—that you apply a specific Name to the emotional valence present in the moment.

The sounds of /d/, /l/, /n/, and /t/ all invoke some nuance of internal mental control that have less to do with an ongoing stream of thought than with some kind of active cognitive process. The /d/ indicates a desire to hold on to control, to keep the feeling that your thoughts or ideas hold importance and validity. The /t/, on the other hand, signifies nonchalance about a mental construct and willingness, or perhaps the intention, to let it evaporate. The /l/ actively lets mental processes flow along in an easy manner without holding on to any idea and without letting go of any, either. Finally, the /n/ represents the ultimate in mental control, void of any voice or stream of consciousness debating the issue. The /n/ generates a strong feeling of being in control.

Because of the dynamic nature of the feelings associated with these sounds they typically do not play central roles in a conventional meditation setting. However, don't shortchange the Names that deal with these mental control constructs. Learning how to deal with these psychological processes can prove helpful in establishing an ongoing state of everyday mindfulness.

## *Sticking to Your Guns with DARR*

Sometimes you feel a need to stand up for an idea, for example individual rights, the rights of others, or something that you have firsthand knowledge about. The Name DARR can facilitate the courage needed to stay the course when encountering such challenges. This simple Name has only an initial feeling and a target feeling. It does not use an intermediate sound to go from the initial desire to hold on to control, /d/, to the target of feeling energetic, /rr/. The double /r/ here indicates the stress placed on the feeling of vigor.

One should take care in picking the situations for using DARR. If you underestimate the power of your idea, using DARR could lead into arguments. Just wanting to be right should not mean that you should invoke DARR. If during a reflective time, you ponder a hypothetical situation where you need to stand up for a notion, then repeating the sequence of DARR with that scenario in mind can help you prepare for the actual time that you need to not back down.

## Traditional Use of DARR

*Darr* translates as *the distressor*. Muslims use *darr* to develop the ability to intimidate and make a viewpoint prevail. The SMY usage of *darr* coincides with this tradition.

## *Absolving with TAWWÂB*

Sometimes you may realize that a path taken has led or is leading in the wrong direction and you regret your actions. On these occasions you need to wipe the slate clean, get rid of the pangs of guilt for the missteps, and begin anew with a positive attitude. TAWWÂB can help you look past mistakes and arrive at a better outlook. The /t/ represents the initial mood of needing to give up on the idea or mental effort that went astray. The target here consists of the /âb/ combination, a relaxed, feel-good mood. In order to arrive at this target you need to purge regret and misgivings by expressing the /ww/. The /w/ appears twice to emphasize its importance. Moving forward cannot happen without relinquishing the shame and remorse, the feeling bad for the error.

Note that TAWWÂB works only whenever you feel bad about something under your control that resulted in a poor outcome or injustice. Without a negative feeling associated with a misdeed the /ww/ in TAWWÂB has nothing to release. TAWWÂB will work as an after the fact practice. That is, when you reflect on something and see its folly, using TAWWÂB can help dispel guilt that the missteps generated.

## Traditional Use of TAWWÂB

The English translation for *tawwâb* is *the acceptor of repentance.* Muslims traditionally use *tawwâb* if they wish to be forgiven. Feeling bad about our actions amounts to repentance. From an SMY viewpoint *Tawwâb* accepts this repentance and lets you start over.

## *Taking a Subtle Approach with LATÎF*

It can often pay to keep a low profile. Needlessly interjecting our opinions at inappropriate times serves little purpose. Letting things flow along whenever they do not appear headed for trouble or problems allows you to stay more mindful than if you unnecessarily vie for attention or control. LATÎF can help you achieve an easy-going approach and avoid meddling with things that do not need it.

The initial feeling, /l/, indicates a willingness or desire to let things flow. You cannot use LATÎF if you do not wish to lets things perk along without your assistance. The target, /f/, specifies the aim of contentedness. You don't just want to let things go. You want to feel satisfied with this approach. In order to reach the goal of the content /f/ you first have to rid yourself of any lingering investment in the present situation; the /t̲/ accomplishes this. This sound differs slightly from the English /t/ (indicated by the underline). To pronounce this sound your lips must round slightly. The result sounds almost like the English combination of /tu/. The feeling associated with the English /t/ consists of letting go of mental control. The Arabic /t̲/ adds another dimension to this release—reluctance.

After the /t̲/ frees your mind from wanting to impose control the /î/ follows, bringing in a feeling of being under external control. This external control can simply be whatever in the environment appears in control at the moment. Of course the Sufis recognize the outside force as Allah. Your desire to let things flow and release mental control should allow this feeling of outside control to percolate without any problems. The recognition of an outside force controlling the situation allows the contented /f/ to manifest.

## Traditional Use of LATÎF

*Latîf* translates as *the subtle, the refined.* Muslims use *latîf* when they want to enhance their ability to express subtlety. The SMY understanding of *latîf* as letting go and feeling content might be understood as leaving a light touch, a subtle spirit.

## *Displaying a Flash of Insight with NÛR*

If you have the opportunity or desire to teach someone, whether in a formal classroom, an apprenticeship, or teaching a child or grandchild, you can use NÛR to enhance the effectiveness of your teaching ability by keeping your ego in check and your focus on the material you teach.

When you assume the role of a teacher you should have developed solid control of the mental ideas and constructs of your material. Solid mental control indicates an /n/ mood. The target of NÛR, /r/, indicates an active level of energy. You cannot expect a student to grasp information if you deliver it in a staid manner. Notice that the target says nothing about the subject matter, since the premise of using NÛR presumes you know the topic. NÛR only concerns the best approach for the instruction, the teaching style.

The intermediate sound/feeling, /û/, sets an austere mood and allows energy generated via the /r/ to focus on the information you want to convey and avoid distractions, such as feeling good about your role as a teacher. The /û/ keeps potential ego trips in check. Although a sense of humor and a lighthearted attitude often prove helpful in establishing a good rapport with students, the approach you need for the actual act of teaching the subject material should stay devoid of pleasantness. Yes, do establish good rapport, laugh at life's foibles as they arise, and take pleasure in the relationships and experiences. However, don't let the pleasure distract from your work. Taking pleasure in your mental control will likely appear as indulgence and in any event will not contribute to getting your point across. You need to learn how to separate the social aspects of the situation from the teaching. NÛR says: to teach, take your mental control and act in an animated but austere manner.

## Traditional Use of NÛR

The English translation of *nûr* is *the light.* Muslims use *nûr* to experience the light of knowledge. The SMY usage of *nûr* concurs in this: a good teacher can be a light unto the world.

## *Celebrating Success with NÂFI'*

A number of Names, including NÂFI', help celebrate good fortunes and auspicious happenings. Choosing which of the celebratory Names depends upon the salient feature of your mood as you appraise the favorable place in which you find yourself. With SHAKÛR the imprint from the surroundings triggered the initial /sh/ feeling. The scenario that fits with the use of NÂFI' occurs when your attention dwells on a strong feeling of internal control, a realization that events have turned out like you wanted and/or engineered. When things go your way you should not gloat or feel prideful. You can use NÂFI' to keep from showing excitement, which might come across as bragging, and stay more mindful of the moment.

The target of NÂFI' consists of an ayin, /'/. This sound responds to that "lump in the throat" feeling with a cathartic release of emotion. In this case the irresistible surge of emotion in response to your fortuity precedes the release afforded by the /'/. The first intermediate sound, /â/, ensures a relaxed state, a way to bask in and enjoy your state of mind without seeming boastful. Following this the /f/ tags on a feeling of contentment that generates the swelling of emotion which gets released by the /'/. Think of the /'/ as a release valve that takes away the surge of feeling before it can infect your ego with potentially poisonous grandiose gloating.

## Traditional Use of NÂFI'

*Nâfi'* translates as *the propitious.* Some Muslims use *nâfi'* when they wish to experience a fortuitous outcome or event. The SMY interpretation fits the traditional meaning in the sense that it suggests the usage of *nâfi'* in propitious times, however, not as a means to engender such times. That is, *nâfi'* can help you acknowledge propitious times in a non-boasting or indulgent, but instead respectful, manner.

## *Chapter Summary*

The psychological issues dealt with by the Names in this chapter take on one of two flavors: being in control and letting go of control. DARR fosters an energetic agenda when you want to keep in control. In a similar vein NÂFI' allows you to accept feelings of strong control in a gracious manner, while NÛR helps you to better manage situations involving feelings of control. On the other hand TAWWÂB helps when you feel a need to release the control of something that has gripped you, and LATÎF facilitates situations when you want to just let things flow smoothly without interfering. Learning how and when to use these formulas can help you gain ground in establishing a lifestyle of mindfulness.

# CHAPTER 9

## ADDRESSING AGITATED, STRESSED, OR VIGILANT STATES

For some the primary intrusions to meditation arise from stream of consciousness, the seemingly ever-present mental churning of the mind. However, for many, a number of other distractions hinder progress of getting into deeper states with perhaps the number one issue centering on posture. Sitting still and holding a comfortable position for a period long enough to enter into deep meditation requires a vibrant, strong, healthy physique. As a result of the physical requirement of mindfulness meditation some programs dedicated to mindfulness, including Mindful Based Stress Reduction pioneered by Jon Kabat-Zinn, include hatha yoga exercises, more commonly just called yoga exercises.[47]

Yoga exercises, popular in today's culture, consist of holding various physical poses and stretches and typically stress duration rather than repetition of the pose. My first yoga instructor told our class the purpose of practicing yoga postures was to make the body strong enough to sit comfortably for the long period necessary for deep meditation. Surprisingly the *Yoga Sutras*, the cited origin of the many flavors and styles of yoga in existence today, has only three sutras dedicated to posture. The first of these states that posture should be steady and comfortable. From early on yogis understood that if you wanted steady and comfortable posture you needed a fit body and a fit body required maintenance—thus the practice of strengthening exercises.

The second sutra on this topic says that steady and comfortable posture comes from relaxation of physical effort and meditation on the endless. Some of the modern schools of yoga do not appear to practice "relaxation of effort," but on the contrary they engage students in quite strenuous workouts. Of course from the standpoint of the *Yoga Sutras* such exercises serve only as a preliminary for actual yoga, and a vigorous workout can make relaxation come easily and thus enhance a meditation session. As for the second part of this sutra, meditation on the endless, most mindfulness schools of today follow this advice when you consider breath as endless.

The third sutra on posture states that achieving steady and comfortable posture will prevent the attack of opposites, although the nature of these opposites and what their attacks consist of does not get mentioned. The SMY interpretation of the pairs of opposites originates from the poles of the dimensions of emotions. Specifically, in regard to Patanjali's pairs of opposites SMY identifies the opposites of relaxed and energized in the arousal dimension of emotion and pleasant and uncomfortable in the pleasure dimension. If you cannot remain steady, one of Patanjali's directives for posture, then an attack comes from opposites of arousal-relaxation. This chapter shows how certain Names deal with situations that arise as a result of such a clash between aroused physical sensations and a desire to relax. In later chapters Names address attack of opposites that occur whenever you cannot stay comfortable and shift between pleasant and uncomfortable sensations.

If you have sufficient strength to sit still for a period long enough to achieve successful meditation, then you might not need to worry about attacks from the pairs of opposites. However, if you do not have such strength your meditation will suffer. Your body requires some form of physical exercise to keep it in good enough shape to endure long sessions of sitting. SMY does not include physical exercises, but it does include a number of sequences that you can use to address the pairs of opposites referred to in Patanjali's sutra. Not everyone can participate in hatha yoga and physical exercises that tone the body and keep it optimally strong. You may have an injury or permanent disability that keeps you from exercising as much as needed for a strong body. As you get older your body will not tolerate as much physical activity. Sore muscles can distract from meditation. Sitting still (recommended for SMY, but not absolutely necessary) can become difficult. Rather than skipping meditation because of any of these physical issues you can use SMY exercises to combat what Patanjali calls the attack of the pair of opposites and extend and even deepen your meditation.

During traditional meditation, uncomfortable posture—an antsy feeling—may occur after you have sat for a while. You want to relax, but your body doesn't want to sit still—the clash of opposites. In these instances a name with an initial /r/ can help to settle you down and extend the productive time of your meditation. Additionally, you can often bring bodily tension into a meditation session, in which case a Name beginning with /r/ can tame these feelings and help your meditation begin on a suitable track.

Besides helping smooth out meditation the Names beginning with /r/ can provide relief in everyday situations, for example, when you feel stressed or angry and wish to relax and chill instead. Names applying in such cases have little or nothing to do with posture but tend more to do with tension, anxiety, and stressful circumstances that induce an innate fight or flight response.

## *Finding Comfort with RA$\underline{H}$MÂN*

The Name RA$\underline{H}$MÂN provides an excellent means for relief from feeling stressed. Perhaps tensions from a high pressure job get your blood pressure up. Maybe you even get a bit angry because you have to do something a second time. The fast-paced lifestyle that many people experience often generates an unhealthy level of stressful arousal. RA$\underline{H}$MÂN gives you a way to step back from omnipresent demands and affords some relief.

In RA$\underline{H}$MÂN the target feeling consists of a relaxing sense of control provided by /ân/. To get there from the aroused /ra/ you need two intermediate sounds/feelings, /$\underline{h}$/ and /m/. When faced with a stressful aroused /r/ feeling, the /$\underline{h}$/ cuts off the flow of arousing energy by draining out the /r/. Feeling the /$\underline{h}$/ in the abdomen as you exhale can enhance the process. The /$\underline{h}$/ should provide some relief from the agitation and let a feeling of /m/ in your heart center come quite naturally when you breathe in. This pleasant feeling allows the subsequent /ân/ to easily seep into awareness. You should feel relaxed and back in control.

While RAHMÂN can help relieve stress and let you feel in better control of your life's struggles, the Name also finds use during meditation, whenever you experience physical discomfort and perhaps need to change position from sitting too long. Using SMY principles with RAHMÂN you can facilitate a smooth transition from the movement of changing posture, stretching, flexing, or whatever physical movement you require at that moment, back to your meditation practice.

## Traditional Use of RAHMÂN

*Rahmân* translates into English as *gracious and beneficent*. *Rahmân* holds the first position in the traditional list of ninety-nine attributes of universal consciousness. When people memorize the attributes by speaking them, *rahmân* traditionally gets pronounced first. Muslims use it to refer to the gracious nature of Allah or God. SMY notes the beneficial nature of *rahmân* to relieve stress. Starting an SMY meditation with *rahmân* can help get you settled into meditation and make yourself comfortable.

## *Finding Physical Comfort and Mental Relief with RAHÎM*

RAHÎM begins like RAHMÂN with /rah/ but RAHÎM differs in its target feeling. Instead of feeling relaxed and in control like RAHMÂN, with RAHÎM you want the relief from the aroused /r/ state to manifest though a pleasant outside force that assumes control of the situation. Like with RAHMÂN when the arousing /r/ feeling comes into focus, make an effort to purge it with the /h/, paying attention to the contraction of the abdominal muscles, if possible. Then, instead of immediately feeling the physical pleasure that expulsion affords, as happens with the /mâ/ of RAHMÂN, you derive a sensation of pleasure by feeling a desired presence of external control, achieved through the /îm/. You can enhance this feeling as you breathe in by letting your awareness rise to the space between the ears as you detect the /î/ feeling. This can automatically generate an /m/ feeling that engulfs your entire being.

One way to use RAḤÎM might be to help release an aggressive impulse triggered by anger. The /ḥ/ releases the /ra/ before you let the /î/ indicate some force has control. This recognition of outside influence allows you to back off from any antagonistic posturing. The subsequent /m/ smooths over ruffled feelings.

The key to effective use of RAḤÎM lies in the desire to feel the presence of external force controlling you. You may accomplish this feeling with a non-theist viewpoint. One way might be to adopt the notion of a universal consciousness that you can tap into. Another way could be feeling the norms of society weighing on your conscience. You may also envision the /î/ feeling as coming through a right-brain experience, a non-rational intuition that guides you, again like a form of consciousness. In any case, to achieve the /î/ feeling, one must abandon the feeling that the self that you identify with has control.

RAḤÎM can prove helpful during meditation as well as other settings. If during meditation you detect subtle physical discomfort you may not need the relaxing remedy afforded by RAHMÂN. Sometimes the expression of the /raḥ/ will rid the body of the annoyance such that you can seek the meditative sanctuary of the /îm/. In daily stressful situations when you have the opportunity to take time for some SMY reflection, you may find that the feeling of letting go of control to a trusted outside force rather than physical relaxation provides a better solution to the situation.

## Traditional Use of RAḤÎM

*Rahîm* translates into English as *merciful* and *compassionate*. This word appears second in the traditional list of the attributes or Names of Allah. Muslims use *rahîm* to refer to the merciful nature of Allah. The SMY use of *rahîm* can help control anger and allow you to develop compassion in anger's place. The Name also brings relief from physical discomfort while allowing you to stay in a meditative state, certainly a form of compassion if thought as coming from an external power, as this word indicates.

## *Compassion, a Different Kind of Comfort with RA'ÛF*

What determines whether you choose the target feeling of /f/ for an uncomfortable or stressed state rather than RAHMÂN or RAHÎM can depend on different factors. The use of an /h/ after a /ra/ agitation induces a pleasant feeling, either of relaxed personal control or desirable outside control, but the /h/ requires an active effort that may not be appropriate or available if your body lacks strength or has an illness or injury that prevents such a strong response as the /h/ requires. These situations might not call for a pleasurable outcome, especially if you have a painful condition. In such times whenever you feel agitated or stressed, work for a target mood of subdued contentment via the Name RA'ÛF. In this Name the contented feeling /f/ gets subdued by the austere, empty /û/.

The intermediate bridge to the target in this case comes through a /'/, a hamza, which you express as a break in the breath. The /'/ doesn't have a sound that you can express by itself. It just breaks off the previous sound. This break after the /ra/ interrupts the agitated state and makes the target of /ûf/ possible. The break afforded by the /'/ does not provide the dramatic relief derived from the /h/, but the hamza does create a separation from the annoyance at hand. The breathing that can augment the positive effect of RA'ÛF consists of a short break at the end of exhalation. This lets you feel a kind of clearing or separation from the /ra/, which then allows you to experience an /û/ feeling, an acknowledgment of the emptiness or lack of pleasure in your current state. Finally, the contented /f/ completes the sequence and you attain the target feeling, not one of pleasure, but of calm acceptance.

### Traditional Use of RA'ÛF

The English translation for *ra'ûf* is *the compassionate, the gentle, one full of pity.* Muslims use *ra'ûf* to help realize compassionate feelings in a situation that calls for gentleness. Certainly, when you experience suffering due to illness or bodily injury you can benefit from compassion. *Ra'ûf* can help you get through those rough times.

## *Staying Alert with RAQÎB*

Since one should stay alert during meditation, some level of arousal proves necessary and beneficial. Although you don't usually consciously register any such vigilance, at times such a focus can occur in a natural fashion, especially when you make an effort to clear the mind. You might have that "wired" feeling of being alive and wide awake. If you notice this type of /r/ state of alertness during meditation, but don't feel any physical discomfort, no aches from sitting too long, then you can transform the energy from the /r/ into a pleasant feeling of external control with the Name RAQÎB. The target feeling in this case consists of the /îb/ combination, a feeling of external control yielding a goodness that you grasp. You attain this target via a somewhat reluctant letting go of control, as denoted by the /q/.

In settings other than meditation you can use RAQÎB to direct or sublimate excess energy from nervousness or boredom by consciously letting go of control via the /q/. In these instances you forego taking initiative to control any aspect of the environment and allow an outside force of your choice—God, Allah, Universal Consciousness, or simply right-brain functions—to take over your awareness, via the /î/. In order for this surrender to an outside force to achieve the goal of feeling pleasure you must have a positive sentiment associated with outside energy.

RAQÎB shares similarities with RAHÎM. Both deal with aroused states and both work toward feeling good about external control. The intermediate stages of the words, which transport the arousal to pleasantness, determine whether the experience of the pleasantness occurs in a basic /m/ manner or a more charged /b/ fashion. The /h/ of RAHÎM drains out the arousal, while the /q/ of RAQÎB yields control of the arousal to the external power. Thus the state of awareness still retains energy, which gets put to use by the /b/ as it holds on to the pleasant feeling generated by the sequence.

## Traditional Use of RAQÎB

*Raqîb* translates into English as *watchful*. Muslims traditionally use *raqîb* to generate an observant countenance, to keep awareness at a high level. Use the Name *raqîb* to maintain a high level of awareness, in which you simply watch things unfold. *Raqîb* helps you control energy when you deem it better not to use your energy to act.

## *Seeking Answers with RASHÎD*

The Name RASHÎD finds use in times of contemplation whenever you have a keyed up desire for specific knowledge. The person using RASHÎD explicitly tunes attention of the senses with an expectation, or at least a desire, to gather insight or direction. The source of that inspiration might be a teacher whom the person respects or follows as a student. The stimulation may also come from internal visions or a reassuring voice.

The initial sound of RASHÎD, /r/, indicates a level of arousal. Typically if you enter contemplation you would push away the arousal with one of the previous four Names beginning with this sound. However, if you recognize the excitement as a drive for understanding or knowledge about something, you can apply the energy to a search for a way forward in your quest. Both RASHÎD and SHAHÎD contain the /sh/ sound/feeling that indicates mental processing triggered by some form of stimulus. In SHAHÎD the /sh/ processing occurs spontaneously and impedes our meditation or protrudes into our everyday awareness. In these cases something from the outside impinges on our consciousness. In RASHÎD the /sh/ works as an intermediate step toward the goal, a step that you initiate. With RASHÎD you invite input.

You can characterize the energetic /r/ state that instigates this desire for outside stimulation as an innate drive to know how to proceed, a yearning for knowledge, when facing choices. Do not confuse this yearning with Wrong Thinking, that is, thinking about a problem. The mental chatter associated with Wrong Thinking, that you soothe with SALÂM, will not occur in this circumstance. Instead you simply feel a drive. For some this might seem impossible, since in our highly verbal society we very naturally attach problems to something that gets expressed verbally, be it with others or to ourselves. If you can forestall that chatter and feel the natural instinct to survive and thrive that all humans possess, then you can take advantage of the Name RASHÎD.

You invoke the intermediate /sh/ of RASHÎD as a form of listening and looking and feeling for the answer to the problem driving you. This can occur quite naturally when you pay attention to a teacher. However, this type of tuning all senses can take place during meditation or contemplative times as well. Sufis and other meditators often report seeing visions or hearing the voice of a teacher who is not present during meditation. RASHÎD can facilitate such mystical experiences. The /î/ in RASHÎD allows the feeling of outside control to happen. This might be the control of a teacher whom you listen to or an outside control of a force that you trust or invoke.

The final /d/ of RASHÎD lands you back with a feeling of holding on to being in control. The final combination of /îd/ works differently in SHAHÎD than in RASHÎD. In SHAHÎD you acknowledge the external control brought on by the unwanted stimulus and then take control with the /d/. In RASHÎD you seek the external control and through it you find control. To state that in another way: you find control in your life by giving up control to an outside force/teacher. In this instance the two sounds work in tandem, making the target an /îd/ combination, whereas in SHAHÎD, the /î/ and the /d/ do not fuse together in this same manner.

## Traditional Use of RASHÎD

The English translation of *rashîd* is *the guide* or *the teacher.* Muslims might use *rashîd* to call on a guide or teacher. The SMY usage of *rashîd* agrees with this interpretation.

## *Getting the Job Done with RAZZÂQ*

RAZZÂQ provides an example of a Name that doesn't fit a traditional meditation setting. The initial sound/feeling of /r/ and the target of /q/ indicate the scenarios in which this word applies, a time when you have energy, an aroused state of some sort, but want or need to let go of controlling how to use the energy. An example might consist of a situation where you have responsibilities dealing with your physical existence and feel reluctant to act because you would rather do something else; however in reality you see no alternative—a job that you feel obligated to do, but do not feel enthusiastic about doing. You still remain in control in that you consciously control the movement of muscles, however reluctantly, with the sense that what you are doing is not cognitively driven or perhaps not voluntarily chosen.

In order to mentally let go of your physical situation you need the help of two intermediate feelings. The first one, the /zz/, sets your mental chatter to a low-key mindset. This keeps you from fretting over your predicament via a flurry of lively stream of consciousness. The /zz/ lets you operate in automatic fashion without debating what's happening. The second intermediate sound, the /â/ relieves you of any anxiety and agitation present and puts you in a relaxed state in order that the reluctant release of control can transpire.

You can see how this flow of awareness doesn't fit a meditation setting. One does not meditate reluctantly. You can use the Name of RAZZÂQ when pondering or meditating on a situation or job that you feel you need to do. In a non-meditation setting where you engage in uninviting work, repeating the name out loud or silently, or better yet, feeling the emotional valence of the name, can help you get through the task in a better frame of mind.

## Traditional Use of RAZZÂQ

The English translation of *razzâq* is *the provider.* Some Muslims use *razzâq* in order to help them realize or take on the attributes of a provider. The SMY interpretation of *razzâq* lends itself to the concept of a provider in the sense that its usage fits in situations where you must complete tasks for which you do not choose, which often occurs for a daily wage earner.

## *Stepping Back in Awe with* RÂFI'

The final Name that begins with an aroused /r/, RÂFI', might find use during a meditation or prayer setting. If you feel energetic about meditation or prayer, RÂFI' can help you take that energy and direct it into a calm, content emotional experience. The /â/ relaxes the energy of the moment and lets the contented /f/ pervade consciousness. This can create an emotional response that gets released with the ayin, /'/.

RÂFI' can also help to guide a response to circumstances that you find touching, something moving, perhaps a work of art or someone's actions or even a presence. The registration of the initial stimulus appropriate for inducing the feelings of RÂFI' should occur at a gut level, a physical feeling, not in the head, as happens with a mental /sh/ that corresponds to a SHAKÛR response of appreciation. In order to register some object in this manner you must be alert and taking in the situation, as expressed by the /r/. The target feeling in this case consists of /'/, an ayin. You feel the /'/ as an emotional burst, a catharsis. In order to get to this target of raw emotion from our alert state you need to first attain a relaxed, contented state through feeling the /âf/ combination. The relaxed, contented /âf/ acts as a check valve on the energy of the initial /r/ state. Going straight from /r/ to /'/ risks losing grip of emotional equilibrium.

Repeating or feeling the Name in real time, i.e., as you feel moved by something in your awareness, can augment mindfulness of the situation. During periods of reflection you might recall a situation of this nature. You can practice the sounds/feelings of RÂFI' at that time in order to engender the response in future scenarios.

## Traditional Use of RÂFI'

The English translation of *râfi'* is *the exalter.* Some Muslims use *râfi'* to praise someone or something. When you witness things that stir an emotional response of appreciation and wonder, use *râfi'* to engage in the appreciation in a mindful way that expresses the awe in a controlled, gentle, yet expressive manner.

## *Chapter Summary*

Psychologists agree that we require some level of stress for optimal performance in this world. However, it is just as clear that too much arousal can produce harmful levels of cortisone and other hormones which generate negative health consequences. The Names in this chapter deal with the energetic /r/ state by either trying to subdue it and provide relief or by recognizing it as a favorable level and allowing it to get a necessary job done.

Three Names aim to reduce stress levels. RAHMÂN affords a good way to reduce stress and feel in control. RAHÎM also reduces stress but instead allows you to let go of control. Both of these Names assume a robust underlying physical core. For situations where you have a physical ailment to deal with and the pleasant /m/ found in the previous two Names can't be reached, RA'ÛF can prove useful in easing the psychological strain such a condition can induce.

Four Names use an energetic /r/ state to accomplish a necessary objective. The simplest of these, RAQÎB, proves useful when you must pay attention, passive but alert. A more engaging RASHÎD can help you focus your energy on solutions to problems, while RAZZÂQ allows you to pursue mundane but necessary tasks in a mindful way. Finally, RÂFI' lets you channel hyped up approval into appropriate appreciation.

# CHAPTER 10
## CEDING CONTROL OF YOUR PHYSICAL ENERGY

The sounds /k/, /kh/, and /q/ have an emotional quality that signifies engagement with the physical environment without a subjective feeling of being in control or working in your physical self-interest. Such activities might include work at tasks not of your choosing or engagement in endeavors for which you do not need to attend due to their automated nature. Nobody controls all aspects of their physical environment all of the time. One must often relinquish personal desires or volition in order to do what is socially mandated as correct or necessary. Sometimes this happens willingly, such as at a task that you do not choose or do not benefit from directly but nevertheless like. At other times action takes place reluctantly, perhaps on a distasteful job, necessary for financial reasons. For typical agreeable exploits a /k/ expresses the feeling, or a /kh/ for more urgent or stressful efforts. An unwilling or reserved release of physical control carries a /q/ feeling.

If you discern no outside entity causing you to engage in physical activity the situation may invoke more subtle shades of ceding control indicated by a /k/, /kh/, or /q/. These circumstances usually involve automatic movement, where your mind doesn't dwell on how to do things. In these instances you relinquish bodily control because you know the procedure so well that no cognitive control need take place.

## *Giving Your Energy to a Cause with KARÎM*

When opportunities arise to do something beneficial for another person or group, you often have to sacrifice your time and energy in a way that has no physical benefit, but in fact costs resources. These things you do willingly with a faith that they will create good, pleasant feelings in those aided, and as a reward, the same emotion simultaneously will occur in you for providing the assistance. Using

97

the Name KARÎM in these situations can augment mindfulness as you observe the process unfolding. You can also practice with KARÎM if you wish to devote your energy in such endeavors.

The goal in this situation consists of a simple pleasant /m/. A selfless act does not need to be painful or unpleasant. Giving up some of your energy, if done with reason and wisdom, should not hurt you, but rather fill you with joy that your abundance could provide assistance to another person. The intermediate steps of /r/ and /î/ move you from the /k/ to the /m/. The /r/ indicates the energy needed for the task at hand. The /î/ marks a surrender of mental control, a necessary step. If you felt that mentally you had control of the venture it could easily amount to self-aggrandizement and an inflated ego, a quality not conducive to mindfulness.

## Traditional Use of KARÎM

The translation for *karîm* is *the generous.* Muslims use *karîm* to increase the capacity or desire to act in a generous manner to others. If you want to develop your generosity you can repeat the name *karîm* out loud, in your heart silently, or feel the sequence of emotional values of the sounds in your entire being.

## *Taking on a Task with Optimism with KABÎR*

Sometimes a person will work without feeling in control, not to help others, but to fulfill an obligation, for example, an occupation which generates income that supports a family. Instead of wanting to help others, the goal boils down to a simple desire to do a good job in order to benefit from the reward for such effort. If you approach these circumstances without reluctance, in a /k/ mood, then the Name KABÎR can help you labor in a mindful fashion.

The goal of /r/ in KABÎR indicates a wish to keep up the energy level, and have stamina to get the job done. The presence of the first intermediate sound /b/ allows you to feel positive about what you do, since /b/ generates a feeling of holding on to a good feeling. The next sound, /î/, acknowledges the outside force for which you work, perhaps your boss, or the company. With KABÎR you can work for someone with an energetic, positive outlook.

## Traditional Use of KABÎR

The English translation for *kabîr* is *the great one.* Muslims use *kabîr* in order to generate a feeling of confidence. Repeating the word KABÎR, or feeling the sequence, can help you develop a positive mindful attitude to a job.

## *Letting Go of Control with KHABÎR*

The previous Name, KABÎR, differs from the current KHABÎR only by the initial feeling, a /k/ vs a /kh/. These two unvoiced stop consonants get articulated in similar fashion, via the back of the tongue. This produces a feeling of releasing control of the physical surroundings. The /kh/'s harder pushing of the tongue against the back of the throat gives the /kh/'s release of control a more urgent feeling than that of the /k/. This difference distinguishes the circumstances for the contrasting usages of these words. The feeling of urgency in giving up control may come for various reasons. Instead of applying to normal routines of acting without control, as in the case with KABÎR, the presence of an insistent drive to surrender control indicates special or unusual circumstances—these call for KHABÎR. Such an occasion might occur whenever you see a more qualified person to do a task and you feel a need to let them take over, or perhaps you just feel a driving need to step back for whatever reason. The target of /r/ indicates that although you have ceded control you remain alert, perhaps so that you can learn from the situation.

The first intermediate sound/feeling of /b/ indicates that the urgent giving up of control generated a pleasant feeling worth holding on to. The subsequent /î/ induces a feeling of being under control of an outside force. For KHABÎR the /î/ blends with the /r/ so that the energy and alert target feeling, the /r/, gets tied to the feeling of external control. This engenders a sense that the stepping back from control was to let something external take charge. To some extent this blend of /îr/ also takes place in KABÎR, but due to the urgent nature of ceding control with KHABÎR, the effect of the /î/ on the /r/ comes to the fore.

## Traditional Use of KHABÎR

The English translation for *khabîr* is *the aware*. Muslims use *khabîr* to facilitate awareness of surroundings and an individual's place in the world. Awareness covers a broad area of consciousness and emotional reality. Connecting the SMY interpretation of *khabîr* to awareness does make some sense, if you consider the urgency of the giving up control as stepping back and the target of arousal as an indication of sustained awareness.

## *Accepting with KHÂLIQ*

The Name KHÂLIQ helps takes the edge off of an urgent need to relinquish physical control, a /kh/ feeling. The target feeling, /q/, retains the feeling of letting go of physical control, but without urgency and instead with an austere quality. KHÂLIQ accomplishes this conversion with the help of two intermediate sounds, /â/ and /l/. The first of these, the /â/, induces relaxation. The /l/ then provides a feeling of letting things flow.

The target of KHÂLIQ, /q/, shares much with the initial letter, /kh/. Both of these sounds correspond to ceding physical control, in the case of /kh/, a feeling of urgency prevails, and in the case of /q/ a lack of enthusiasm. Thus, this Name takes you from a pressing need to relinquish control to an austere release. This transition might fit a scenario where you feel it urgently necessary to make a change in protocol or plans of some sort, but don't really see any ideal alternatives. Perhaps you have to hand over the reins in a project because of pressing needs elsewhere, but you don't see the right person to take over. If you relax, as indicated by /â/, and let things flow smoothly, via the /l/, then you can let go in a more mindful fashion, not with any pleasure, but at least without nervous tension.

Sometimes KHÂLIQ can prove useful in a meditation setting. The act of sitting still during meditation can mandate ceding physical control in certain instances. This happens to me whenever I have a muscle that feels in need of massage or some kind of movement. In order to exorcise the urge to stretch the muscle I use KHÂLIQ to settle into my meditation. The urgent need to give up physical control expressed by the /kh/ corresponds to my dilemma. With KHÂLIQ I control this desire by relaxing and letting things flow. This leads me to the point where I have conquered my desire to move and can enter into meditation.

## Traditional Use of KHÂLIQ

The English translation of *khâliq* is *the creator* or *the planner*. Muslims traditionally use *khâliq* to enhance their ability to create or plan things for which they have responsibility. The SMY interpretation does not seem to fit easily with the traditional one. One would think that creating and planning need to happen with control. The initial state and target of KHÂLIQ indicate release of control. Relaxing and letting things flow (/âl/) would indicate a lack of concrete plan.

## *Gladly Ceding Power with KHÂFID*

In some circumstances pushing a point of view leads to conflict or disappointment. This might occur when you disagree with another person who has a stake in the situation. In order to avoid a confrontation at these times, stepping back and letting somebody else take over can often be the wise decision. A similar stepping back happens with KHABÎR but with a different target. With KHABÎR the goal is awareness or alertness generated by the /r/ because you want to stay observant. With KHÂFID the /d/ indicates a desire to hold on to gain control of your thoughts and keep it. In this case you don't need to observe but rather need to avoid a feeling of being dominated by letting another take over. Giving up physical power in an urgent manner with /kh/, although deemed necessary in these instances, can still humble you. You want to hand over power without generating self-doubt, thus the target of /d/. Two important intermediate sounds/feelings get us to that confident /d/. First comes the relaxing /â/. It dials down the worry and stress usually present in /kh/ moments. The /f/ follows for further mellowing before finally arriving at the target.

## Traditional Use of KHÂFID

The English translation of *khâfid* is *the humbler* or *the debaser*. Muslims use this word to bring humility into one's life. The SMY understanding of *khâfid* fits with this in the sense that you can use *khâfid* to humbly step back and let another take over in a physical enterprise. However, this does not cede mental control or confidence.

## *Enhancing Reflective Times with QUDDÛS*

I find it significant that only one of the ninety-nine Names ends with an /s/. Experiencing the strong stream of consciousness, an /s/ state, rarely lends itself to mindfulness. The /û/ preceding the /s/ provides the key to making the /s/ work in a mindful manner. This effectively makes the target in QUDDÛS a /ûs/ instead of a simple /s/. An /ûs/ feeling means no pleasure in our thought stream. It corresponds to serious thinking, pondering devoid of any kind of pleasure.

Likewise to understand the initial sound/feeling for QUDDÛS, that which dictates the appropriate times for its use, you need to consider the /qud/ sequence. This involves a feeling of letting go of physical control, but retaining mental control. This occurs when you study printed material, books, diagrams, etc., since in these instances you ignore the physical surroundings and ramp up mental focus. The /qud/ also describes how one might approach reflective moments. When you reflect on a problem of life or what has transpired that day, you are not exercising any physical control but just thinking.

Putting together the above described initial and target situations you can see that QUDDÛS finds its niche as a Name that facilitates intellectual pursuits. Repeating this Name or its emotional sequence can enhance time spent philosophizing, studying, or reflecting.

## Traditional Use of QUDDÛS

The English translation for *quddûs* is *the holy*. Muslims use *quddûs* when they wish to feel a holy presence, as though in a sacred ambiance. In order to feel holy or the presence of something holy the ego needs subdued. The SMY interpretation of *quddûs* lends itself to such a toned down version of the self, to somebody in search of answers to the mystery of existence, to a sacred understanding.

## *Acting with Confidence with QÂDIR*

In our society everyone faces many situations where they must act in an environment where they cannot control all of the physical elements. For example, an individual drives a car in the midst of many, many other cars that others control. People work in teams on projects where one person's efforts join those of many. If you have trepidations in these types of circumstances then you can use QÂDIR to help you act with confidence.

The initial /q/ reflects unease with the inability to control everything. The intermediate, /â/, eliminates agitation and induces a relaxed state. Once you have removed the tension due to the lack of physical control you can achieve the target of /dir/. These two sounds, /d/ and /r/, work together. The /d/ generates mental control that allows you to focus and the /r/ represents the energy you need to apply in order to get your part of the job done.

Paying attention to the contraction of the abdominal as you breathe out and feel the final /r/ will enhance the effect of QÂDIR. Repeating or feeling QÂDIR can help in situations where you need to confidently do your part in a team activity. QÂDIR doesn't often work during mindfulness meditation. However, if you have a practice of reflecting on how you might improve things in your life, you may use QÂDIR while pondering on ways to act more self-assured, so that when faced with those circumstances you will have a better chance to act in an assured manner.

### Traditional Use of QÂDIR

The English translation for *qâdir* is *the able*. Muslims use *qâdir* when they want to develop confidence in their ability to perform a task or fulfill an obligation. The SMY analysis concurs with this traditional usage.

## *Stepping Back with Caution Using QÂBID*

The Name QÂBID can provide help whenever stepping back and not trying to dictate actions or drive forward into a daunting challenge seems prudent. Whenever you can't decide whether or not you should act, pushing ahead can prove disastrous if you harbor mental doubts. Reining in the impulse to proceed makes sense under these conditions. QÂBID can help you accomplish this in a mindful manner.

QÂBID's initial sound, /q/, acknowledges the reluctance of letting go of control and engaging in a physical task. The target feeling, /d/, engenders a feeling of mental control. You get to this target emotion via the intermediate sounds. The /â/ brings relaxation and relieves the apprehension fostered by your dilemma of whether or not to act. The /b/ follows and lets you hold on to the good feeling afforded by the reduction of tension. With this good feeling replacing the tormented one the target, /d/, of feeling in mental control can find traction.

QÂBID and QÂDIR provide contrasting strategies for facing potentially difficult tasks. Deciding which Name to use can take place as you size up a situation. If you step back a moment and take a deep breath and experience a hesitant /qâ/ feeling, a gut check can tell you whether to proceed with QÂDIR or QÂBID awareness. If the pause affords a confident /d/ then QÂDIR works. However, if self-assurance doesn't come and the pause itself feels good, then QÂBID would apply. When you deem action necessary but don't feel a high level of confidence, then using QÂDIR could make sense as a way to bolster poise. The key to knowing when to use QÂBID rests in recognizing the presence of an intuitive foreboding feeling at the same time you have an itch to swing into action. Experience can provide the teaching. We learn from our mistakes. QÂBID can help you avoid repeating them.

Having the ability to apply a Name while in an everyday situation can prove challenging. It may appear as an afterthought that such a practice would have helped. Certainly for someone just beginning to practice SMY this seems likely. However, as you develop familiarity with the various Names your skill at applying them at such times will improve. Taking time during a daily meditation or period of reflection to ponder how you could have made use of a particular Name such as QÂDIR or QÂBID can help you reach a point where the practice becomes more automatic.

## Traditional Use of QÂBID

The English translation for *qâbid* is *the constrictor* or *one who holds back.* Muslims use *qâbid* when they wish to curtail their actions in some manner or perhaps the influence of another person or idea. The notion of holding back fits the SMY interpretation of *qâbid.* When practicing SMY it seems wise to apply the exercises on oneself. Constricting your behavior when necessary or judicious makes sense, but using SMY in an attempt to modify the emotions or actions of others does not.

## *Staying Strong and Not Faltering with QAWÎ*

The SMY sequence of QAWÎ provides a good way to face adversity without fear. QAWÎ can also help you deal with a nagging but not life-threatening physical problem by ignoring the irritation. Additionally, QAWÎ can help you ignore little aches and pains that often arise during meditation sessions. The proper practice of QAWÎ can result in a feeling of physical strength and confidence.

In adverse situations, during illnesses, and perhaps after a half-hour of sitting still a /q/ feeling of lacking physical control can often prevail. One target feeling in these circumstances that makes sense consists of a /wî/ combination. The /î/ part acknowledges the presence of control from an outside force, but the /w/ modulates that feeling by taking all of the unpleasant aspects out of that initial /q/ feeling. If you were to go straight from the reluctant giving up control to feeling the control of an outside force, it could lead to negativity and start your feelings spiraling downward into depression. However, whenever the /w/ effectively disregards the unpleasant nature of the problem you face, you can associate the feeling of being under the control of an outside force with a feeling that some power watches over you, or perhaps lose your sense of self to a feeling of belonging to a universal consciousness.

This feeling of lack of internal control, associated with /î/, helps complete the successful dismissal of the physical inconvenience. With QAWÎ you sense that you have overcome a physical discomfort because you have tuned into a higher source of energy. However, do not misconstrue the above to mean that QAWÎ will treat serious illness by itself, though you could augment the effectiveness of other treatments with QAWÎ.

## Traditional Use of QAWÎ

*Qawî* translates into English as *inexhaustible strength* or *supremely strong*. Muslims traditionally use *qawî* to engender a feeling of physical strength. When you practice the SMY pattern of *qawî* you can feel strong in the face adversity.

## *Adding Physical Control with QAYYÛM*

QAYYÛM offers another SMY approach for situations similar to those for which QAWÎ proves effective—adverse times, nagging but not life-threatening physical problems, and little aches and pains that can arise during meditation. Whether you choose QAWÎ or QAYYÛM to combat such unpleasant situations depends on how vital you feel at the time. QAWÎ applies whenever you have adequate energy. Use QAYYÛM for times when you feel less energetic, or somewhat depleted.

You arrive at the target feeling of QAYYÛM, a positive outlook delivered by /m/, through a process consisting of two separate, but linked, intermediate stages. The first step, /yy/, works like an energy pump. Where the /w/ in QAWÎ uses energy to push out negative feelings, the /yy/ actually brings in energy to use for physical control by the way it gets articulated. You take the energy that the /yy/ gathers and apply it to your negative, adverse physical mood by turning the /û/ feeling into a positive /m/.

QAWÎ ignores a problematic feeling, while QAYYÛM attempts to overcome one. Deciding which one of these Names to use can happen on an ad hoc, run-time basis. You may sense through experience which one will follow the /q/ just before beginning using the Name. If you have enough energy you can push the problem away with QAWÎ. You can feel this repulsion whenever you exhale a /w/ sound and feel your diaphragm pushing out air. If you lack sufficient energy when you launch the attack on the problem with a /q/, then you must build up your reserves with QAYYÛM to rid yourself of the issue facing you and get back to meditation or your task at hand. You can feel the energy of the /yy/ surging into the back of your throat as you inhale and focus on the sound. You should take care to bring in the energy from the /yy/ into emptiness and let it fill up as you breathe in. This forms the final /ûm/ combination of QAYYÛM and represents the transition from empty to full. By expressing or feeling QAYYÛM you replenish your energy supply.

## Traditional Use of QAYYÛM

*Qayyûm* translates into English as *self-existing* or *self-subsisting*. Muslims traditionally use *qayyûm* to promote self-reliance. The SMY pattern of QAYYÛM helps you gather the energy needed to deal with a physical problem. This process generates a feeling of gathering physical control to fill up a positive emotional reservoir. It involves work done by the self for the physical self and thus in a sense helps you be self-existing.

## *Getting into Action with QAHHÂR*

Sometimes a person needs to just act rather than worry about the details of how to proceed. For these times the giving up control, denoted by the /q/, may indicate that you have ceded control to another person, or that you have just been passive and have given up control of your physical environment for at least a temporary period. If you recognize this surrender of authority and realize a need to act then QAHHÂR can provide assistance.

We reach our target of action, /r/, via two sounds. First an /h/ drains away the giving up of control and returns our volition. An /h/ which follows a sound, rather than leading a syllable, will flush out, or exhaust the previous sound. The first /h/ clears the /q/ while the second /h/ expresses our idleness. Then, that sitting on the sidelines feeling of relaxation, /â/, present because of our stepping back from wielding influence, comes to the fore. This relaxed feeling gets jettisoned via the target /r/, which generates an abrupt swing from inactivity to action.

To enhance the use of QAHHÂR as you exhale, try feeling the air flowing out as you exhale as part of the process of flushing out the /q/. Then continuing to breathe out, first feel the abdomen change from a relaxed state as muscles contract and push out the last bit of air as you feel the /r/. Take care in choosing this Name due to its volatile nature of swinging into action from inaction.

## Traditional Use of QAHHÂR

*Qahhâr* translates into English as *the conqueror* or *the one who prevails*. Muslims traditionally use *qahhâr* to engender feeling indomitable. Based on the SMY breakdown *qahhâr* eliminates the feeling of being physically controlled by an outside force and sets you into action. This points to a determined, indomitable sense of being.

## *Chapter Summary*

The eleven Names found in this chapter offer a wide variety of options to help you mindfully participate in physical activity in which you have relinquished your sense of control or self-interest. Everyone does some form of physical activity of this nature, often quite freely. If you use your energy to help others, the Name KARÎM can help you stay focused. For potentially difficult tasks you can use KABÎR to stay balanced. If you face a troubling situation and would rather let someone else take over the challenge, then KHABÎR offers a useful emotional pattern to apply. KHÂLIQ lets you accept necessary, but difficult, transitions of control, while KHÂFID lets you retain confidence when relinquishing influence.

At times ceding control happens with reluctance. Some Names can help us conquer this lack of enthusiasm. When facing a chore with wavering confidence, QAHHÂR gets rid of doubt and presses ahead. In contrast, QÂDIR lets you first step back and gain self-assurance before proceeding. And if discretion dictates retreat instead of rushing ahead unprepared, then QÂBID can prove useful. QAWÎ lets you face adversity without fear, but if you sense waning energy in tough times then you would do better with QAYYÛM which allows you to retreat in order to rejuvenate. Finally, you can employ QUDDÛS to enhance reflective moments, when you give up physical activity to just think and ponder.

You should note that two pairs of Names provide contrasting strategies for facing potentially difficult tasks. If you step back a moment and take a deep breath to experience a /qâ/ feeling, a gut check can tell you whether to proceed with QÂDIR or QÂBID awareness. If the pause affords a confident /d/ then QÂDIR works. However, if the confidence doesn't come and the pause itself feels good, then QÂBID would be called for. In a separate strategy, before diving into a possible onerous situation you might try to expel the nervous doubt with QAWÎ, which requires the active expulsion via a /w/ after the initial /qa/. In this instance, if the energy required to generate the /w/ does not flow freely, regroup with QAYYÛM.

# CHAPTER 11
## WANTING TO KEEP PHYSICAL CONTROL

The three Names in this chapter begin with the /gh/ sound which indicates a strong desire for physical control. Virtually all people face times in which they have to have control over their physical surroundings in some capacity, unless a person requires around the clock assistance. For some their livelihood requires them to work with their hands in creating or fixing physical objects. Still even if you have a cerebral job you need to have control over objects necessary for daily living. The typical mood for normal instances of manipulating and otherwise controlling things does not equate to the /gh/ sound. Rather the feelings associated with /gh/ have desire and urgency that do not appear under most normal functioning. If you have to struggle to get something done, or if you find yourself in a situation where you want to control something physical in a harsh or aggressive manner it would correspond to a /gh/ moment.

## *Developing Self-Reliance with GHANÎ*

While most people function quite well in their environments, some face challenges that make certain tasks problematic, and others would like a chance to meet more challenges and require less outside assistance. GHANÎ can prove useful for those who have an urgent desire to depend on their own abilities more and on the assistance of others less. The initial sound, /gh/, corresponds to the person's strong yearning to hold on to physical control, to do the job themselves. The /n/ provides the strong mental control necessary whenever you need to focus your mind on a task, particularly for someone struggling for physical control. Such folks wrestle with insecure feelings. The /ghan/ combination works together to provide optimum control of both the environment you wish to master and the insecurities in your mind. However, by itself /ghan/ would prove unsustainable. You can't keep up such intense focus without burning out. You need to find a way to make the task routine. The feeling of outside control provided by /î/ indicates a move to autopilot or a petition to a higher power for guidance.

## Traditional Use of GHANÎ

*Ghanî* translates into English as *the self-sufficient*. Muslims traditionally use *ghanî* to promote a feeling of not needing help from others. The SMY breakdown of *ghanî* fits this understanding.

## *Asking for Forgiveness with GHAFÛR*

Whenever you have an urge to control something physical in a forceful manner that has a negative impact on a person or a person's possessions, the act of transgression appears as a /gh/ moment. Likewise whenever somebody impinges on a physical aspect of your life and exercises some control or leverage on your physical space it will automatically generate a reaction of wanting to keep your control in direct response to the intrusion. That grasping of control of something physical in our environment, whether generated by our own actions or in response to another's, comes from a territorial instinct one must learn to manage in order to fit in socially. Unfortunately, everyone has times when this instinct lashes out and does something to another they regret. Likewise, everyone experiences times when another person encroaches on them. With the Name GHAFÛR you can deal with these behaviors and proceed in a steady, vigilant manner.

A contented /f/ appears as the immediate response to the emotional /gh/. The /f/ smooths out the ruffles associated with the disconcerting /gh/. You need to find contentment in response to the controlling /gh/. The /f/ eliminates the contention brought on with our expressing the territorial /gh/. The austere /û/ follows and presents a clear-eyed view of the incident. It indicates a lack of pleasure with the affair. Finally, the /r/ generates an alert state. You don't have to, or even want to, relax in these situations. You need to pay attention when instinct instigates a /gh/ reaction. Keep the "eye of an eagle."

The three letters of the /fûr/ combination work together to furnish the response to the /gh/. In a sense the /fûr/ comprises the goal. You do not just want a simple goal of an arousing /r/. Arousal without first gaining the contentment afforded by the /f/ and the austere mood generated by the /û/ could prove problematic. You need to feel empty of pleasure as a result of the deed, content but not happy, and alert to go about your business and try either to avoid being crossed, if another initiated the problem, or try not to slip up again, if it was you who erred.

The time for using GHAFÛR comes after a transgression on the physical space of another. To get the maximum benefit of a clean conscience, the practice of using GHAFÛR should take place at a time where you can focus on the Name and its meaning.

## Traditional Use of GHAFÛR

*Ghafûr* translates into English as *the all-forgiving*. Muslims traditionally use *ghafûr* when they wish to ask forgiveness for a particular instance of transgression. This syncs with the SMY interpretation.

## *Forgiveness and GHAFFÂR*

GHAFÛR and GHAFFÂR have very similar patterns. They share initial and final sounds, as well as an intermediate /f/. With the leading /gh/ feeling it means that the Names both pertain to situations associated with extreme desire to control a physical aspect of the world. The /r/ target sets alertness as the goal of each Name. Their two differences, a double /ff/ and an /â/ in GHAFFÂR instead of the single /f/ and /û/ in GHAFÛR, determine the contrasting situations for which they each apply. The /û/ in GHAFÛR indicates penance in a way. It guarantees the absence of pleasure, whereas the /â/ GHAFFÂR lacks this flavor of atonement, but instead suggests a cooling off or total relaxation, as it follows the double /ff/ of contentment. So instead of asking for forgiveness for an act of transgression as happens with GHAFÛR, with GHAFFÂR you desire something else. Through the /ffâ/ GHAFFÂR removes the desperation of wanting to have physical control and replaces it with contented relaxation before ending in a state of alertness. To summarize, use GHAFFÂR to combat the unhealthy /gh/ urge to take control of the physical aspects of the world. This does not mean that all /gh/ moods need to be combated with GHAFFÂR. The example provided with GHANÎ points to some appropriate /gh/ states. However, you should recognize the existence of /gh/ states which have crossed a line from fighting for self-sufficiency to illicitly intruding on someone else's space, and use GHAFFÂR to adjust your attitude toward such moments in a mindful manner. Does this constitute asking for forgiveness? Perhaps, if you know that you have crossed that line in ways in the past and want to keep from acting in that fashion again. GHAFFÂR does not apply for a specific instance of wrongdoing, as the case with GHAFÛR, but instead as a wide-ranging plea for adjusting one's behavior and atoning for a general pattern of improper conduct.

## Traditional Use of GHAFFÂR

*Ghaffâr* translates into English as *the great forgiver*. Muslims traditionally use *ghaffâr* to ask forgiveness for a repeated pattern of transgressions. The SMY interpretation of *ghaffâr* is compatible with the traditional usage.

## *Chapter Summary*

The small number of Names dealing with holding on to physical control stands in contrast to the large number of Names that give in to yielding such power—three versus eleven. The relative paucity of Names that address the desire to be in charge seems to indicate the lack of subtlety in this realm, and perhaps reflects the darker nature of such aspirations. The Sufi ideal and wider Muslim conviction of submitting to the will of Allah reflects the narrower lane for ruling the environment and being the one to call the shots. Yes, one Name, GHANÎ, reflects the innate need to provide for physical needs but the other two offer only a way to subdue and overcome the urge to dominate. Both GHAFFÂR and GHAFÛR want to induce contentment, the /f/ and /ff/, and reduce the push for being the one who dictates what happens.

# CHAPTER 12
## GRASPING PLEASURABLE MOMENTS

If you have good fortune you will find many things in life that afford pleasure, many things that make life worthwhile. Sources of happiness come from physical amenities, emotional relationships, and mental impressions. The genetic design of our bodies impels us to seek out the pleasure of sex, food, and a warm place to stay. The physiological makeup of our emotions pushes us toward loving relationships and away from bad ones, and if not innate most of us learn to pursue ideas that provide intellectual pleasure. Although such pleasurable things afford reasons to live, the feeling of holding on to pleasure can distract from a mindful presence and even lead into bad habits and/or addictions. The Names in this chapter all begin with the /b/ feeling and thus provide various ways to deal with pleasurable moments or potentially pleasurable indulgences. They can help celebrate pleasure in an aware and enlightened manner when deemed appropriate and desirable, and eschew the pursuit of the pleasure when it comes from an unsuitable source.

During moments of pleasant experiences you can use SMY to incorporate a worthy pleasure into a mindful awareness or help expel an illicit pleasure. You can also take advantage of some Names beginning with /b/ during moments of reflection and meditation. During reflection you can envision pleasant scenarios and develop a response that can then be available when a real incident takes place. If you experience times of spontaneous emotional pleasure that grab your attention while meditating, you can learn how to integrate these into a more mindful meditation session.

One final usage of some Names in this chapter centers on devotional practices—acknowledging an outside power that invokes a feeling of awe by expressing emotional energy toward that entity or idea. For some the feeling of love and gratitude to the powers that they perceive to be connected to a deity or higher, perhaps universal consciousness, or panpsychism, looms as a strong force in their awareness. Names beginning with /b/ can harness these emotions and enhance the connection to this force.

## *Avoiding Illicit or Immoral Pleasures with BÂ̱TIN*

If you recognize a physical attraction to a form of pleasure that you regard as inappropriate, perhaps a drug or alcohol or sexual attraction, you can use BÂ̱TIN to help keep the fixation at bay. The allure of improper physical gratification can generate a /bâ/ feel-good, relaxed sensation. You don't just feel good, but the good feeling relaxes you and lets you put your guard down, thus the /bâ/, not just /b/. The target in these instances, /n/, puts us in position of strong mental control. In order to reach this target you must first purge any grip the pleasant object has on your cognitive processing via the intermediate sound/feeling of /t̲/. The somewhat unpleasant feeling of releasing control evoked by /t̲/ might reflect reluctance to give up the pleasure, or regret that you find something unacceptable attractive, or a combination of these factors. Whatever the case, the /t̲/ roots out the attraction before the control afforded by the /n/ can take over.

You can take advantage of the power of BÂ̱TIN when directly faced with a tempting illicit gratification by simply repeating the Name aloud or under your breath or by feeling the emotional sequence denoted by the Name. You may also find BÂ̱TIN useful during times of reflection when pondering situations in which you have succumbed to desires that you have later regretted. By practicing BÂ̱TIN in such milieus you prepare yourself for facing the real temptation.

### Traditional Use of BÂ̱TIN

*Bâ̱tin* translates into English as *the hidden*. Muslims traditionally use *bâ̱tin* in various ways, sometimes to find what lays hidden, sometimes to avoid an undesirable situation. Since the SMY usage of *bâ̱tin* corresponds to avoiding a bad habit, it matches this second traditional interpretation well.

## *Staying Mindful with BÂRI'*

The /b/ feeling of holding on to pleasure will often naturally bring on a relaxing /â/, signifying a reveling in pleasure afforded by an accomplishment. In other words the two feelings combine into a single feeling of /bâ/. For example, if you have attained a goal, the achievement can generate a satisfying good feeling that you like to savor. As you experience this /bâ/ you may have an urge to celebrate by breaking out of the relaxed part of the /bâ/, or at least express some enthusiasm—acts which carry arousal, an expression of /r/. In order to deal with this desire you can express the presence of the energy with /ri/ and follow it with a /'/, a hamza. The /'/ defuses the /ri/. It muffles it and in effect removes the arousal. Keeping our cool and not overreacting, like shouting and gloating, allows you to enjoy a feeling of success without creating a prideful display that disrupts mindfulness. Using the Name BÂRI' can help you avoid arrogance and haughty displays and let you take pleasure in your good fortune in a mindful manner.

In addition to using BÂRI' whenever you want to hold on to a good feeling and wish to suppress any unattractive or immodest rejoicing, you may also ponder BÂRI' during times of reflection when you recall situations where you lost your dignity by reacting in an arrogant way to favorable circumstances. Reliving the feelings of such an experience in a manner that lets you control your /r/ reaction can condition your behavior for the next time you encounter similar circumstances.

You can also use BÂRI' during quiet meditation if you experience a good feeling that you wish to savor without disrupting your session. Meditators often report feelings of spontaneous joy while meditating, consisting of a deep engulfing emotion. BÂRI' allows you to distance yourself from an energetic reaction to the pleasantness and let you remain in a nourishing, refreshing sense of stillness.

## Traditional Use of BÂRI'

The sources I have seen for translating the Names of Allah into English include a wider range of translations for *bâri'* than most of the other Names. The various translations include *the evolver, the maker, the creator of harmony, the originator of individuation, the one who shapes,* and *the one who brings into existence.* Some Muslims traditionally use *bâri'* to encourage personal growth. Characterizing the SMY understanding of *bâri'* as a form of evolving does make some sense, if you consider acting modestly as a form of social evolving.

## *Acknowledging Pleasure from an Outside Source with BÂQÎ*

You can experience pleasure that does not fit into scenarios described for BÂṬIN and BÂRI', i.e., not alluring, illicit pleasure and not pleasure that might make you want to gloat. Pleasant emotions that you wish to savor can occur not from individual action, but from something outside of your control. This can happen when you experience a strong feeling of love in a relationship, or feel blessed by some perhaps unexpected good fortune. BÂQÎ can help you move the strong positive pleasant feeling into a deeper mindful recognition of your providential situation.

The target feeling, /î/, lets you acknowledge the outside influence that afforded you the satisfying emotion. For Sufis the feeling of outside control points to Allah. A non-religious person using SMY can think of the /î/ as their non-rational side or their unconscious or perhaps universal consciousness or even another person. In any event, the only intermediate sound/feeling that gets us to the /î/ from the pleasant /bâ/ comes from /q/. With the /q/ you release physical control in an austere manner. This stepping back from physical control allows the external control expressed by /î/ to follow smoothly.

BÂQÎ can sometimes work in situations where SHAKÛR might apply, i.e., when a feeling of gratitude seems appropriate. Which of these two Names you choose depends on whether you mentally or emotionally process the incident. Mentally recognizing your good fortune calls for SHAKÛR, while emotionally experiencing it indicates BÂQÎ. After using BÂQÎ to move your experience into a meditative state you might use SHAKÛR as your mind catches up to the reality of the experience.

You can practice BÂQÎ during times of reflection as you ponder situations where the Name would apply. For example, whenever you feel fortunate about things that bring you joy for which others played a significant role, BÂQÎ can help you stay mindful of the fact that the web of life and society that surrounds you gives you this pleasure. Although BÂQÎ does not express thanks per se, it does help keep us aware of how our pleasures fit in the realm of existence.

Additionally, BÂQÎ can prove useful during meditation sessions. Sometimes you can spontaneously feel a /bâ/ moment. Perhaps you have an urge to lift your hands with palms up in a /bâ/ expression of joy or maybe you just feel a powerful surge of energy coursing through your body. In these instances it may seem that you have let go of physical control, but not in a voluntary manner, rather an austere /q/ release of physical control. As this proceeds it feels as though an outside force has taken control, thus the final /î/. The carrying out of a non-vocal, emotional BÂQÎ sequence can provide a powerful experience, if you succeed in attaining the final strong /î/ feeling. The pleasant /bâ/ and the involuntary movement or feeling of energy get tied to an outside force giving this sequence a dimension of mysticism. The potent nature of this practice gives it an almost addictive form of devotional or Bhakti yoga.

## Traditional Use of BÂQÎ

*Bâqî* translates into English as *everlasting* or *eternal*. Muslims traditionally use *bâqî* in efforts to strip away the ephemeral aspects of consciousness and experience its eternal nature. The powerful feeling produced when using SMY to practice a BÂQÎ sequence can feel as though an eternal force is coursing through you.

## *Accepting Pleasure Without a Debate Using BÂSIT*

Some people do not let themselves enjoy simple honest pleasures. This happens for various reasons, perhaps a feeling of guilt intrudes, or nervousness or anxiety, or you believe you don't deserve the positive experience. In any case a good feeling that comes to you via a wholesome lifestyle does not need to be eschewed. If the feeling does not make you feel like bragging or feels like it comes from an outside force, but rather generates an internal debate about its origin or quality or worth, you can use BÂSIT to shut off the internal dialogue and simply let the goodness resonate throughout your being.

In the situations in which BÂSIT applies, the pleasurable, relaxed /bâ/ leads into stream of consciousness, /s/, mental questioning and debating. The /s/ in this case doesn't play the role of an intermediate feeling as much as it stands as part of the initial condition. The only other significant sound/feeling remaining consists of letting go of control, /t/. This letting go of control frees you from the mental agonizing about how to categorize the pleasure and simply lets the good feeling resonate without any fuss.

In daily living situations the use of BÂSIT may allow you to enjoy things in a mindful manner rather than getting lost in a stream of consciousness debate on the merits of the pleasure. The difficulty with applying BÂSIT directly at the time of such denials lies in the pernicious nature of habits. Once you have an established habit of internally debating pleasantness, by the time you recognize yet another debate you may already have passed the pleasant stage. This makes the use of BÂSIT problematic. SMY requires that in order to generate positive effects the beginning letter of a Name must match the current mood/feeling. If you have left the pleasurable feeling behind and find yourself debating it, you will benefit from SALÂM to correct the stream of consciousness problem. BÂSIT will not produce the desired results unless and until the pleasant feeling has returned. Thus, it behooves someone who senses that BÂSIT will prove beneficial to use times of reflection to practice BÂSIT.

During times of reflection you may wonder about the legitimacy of the gratifying pleasures. Although you should exercise restraint and moderation in your sources of delight, it does not mean that you must avoid pleasure derived from properly maintaining your body. Reasonable enjoyment of the physical and emotional aspects of your existence promotes health. You don't need self-flagellation. When used in times of reflection BÂSIT can help you remove any internal debate about your enjoyment of life.

Finally, BÂSIT can also be used for devotional purposes. A person who desires to express appreciation for what could be called a source of goodness for the spirit expresses a strong feeling they attribute to this force via /bâ/. Thoughts concerning this goodness wash through them in a stream of /s/ energy. In order to refrain from getting caught or fixating on these thoughts, they get washed away via the /t/. This release keeps the devotional energy free from any attachment that the stream of consciousness might try to interject into the devotion.

## Traditional Use of BÂSIT

*Bâsit* translates into English as *expand* or *enlarge*. Muslims traditionally use *bâsit* in an effort to expand personal boundaries—physical, emotional, mental. The SMY understanding of *bâsit* does allow you to enlarge your life by removing nagging deliberations that impede legitimate enjoyment of pleasure.

## *Release Through BÂ'ITH*

Another Name beginning with /bâ/, BÂ'ITH, finds use in situations where a pleasant sensation or circumstance threatens to sour and/or fade away. The pleasantness in these instances can ensue from physical or emotional sources. I will get to some examples shortly, but first consider the psychological processes involved in the Name BÂ'ITH. The /b/ indicates the pleasant feeling that you wish to keep and the /â/ acknowledges the relaxation derived from this pleasure. The impending loss of this pleasure engenders an ayin, /'/, a cathartic expression that releases your inner turmoil. The resolution of this emotional appeal comes with the gentle mental control of /th/, a way of saying take it steady. The /th/ gets articulated by placing the tongue on the teeth. With the tongue thus situated you cannot close the jaw and therefore you cannot bite, which rules out any aggression and thus neutralizes arousal. Thus the /th/ feeling corresponds to one of internal mental control (due to the use of the tip of the tongue) that dictates physical restraint. Therefore after the /'/ expresses the release of the pent-up feelings and anguish due to an impending loss, you grab mental control while soothing the physical dimension of your emotions with /th/.

For a physical example appropriate for BÂ'ITH consider the situation in which a physical ailment plagues you, perhaps a sore muscle keeps you from participating in an activity. BÂ'ITH can help when pondering the loss of the pleasure derived from taking part and enjoying yourself. Please understand that BÂ'ITH serves as a way to bring emotional equanimity and mindfulness, and not as a way to cure a physical aliment. BÂ'ITH can work in conjunction with other healing methods that you employ by keeping your mind and emotions on an even keel while physical healing takes place. One way to work with BÂ'ITH in relation to physical ailments involves breathing in on the BÂ segment of the Name with the intention of filling up the physical soreness with a good sensation. Then as the pain or soreness takes over awareness, exhale the 'ITH portion of the Name to release the emotion associated with the pain and gain subtle control.

The possible breakup of a relationship provides an example of an emotional scenario where BÂ'ITH may prove useful. Because successful relationships most often center on shared good feelings, whenever those feelings suffer a setback or appear to be in jeopardy, you can use BÂ'ITH to help work through the issue. This should prove most effective when contemplating the problem. Let the memories of the good feelings you associate with the relationship fill you up with the BÂ feeling. Then as you recognize the trials that the relationship faces, exhale the 'ITH feeling. This affords a therapeutic, cathartic expression of the troubles facing the relationship and leaves you in a tender non-combative mood.

Additionally, BÂ'ITH can work in a devotional manner. The good /bâ/ feeling proffered as devotion can sometimes generate an emotional buildup, a lump-in-the-throat type of response that requires an ayin for its release. This may occur whenever a person feels lost or remote from a familiar force to which they express their love. The /ith/ response to the ayin then allows for a gentle control to soothe the situation.

## Traditional Use of BÂ'ITH

*Bâ'ith* translates into English as *awakening* or *resurrection*. Muslims traditionally use *bâ'ith* to awaken a dying or dead spark or spirit within. The use of the SMY pattern of BÂ'ITH creates a cathartic feeling of physical or emotional rejuvenation.

## *Embracing Goodness with BARR*

When you have a pleasant experience you wish to relish, i.e., a /b/ moment, you do not always relax into the feeling. Although the previous four Names began with /b/, followed immediately by the relaxing /â/, BARR and the remaining two Names beginning with /b/ have a less relaxing /a/ as the subsequent sound. The /a/ has qualities of relaxation, but it also carries some austerity from the partial /û/ inherent in its nature. This subtle sound does not have much influence in establishing the emotional valence of these or any other Name, and typically gets ignored. Thus the sound/feeling following the /a/ determines how the Name reacts to the pleasantness signified by the /b/. For BARR the reaction occurs through the arousal dimension. The other two Names beginning with /ba/ respond via the control dimension of emotion.

You might ask why one would have to deal with emotional situations . where the /b/ feeling pervades. Does holding onto pleasantness need a resolution? Indeed some Names exist that end with a /b/, indicating that /b/ can work as a resolution in some instances. Likewise it does seem logical that a simple /b/ feeling needs no attention given it in order to modulate to another state. However, that does not imply that every /b/ moment stands alone. If grasping a pleasant moment seems open-ended, or leads to anticipation of action or contemplation, then staying with the /b/ will not occur. You can use a Name to help guide you through appropriate follow-up.

In the case where you recognize the source behind the pleasant /b/ and want to embrace it then BARR works as an excellent way forward. The double /rr/ sound at the end indicates a strong increase in the arousal level. When you put such an increase after the /b/ it connotes an enthusiastic embrace of the good feeling. You would use BARR whenever the goodness generating the /b/ feeling came from something in which you wish to invest energy, for example, a good feeling from a familial relationship, or a spiritual commitment.

The /r/ appears twice in this formula, indicating that you should stress and sustain this feeling. To generate this feeling you can focus on the abdomen while exhaling and apply energy to the feeling /r/. You could even apply this breathing pattern during simple yoga stretching exercises. While you stretch muscles and inhale, feel and hold on to pleasantness. Then when you exhale, release the pleasant feeling and squeeze air out with the abdominal muscles while you feel the energy and vitality needed for the exercises. Let the /rr/ contribute to your feeling of overall well-being derived from the yoga exercises. The oft-heard instruction from a yoga teacher of "Inhale deep, and exhale hard" mirrors an SMY manner for breathing BARR.

## Traditional Use of BARR

*Barr* translates into English as *source of goodness*. Muslims traditionally use *barr* to instill a feeling of deriving goodness from the one source of all goodness for them, i.e., Allah. The SMY way of looking at *barr* points to the source of something good as something to embrace.

## *Validation of Goodness using BASÎR*

In situations where you instinctively or automatically recognize the source of a pleasant feeling as stemming from something of value, the Name BARR will allow you to accept the goodness and devote your emotional energy to it. However, whenever you encounter a good feeling that does not generate automatic recognition, your inherent nature dictates a mental evaluation of some sort. In such circumstances you can use BASÎR for emotional equanimity. The /s/ indicates the engagement of mental stream needed to process and register the nature of the good feeling. This mental processing then gets suppressed via the /î/, as you yield to the outside control, the control exerted by the new stimulus that has engendered the pleasant sensation that has you in its grasp. The final target feeling, /r/, comes and increases the arousal level present in the situation. This essentially imparts a wake-up jolt that allows an embrace of the fresh pleasure.

A word of caution needs to be added about the use of BASÎR. Not every new experience of a good feeling comes from a wholesome source. If the /s/ portion should identify an illicit pleasure, continuing with surrender to an outside force should not occur. Instead you should recognize the situation as problematic and switch to an alternative Name. If, however, the good feeling derives from a reputable source, then enjoyment should not present a problem. You can open up to new experience with BASÎR, new foods, new forms of visual art, new music, new people.

## Traditional Use of BASÎR

*Basîr* translates into English as *all seeing*. Muslims traditionally use *basîr* to develop the ability to see things that they might otherwise miss. The term "see things" refers to more than just physical objects in the environment. It also refers to seeing patterns of behavior and motivation and other abstract notions. This interpretation of "seeing" fits with the SMY understanding of *basîr*, if you add the notion of wonder to the seeing. That is, from the SMY viewpoint *basîr* does not refer to seeing, or rather experiencing, everything all the time, but only when that experience prompts some positive good feeling that you grab on to.

## *Living with Your Full Self Using BADÎ'*

So what do I mean by "your full self"? I refer to those moments when you feel full of a good feeling that belongs to you or that you attribute to your own doing, i.e., when something you did makes you happy or proud, or at least makes you self-conscious. Successful comedians know how to take these self-aware moments and through self-deprecation create humor. The use of the Name BADÎ' does not make you a comedian, but it can help to avoid coming across as an egotistical blowhard. Developing the quality of BADÎ' can keep you from trying to impress people with your accomplishments. When you have an impulse to expound on one of your accomplishments or adventures, carrying through on the urge can make you look or sound arrogant or self-centered. Rather than boasting, use BADÎ' and step back from the spotlight.

Feeling good about oneself does not make you a bad person. Everyone should strive for a high level of self-respect. This good feeling only becomes a problem when you try to impress others with your knowledge or deeds. When you experience a good feeling about yourself and cling to it, it exists as a /b/ feeling. Whenever you feel responsible for this feeling it will generate a feeling of being in control, a /d/ feeling, if you do not let the feeling flow on unattended. The solution that keeps a /bad/ combination from putting you in a bad (no pun intended) light involves feeling the presence of external control, /î/. In order to feel under external control you must recognize that you can never take full credit for your achievements. You benefit from circumstances that the universe has afforded you. Yes, you get to contribute, but other forces always play a part. A religious person should find it easy to generate a feeling that something external to them, specifically God or Allah, has played a significant part in enabling them to accomplish something noteworthy. A non-religious person (who is not a narcissist) should not have to look too far to realize that nobody can take full credit for an endeavor.

Generating an /î/ feeling can prove difficult at a time where you have just experienced a good feeling about something you did. Attributing what you deem as the fruit of your hard work to an outside force may not come easily or naturally. The ayin, /'/, that follows the /î/ reflects the emotional cost of expressing the /î/ feeling. With the /'/ you articulate how hard but at the same time, in some way, how relieving it feels to give credit to an outside force.

Practicing BADÎ' in daily life can prove beneficial once one has learned to recognize the situations where it should apply and how to engender the proper mental state that accompanies the Name. Prior practice of BADÎ' during times of reflection will make this task much more practical. If in your daily times of reflection you recognize a need to rein in a boastful tendency, you will benefit from working with BADÎ'.

## Traditional Use of BADÎ'

*Badî'* translates into English as *the incomparable, the one who starts anew,* or *the originator.* Muslims traditionally use *badî'* to develop individuality or originality. The SMY interpretation puts a slight twist to this traditional interpretation. That is, the SMY recommends using *badî'* whenever you have already accomplished something original. By using *badî'* at such times it keeps your success from going to your head.

## Chapter Summary

The Names in chapter six worked with certain pleasant situations; however, that group did not exhaust all possible scenarios of pleasure. In this chapter the Names all begin with the /b/ sound in order to address times when you desire to retain pleasantness and relish the sentiment. These Names have a way to manage good strong feelings of pleasure as well as negative attractions to pleasures, such as addictions. As with the pleasant /m/ you can differentiate Names beginning with /ba/ versus Names beginning with /bâ/, with the former Names useful in non-relaxation pleasure and the latter with relaxing pleasantness.

We can differentiate between the /mâ/ psychological state and the /bâ/ mood. The pleasure in /mâ/ triggers relaxation and the tendency to lose oneself to the source of the enjoyment. In contrast with /bâ/ the pleasure remains the focus—you hold on to the feeling. This retention of a pleasing sensation can prove problematic if the bliss carries potential harms, e.g., addictions. You can use BÂTIN to help overcome temptations of such illicit pleasures. Some good moments don't have the potential of physical harm. However, extreme emotional reactions risk making you appear shallow. BÂRI' can help to keep you from seeming indulgent in response to providential circumstances.

We can attribute some /bâ/ moments to a force outside of ourselves. In these instances BÂQÎ allows you to feel grateful for such good fortune. At other times of simple delights BÂSIT lets you enjoy an honest pleasure without fretting about being worthy. In a final example of /bâ/ incidents, whenever you experience a fleeting /bâ/ moment where the source of pleasure seems to be slipping out of reach, you can use BÂ'ITH to help keep your emotional equanimity.

These same three, BÂQÎ, BÂSIT, and BÂ'ITH also prove useful in devotional practices.

Experience of a /b/ mood doesn't have to have the relaxation aspect. Three Names deal with such times—one with a physical response, the other two with mental reactions. When you perceive genuine goodness in the physical realm you can use BARR to foster an active embrace of such wholesome goodness. Whenever good times trigger a strong /ba/ response BADÎ' can prove useful in keeping your ego in check. Finally, if a novel situation generates a good feeling which in turn triggers a mental evaluation BASÎR can help you experience the newness with open optimism.

# CHAPTER 13
## SMY APPROACHES TO FATIGUE

A number of Names help to cope with tiredness or fatigue. Everybody can experience physical as well as mental weariness. In these circumstances the Names that provide relief begin with the sound of /h/ or /ḥ/. The relationship between the sounds of /ḥ/ or /h/ and a tired state seems intuitive. Think about times when you feel tired and need to rouse yourself to get up and do something that needs done. Do you let out a sigh? The sound of that sigh mimics the /ḥ/. It comes as an automatic expression of your low energy. A total of nine Names deal with tiredness and weariness. These cover differing approaches to physical lassitude and varying nuances of mental fatigue, or boredom. If the /ḥ/ or /h/ feeling does not resonate with your current condition or that which you contemplate, then using a Name in this group does not make sense. Only when you recognize the nagging sense of fatigue should you decide which of these will best serve to treat the issue and help you regain a feeling of physical or mental vigor.

### *Revitalizing with ḤAYY*

Perhaps the best response to a feeling of low physical energy comes with the Name ḤAYY. This simple Name consists of two basic salient sounds/feelings. The first, the /ḥ/, equates to the tired feeling. You generate the other sound, the double /yy/, through a constant stream, a glide, articulated with the back of the tongue. The doubling of the /y/ sound in ḤAYY emphasizes this attribute of physical control. All glides get expressed as an independent constant sound, and not like a stop consonant which either holds on to or releases a quality and must get articulated with a burst. The glides, including /ḥ/, will express their quality in a sustained, but not grasping manner. The /yy/ sound corresponds to the generation of continuous physical control.

We can create a /y/ on an inhalation as well as happens in normal speech, i.e., while exhaling. When inhaling and making the /y/ sound the process works akin to a physical energy generator. In fact you may be familiar with this type of gasp for breath. Try inhaling through the mouth with the tongue relaxed, and then compare that to inhaling through the mouth with the mouth in position for generating a /y/ sound, i.e., raise the back of the tongue to somewhat constrict the airway. This process slows down the inhalation and gives you control in bringing the air into the lungs. It's this feeling of physical control that makes such an inhalation an effective manner to address a physical lack of energy. Thus the mechanics for breathing of HAYY involve a hard exhale with the /h/ with focus on the abdomen, followed by the intake of energized air with the /yy/ as you focus on the sensation of air coming in through the windpipe. Some people describe the feeling associated with breathing HAYY in this fashion as energy coming in through the back of the neck. You need not dwell on the mechanics of HAYY other than to notice both emotional and physical aspects of the breath. Also you do not need to vocalize HAYY, either out loud or silently to yourself, whenever you use this breathing technique.

Repetition of the breathing pattern for HAYY can prove beneficial. A single breath of HAYY can only provide a small amount of energy. If your supply of energy has reached a low ebb, then one round of HAYY will likely not boost your reserves in a significant enough manner to stave off the need for another dose for an appreciable amount of time. In most instances you will need repetitions, possibly a dozen or even more. The repeating of the HAYY breathing pattern mirrors another popular yoga breathing exercise called kapalabhati. In both cases air gets forced out by contracting the abdominal muscles and rushes back in automatically.

The rate of repetition during kapalabhati equals about one breath per second. Repetition for the SMY pattern of HAYY does not have to occur at that pace, but it may if you prefer that speed. You may also repeat HAYY in a slower more deliberate manner. How fast you repeat a HAYY breath depends only on personal preference which you will develop as you use it. How many times you should repeat the breathing of HAYY depends on a couple of factors, including how low your energy level reached prior to initiating the practice, the capacity your body has for storing energy acquired in this manner, and the level of fitness of the body parts responsible for the mechanics of the breath. The first two of these factors take care of themselves. You don't have to worry about the level of energy when you start and you should stop when the exercise no longer feels as though it adds to your vitality. Don't try to control either of these subjective feelings. The final factor, the level of fitness of the breathing apparatus, deserves attention and respect. Don't try to overdo things. You may see videos online of demonstrations of kapalabhati that include dozens of repetitions. It takes time for your body to work up to this kind of capacity. Know your limitations.

## Traditional Use of HAYY

*Hayy* translates into English as *alive*. Muslims traditionally use *hayy* to generate physical energy and a vital feeling. The SMY breathing sequence of HAYY fits the traditional usage quite well.

## *Soldiering On with HALÎM*

While HAYY works in general situations of physical tiredness you may need other options for responding to a tired feeling, particularly if the tired feeling stems not just from a physical source, but also from some mental fatigue. In many situations a task can draw you out and feel oppressive, perhaps from boredom or lack of mental stimulation. Yet, you may still feel that you have to persevere to complete a task seen as a duty. HALÎM provides relief in such situations. A pleasant /m/ serves as the goal in such circumstances; it expresses the desire for enjoyment instead of feeling drawn. Getting to this goal involves two intermediate sounds/feelings. First, you let things proceed without trying to makes waves or cause interruptions by expressing the /l/ feeling. Letting things flow sets the stage for the /î/, the feeling of external control, the idea that you must continue due to a commitment to your job. Once established, the feeling of outside control will bring on the goal of pleasantness, /m/. Of course this assumes that you have a positive attitude to feeling under outside control. The Sufis will point to Allah. If you attribute the outside control to a hated boss, then HALÎM will fail to soothe. Don't think about the evil boss. Think about fulfilling your obligations.

Using a specific breathing pattern in a silent manner for the Name HALÎM can augment its effectiveness above a simple vocal usage. Think the sequence for HALÎM as you synchronize your thoughts with your breathing. As you recognize fatigue, forcibly exhale while focusing on the abdomen. This simple act of feeling the /h/ allows you to settle your mind. Then as you inhale bring your awareness slowly up from the abdomen and feel the loose, flowing form of the /l/ as the lungs begin to take in air. Slowly let your awareness rise to your head and feel an outside force taking over control, the /î/, as the lungs fill. Let this engender the target pleasant /m/ which you feel throughout your being.

You can use HALÎM in day to day situations in which boredom accompanies fatigue. Practicing HALÎM when reflecting on such boring and fatiguing situations can help solidify the practice and make it more accessible and automatic whenever an anticipated real-life need for the Name arises.

## Traditional Use of HALÎM

*Halîm* translates into English as *forbearing*. Muslims traditionally use *halîm* to develop the ability to withstand hardship facing them. The SMY usage of *halîm* parallels this usage.

## *Feeling Tired but Content with HAMÎD*

Often during a day's work you may feel tired, but at the same time know that in a few hours or so you will have the chance to rejuvenate when you finish your work and/or reach home. Using the Name HAMÎD can help you keep an even mindful focus in such circumstances. A target feeling of holding on to mental control, /d/, for occasions like these can make sense. You want to stay mentally tough knowing that you must continue even though fatigue besets you. Two intermediate sounds/feelings help you reach this target. First, the pleasant /m/ reassures you that what you do matters, that your tired state resulted from worthwhile work. Feeling good about your efforts allows the acceptance of outside control, /î/. You can think of the outside control as the force pushing you to continue working, maybe the boss will not let you stop, perhaps you feel the weight of responsibility as a provider, but perhaps even better results can emerge if you consider the outside force to consist of a higher power, i.e, God/Allah. The combination of the /mî/, a pleasant mood even though not under your control, paradoxically can let the feeling of holding on to control, /d/, materialize. It feels as though by letting go of control you have gained it—a special dilemma worth aspiring to.

You can use HAMÎD in daily living to dispel fatigue brought on by ordinary work. You can also practice HAMÎD in times of reflection as you ponder situations where your energy has flagged in the past. The use of HAMÎD during private meditation sessions seems rarely appropriate. Simply pushing through a tired state gains little. However, during group meditation you may find HAMÎD useful, if you wish to stay in the session and not distract the group by breaking out due to fatigue.

To help feel the emotional sequence for the Name HAMÎD you can exhale hard with focus on the abdomen to generate the /h/ feeling. Then as you begin to inhale, feel the pleasant /m/ in the chest before bringing the focus to the head with the powerful /îd/ combination.

## Traditional Use of HAMÎD

Hamîd translates into English as *praiseworthy* or *laudable*. Muslims traditionally use *hamîd* to encourage the growth of character, to make one's actions more commendable. The SMY understanding of *hamîd* fits with this traditional usage when you consider that using it in the SMY fashion can help you keep applying yourself at a job whenever you tire.

## *Pushing Through with HAFÎZ*

At times you may engage in a task that you need to complete but grow tired and have trouble focusing on aspects of the work that require attention to details in order to avoid injury or damage to materials. In such situations you can use H̲AFÎZ to push past the tired feeling and let automatic instinctual functioning take over. Some might refer to this feeling as cruising on autopilot. It involves background mental processing that doesn't engage directly with the task at hand, as though things happen by themselves. You might characterize this as feeling under outside control, /î/, but with a twist. The outside force has a semi-dormant monitor, a subtle stream of consciousness that corresponds to the /z/. This /îz/ combination forms the target feeling of H̲AFÎZ. In order to get from the tired /h̲/ feeling to this desired auto-functioning /îz/ state, use the intermediate contented /f/. You could describe the manner in which the Name H̲AFÎZ works as taking that tired, having-trouble-focusing feeling, and staying content and switching to automatic processing.

You may find H̲AFÎZ useful in everyday situations where needed focus begins to wane. Repeating this Name out loud, when practical, or silently if prudent, or perhaps just feeling the emotional pattern can give relief and let you proceed confidently. You can also practice H̲AFÎZ during times of reflection in order to become familiar with the pattern and let its quality take over whenever you face situations that call for it. H̲AFÎZ does not present much opportunity for use during periods of meditation.

## Traditional Use of H̲AFÎZ

The English translation of h̲afîz is *the preserver*. Muslims typically use h̲afîz in order to develop the quality or ability to preserve something or be protected during certain endeavors. SMY calls for the use of h̲afîz in order to help bring focus to a task. Without focus you can cause injury to yourself or others. Thus, h̲afîz can be useful in preserving oneself from harm.

## *Settling a Dispute on Another's Terms with H̲AQQ*

Three Names seem appropriate for addressing fatigue or impasse stemming from a disagreement among persons. It makes sense to deal with differences in a cordial way before reaching a tired state. You will arrive at better solutions to problems whenever you command sufficient mental energy to focus adequately. However, some problems appear when few reserves remain. While in other problematic situations you might start with what seems like adequate energy, but the issue persists until mental resources run low. When these situations arise you can benefit from one of three Names: ḤAQQ, ḤAKAM, or ḤAKÎM.

The key to all three of these Names rests on the surrender of physical control. For ḤAQQ the surrender happens with a /q/, making it a reluctant yielding. For the other two the release of control occurs with a /k/ and holds no reluctance. To decide which of these Names to use, first consider your relationship to the other person or persons in the dispute. If you do not have clear authority, not the boss or the ranking person in a hierarchy, then ḤAQQ will prove the best choice. If your status stands out as the dominant person, then you should not have to worry about releasing physical control, however, if you exist on equal position or a lower position to the others, then surrendering will result in some lack of enthusiasm that the /q/ connotes.

ḤAQQ brings a simple solution to a dispute. If you forsake physical control, the others present in the confrontation have nothing to fight against to disprove. You should recognize this tactic to disagreements as one similar to those offered by sages such as Christ, Ghandi, and Martin Luther King, Jr. I refer to non-violence or turning the other cheek. The translation of this Name adds an aspect to this approach. The Name means "truth" in Arabic. How do you reconcile the meaning of truth with giving up physical control? Think about it. Let the answer come on its own terms.

In addition to using ḤAQQ for confrontations and during times of reflecting on tense interactions and disagreements, ḤAQQ can also work during meditation. Sitting for a lengthy time during meditation can bring on a kind of fatigue that has less to do with physical tiredness than it does with boredom. You may not need to reenergize with a ḤAYY breath, but instead just need a hard exhalation to generate an /ḥ/ feeling to express the boredom. Then just let go of physical control, the physical urge to move or do something else, to experience the /qq/. This simple breathing of the feelings for ḤAQQ can serves as a wake-up call, something to dispel the mental fatigue. It takes experience, self-study, and time in order to get to know your body and recognize which state of fatigue faces you. Sometimes you might exhale an /h̲/ feeling with the intention of continuing with H̲AYY and realize at that instant that you really do have enough energy and do not need H̲AYY, but rather have some form of mental fatigue. With experience you can recognize mental fatigue and know that instead of breathing H̲AYY you need the alternative H̲AQQ breath.

The doubling of the letter in the written representation indicates that you should hold the /q/ feeling longer than usual. So do not try to experience both the /h̲/ and the /qq/ on every breath. After feeling the /h/ through an exhalation, the /q/ feeling should begin and then continue through the intake of air on the next breath and not end until the final release of air in the second breath at the earliest.

## Traditional Use of H̲AQQ

H̲aqq translates into English as *truth*. Muslims traditionally use *haqq* to cast aside doubt and to realize spiritual truths. If you see the truth, that is ultimate truth, as something that you can physically control then *haqq* would not fit your definition. However, if you understand that ultimate truth cannot be physically manifested, then you know that you cannot dictate truth through any physical means, and in fact, only by giving up physical control can you approach real truth.

## *Settling Disagreements Using H̲AKAM and H̲AKÎM*

Disagreements often create frustration that manifests in an /h̲/ feeling. If you hold a position of authority and a dispute arises that fails to resolve in an easy manner, you can use H̲AKAM or H̲AKÎM to keep a mindful awareness as you work through the difficulty. Which of these two Names you should choose depends partially on the type of authority you command and on the method of resolution that seems appropriate. These conditions stem from the presence of the /î/ in H̲AKÎM and the lack of it in H̲AKAM. An /î/ denotes outside control. If you attempt to settle a clash by invoking some type of external control then use H̲AKÎM. External control in this situation might mean citing research or backing up a statement with indisputable facts or even using knowledge gained through personal study or experience, provided you treat such knowledge in an impersonal manner.

For ḤAKÎM the release of control afforded by the /k/ goes a long way in moving the problem at hand toward an agreeable conclusion, the target /m/. If you, as the person of rank, get perceived as having released physical control it makes it easier for everyone to drop their guard. The addition of the /î/ allows the natural arbitrator of external control to enter the picture, giving the resolution a form of authority in instances where you might lack legal or cultural standing. You may find ḤAKÎM beneficial when faced with an immediate confrontation as well as during times of reflection. If you ponder disagreements or competing ideas that you have encountered in the past, using ḤAKÎM can give you peace of mind over these incidents and help you prepare for such situations in the future.

If you possess a position of authority, such as an arbitrator or judge, someone who gets looked upon as having legally or culturally recognized power, you should use ḤAKAM if the position wields more power than the knowledge or facts you might use to resolve the situation. The release of control afforded by the /k/ in ḤAKAM provides the only necessary intermediate feeling to obtain the goal of resolving the issue, i.e., the pleasant /m/. A person of apparent authority who adopts an attitude of releasing physical control allows others to feel more at ease.

Like most of the Names beginning with /ḥ/ a specific breathing pattern can help generate the feelings of ḤAKÎM and ḤAKAM. Begin to let out air with an emphatic /ḥ/ and then switch to the /k/ while still exhaling. As you begin to take in air let the awareness rise from the abdomen. For ḤAKÎM bring your focus to the head to experience the /î/ before letting awareness expand to include the entire upper body as the /m/ fills you with a pleasant feeling of external control. With ḤAKAM as you inhale let your awareness focus on the chest and feel the pleasant /m/.

## Traditional Use of HAKÎM

*Hakîm* translates into English as *wise* or *most knowing*. Muslims traditionally use *hakîm* to develop their sense of understanding of the world and the true self. The SMY understanding of *hakîm* points to the benefit of its usage when you need wisdom to solve a problem.

## Traditional Use of HAKAM

*Hakam* translates into English as *judge* or *arbitrator*. Muslims traditionally use *hakam* to encourage the development of discernment of the senses and of the mind itself. The SMY usage of *hakam* coincides with the idea of acting as a judge.

## *Checking up with HASÎB*

Sometimes a person feels frustrated by ordinary routine. Mental life may seem like an endless stream of consciousness, that "monkey mind" that goes on and on. This may present as a yearning for something missing, and perhaps as a desire to take an objective inventory, to search for something unnamed, unknown. Describing this ennui in terms of sounds would require the /h/, but not just the /h/ alone. The stream of consciousness /s/ needs to be added to create the combination of /has/. The solution for fatigue brought on by this spinning of the wheels, this overabundance of mental chatter, lies in letting the feeling of an external force take control, i.e., opening up to the /î/. Some might describe this as abandoning left-brain thinking for right-brain thinking. Sufis might describe this as turning toward God. However you choose to portray it the /î/ enables the frustration to disappear and allows a pleasant feeling to takes its place, a feeling which you hold on to, as indicated by the /b/.

The appropriate times for using the Name HASÎB have some similarities to those when SALÂM applies. Both deal with perceived problems and stream of consciousness. SALÂM involves mental processes associated with analyzing or pondering a problem. For HASÎB the problem is the endless mental chatter itself. With SALÂM the solution involves letting go of the issue and relaxing, with the /lâ/, to avoid frustration. With HASÎB the answer lies in letting in external control, denoted by the /sî/. Both Names lead to a pleasant resolution; however, ḤASÎB uses a stronger form of pleasure to overcome the initial frustration.

## Traditional Use of ḤASÎB

*Hasîb* translates into English as *accounting* or *reckoning*. Muslims traditionally use *hasîb* to develop the ability to know and understand details of a particular aspect of their lives. The SMY analysis of *hasîb* recommends using this Name to ease the mind from mental gyrations. Anyone who does accounting or any job requiring attention to details and prolonged mental focus could find *hasîb* beneficial in granting them reprise from the grind of their task. Paradoxically, then, the SMY interpretation suggests using *hasîb* to counteract potential mental effects due to accounting, or similar mental efforts, rather than to develop the ability or capacity for such tasks. However, one can hardly become good at something if they do not know how to deal with the stressful nature of the undertaking.

## *Teaching with the Help of HÂDÎ*

HÂDÎ begins with the letter /h/, not /ḥ/ like the previous eight Names. This sound, /h/, carries a softer form of tiredness or exhaustion because the constriction in the throat to form the /h/ does not involve the back of the tongue like the /ḥ/ and requires less force to create. The /h/ in the Name HÂDÎ works in combination with the subsequent /â/. This /hâ/ takes away any tension present and engenders relaxation, a blend of feelings signaling patience. Thus HÂDÎ finds use for moods in which you need to exhibit patience; teaching represents an ideal scenario. Effective teaching occurs perhaps best whenever the teacher demonstrates both personal command and control of the situation and also points to a higher authority, perhaps a text, or a website, some external source, to back up the position the teacher posits. HÂDÎ has both of these elements as the goal. The /d/ represents the personal control and the /î/ the external source. This /dî/ combination supports a teacher's authority by merging the teacher's control with a higher, external control.

You can practice the pattern of HÂDÎ when you need patience, as in teaching, or during times of reflection whenever you contemplate how you could improve your behavior when facing situations that need patience.

## Traditional Use of HÂDÎ

*Hâdî* translates as *the guide*. Muslims traditionally use *hâdî* to seek guidance for daily living or a specific issue in a personal situation. The SMY interpretation of *hâdî* concurs with the translated meaning. The SMY usage takes a slightly different flavor than the traditional one, however. Instead of using *hâdî* when seeking guidance, the SMY recommends its usage for instances when you take on a guiding role.

## *Chapter Summary*

You can experience emotional tiredness through physical exhaustion, mental weariness, or pure emotional distress. The Names in this chapter can help you face these feelings of being drained by either bringing more energy, unblocking already present energy, helping use your current supply in a more efficient way, or helping you adapt to your situation. HAYY brings in physical energy whenever you feel lethargic, while HALÎM adjusts your attitude to allow you to endure physical drudgery. To help you feel good about demanding physical efforts, use HAMÎD. To bring focus whenever you face a mundane task try invoking HAFÎZ.

In the realm of mental tiredness HAQQ facilitates the resolution of interpersonal conflicts whenever resources lag; however, whenever you hold a position of authority HAKAM works better. HAKÎM proves helpful whenever mental efforts fail and you seek wisdom. When fatigue results from a mental overload then HASÎB can provide relief. Finally, HÂDÎ can help whenever you need mental energy to provide leadership.

# CHAPTER 14
## PHYSICAL RESPONSES TO FALLING SHORT OF A GOAL

One of the more common types of problems that people face involves inability to obtain something desirable. The /mu/ sound combination expresses this sentiment. The /m/ represents that favorable feeling associated with achieving an objective, while the /u/ represents the feeling resulting from not getting what you desire. The /u/ corresponds to a short-duration vowel sound as in *put*, and differs from /û/, which indicates emptiness on the pleasure dimension of emotions. The /u/ carries a weaker valence than the /û/ because to speak the /u/ the jaw drops slightly. This contributes a somewhat relaxed edge to the emotional quality of /u/, but it still carries a degree of unpleasantness. A /mu/ feeling indicates falling short of a goal.

Some situations in which a /mu/ feeling pervades can be thought of as an attack from a pair of opposite feelings, which according to Patanjali occurs due to improper posture. In chapter nine Names beginning with /ra/ and /râ/ dealt with opposites on the physical dimension. The /m/ and /u/ lie on the opposite end of the pleasure dimension. While the physical dimension impacts the issue of posture directly, the /mu/ opposites can have subtle effects on position during meditation. That is to say, some of the Names beginning with /mu/ will be useful during a traditional meditation setting in an effort to facilitate sitting still in a comfortable manner, as you shall see. However, a more common usage of Names beginning with /mu/ revolves around issues that one might face in daily living where something desirable falls out of reach.

The category of Names beginning with /mu/ makes up the largest single group of initial patterns in the traditional list of Ninety-nine Names. This plethora of such Names reflects the human condition where falling short of a goal or ideal happens on a regular basis. The twenty members of this collection fall into several subcategories, based upon the immediate reaction to the /mu/ feeling, i.e., the feeling/sound that follows the /mu/. These include seven physical control or energy-related reactions, six mentally-oriented approaches, three with an initial rejoinder related to pleasure, and four that have a general response to failure to obtain a goal. This chapter will only deal with the /mu/ Names that impact the arousal dimension. The other three groups will get addressed in later chapters.

## *Overcoming Feelings of Inadequacy with MUHAYMIN*

The Name MUHAYMIN works for times when a /mu/ feeling arises as a result of feeling that you cannot reach a particular physical goal because you lack confidence in yourself. In order to overcome this feeling of inadequacy MUHAYMIN responds to the /mu/ feeling with a string of three intermediate sounds before arriving at the target of a strong feeling of internal control. The follow-up sound to the /mu/, the /h/, acts as a way to eject the doubting or troubling /mu/. The /h/ exhausts or flushes out the /mu/ to give you a fresh start. With the /mu/ gone, the /y/ brings in energy for physical control. The subsequent /m/ then brings back the pleasant feeling you initially had for the situation, but this time without the troubling /u/. This resurgence of untainted pleasantness along with the boost in the physical realm affords the confidence needed for the strong feeling of control that comes with the /n/.

Even though MUHAYMIN deals with confidence issues it gets grouped with the physical reactions to the /mu/ feeling since its response to the issue involves increase in physical energy. MUHAYMIN can prove useful in everyday situations when your self-assurance falters, as well as when you reflect on times when your lack of resolve or initiative failed to achieve something important. It also can help during meditation when you experience discomfort sitting but wish to have the mental toughness to not let the discomfort grab your attention and cut your meditation time short by affording an infusion of energy. However, don't try to push boundaries of pain with MUHAYMIN.

## Traditional Use of MUHAYMIN

*Muhaymin* translates into English as *protection* or *security*. Muslims traditionally use *muhaymin* when they wish to have protection from potential adversaries or difficult situations. Using *muhaymin* in the SMY prescribed manner, i.e, to boost confidence for a trying task, seems quite similar to the traditional usage.

## *Infusing Energy with MUḤYÎ*

The Name MUḤYÎ shares some similarities with MUHAYMIN. Both effectively flush out the /mu/ with either an /h/ or /ḥ/ and both bring in physical control and energy with a /y/. However, the stronger /ḥ/ and the target of /î/ in MUḤYÎ establish significant differences between the usage and effect of the two Names. The /ḥ/ provides a dramatic, more energetic elimination of the /mu/ than an /h/. With the emphatic elimination of the /mu/ through the stronger /ḥ/ the incoming energy brought through the /y/ proves more invigorating than the more gentle energy from the /hy/ combination. The /ḥy/ pair works just as it does with the Name ḤAYY, i.e., it engenders a robust, energized feeling.

The final sound of MUḤYÎ, /î/, lets you feel as if an outside force controls you. Feeling as though not under your own control helps you to better integrate the energy from the /y/ by distancing yourself from the newfound energy and letting the energy permeate your being as a gift from the universe, or as the Sufis would say from Allah. The goal of MUḤYÎ, the /î/, speaks to the different circumstances for using MUḤYÎ, compared to the uses for MUHAYMIN. Use the latter for boosting confidence and generating a feeling of control for a task, but use MUḤYÎ when falling short of a goal due to lagging energy and when you seek help from a force outside your control.

MUḤYÎ, as is the case with MUHAYMIN, can find use during traditional meditation. Both Names shore up fading vigor. Which one you choose to help you feel more comfortable while you sit depends primarily upon the approach, i.e., how you breathe in the /mu/ feeling of not enough energy. A tentative response to the disconcerting /mu/ should lead to MUHAYMIN, whereas a more confident answer requires MU<u>H</u>YÎ.

## Traditional Use of MU<u>H</u>YÎ

*Mu<u>h</u>yî* translates into English as *revival* or *giving life*. Muslims traditionally use *mu<u>h</u>yî* to suffuse a person with needed energy and to overcome physical ailments. The SMY sequence of MU<u>H</u>YÎ can provide a needed boost when frustrated from lagging energy.

## *Taking Control with the Mind Using MUQADDIM*

The Name MUQUADDIM can help whenever you have a /mu/ feeling due to things unfolding counter to the way you wished but you see no practical alternative at the moment. The times for pushing on with the help of MUQUADDIM differ from those where <u>H</u>ALÎM applies. The instances for which <u>H</u>ALÎM works involve fatigue. With MUQADDIM, ennui rather than fatigue should trigger its use. For example, maybe a group to which you belong has decided to engage in an activity that was not your first choice. Rather than stewing over doing something you would rather not, you can use MUQADDIM to keep a mindful, in the present moment, attitude.

In such situations you reach the target of feeling the positive, pleasant /m/ through two main intermediate sounds/feelings. First, let go of physical control with the /q/. This release of control comes reluctantly, thus a /q/ and not a /k/. You don't really want to give up control, but see it as the best option. This release of physical control gets followed by a strong desire to hold on to mental control with the double /dd/. You need to control your mental processes and not let a /mu/ feeling return. Finally, with the proper frame of mind established by the /dd/ you can now bring back the /m/, this time without the /u/.

MUQADDIM works well in everyday situations where you need to avoid moping because you did not get your way. You can also practice MUQADDIM in times of reflection to prepare or enhance your ability to have a good attitude when doing obligated tasks. During meditation sessions MUQADDIM would not serve much purpose, unless you really wanted out of the session but felt obligated to continue in order to avoid making a disturbance for others in a class.

MUQADDIM doesn't apply automatically whenever things don't move in the way you wish. Certainly whenever you feel things are proceeding improperly you should try to change directions if you have the wherewithal. However, sometimes you must accept things you do not have the power to change. MUQADDIM facilitates this acceptance process.

## Traditional Use of MUQADDIM

*Muqaddim* translates into English as *the expeditor, the one who fosters,* or *the one who puts first.* Muslims traditionally use *muqaddim* to help fight impatience, among other reasons. Through the SMY usage of *muqaddim* you can find patience by developing forbearance.

## *Stop Fretting with MUQSIT*

The best way to understand the mood for which the Name MUQSIT addresses comes from looking at the two sounds that follow /mu/, the /q/ and /s/. What does giving up physical control (/q/) and getting the mental wheels churning (/s/) signify? Most people often face situations where they feel that something falls short of what they would like but see no easy option to change things on the physical level, yet that doesn't stop them from worrying about the matter and trying to think up something. For an example, think of situations when the political party in charge advocates for or enacts legislation that you oppose. Essentially, you have reluctantly yielded physical control to the opposing party, but your fretting about the opponent's agenda means you have not stopped expending mental energy. This /qs/ combination tags on to the gloomy /mu/ framework formulating the feeling of /muqs/. The only sound left in the Name, /t/, indicates the solution to this dilemma lies in the reluctant release of mental control.

The relinquishing of control offered by MUQSIT does not mean abandoning all hope. Rather MUQSIT simply allows you to let go of the mental effort associated with worrying about the problem. Looking for answers while caught in an anxious /mu/ mood does not usually prove productive. You need to free yourself from worry first. Not all problems exist for individuals to keep pondering and fretting over until solved. Using MUQSI**T** does not mean you relinquish responsibility. It just means that you don't have to carry the weight of the world on your shoulders all the time.

Understand that the above does not suggest abandoning political action as a solution when you do not realize a political goal. Act when times call for it, but don't needlessly suffer when no practical action appears in the present moment. Both MUQADDIM and MUQSI**T** adhere to the adage of "accept what you cannot change, have the courage to change what you can, and the wisdom to know the difference." Later in this chapter you will encounter the Name MUQTADIR, which helps whenever action in similar circumstances makes sense. However, practice MUQSI**T** whenever your wisdom rules out action in a real-life situation as described above, or in times of reflection in which you ponder such situations and wish to enhance your ability to better deal with them.

## Traditional Use of MUQSIT

*Muqsit* translates into English as *equitable, impartial,* or *just.* Muslims traditionally use *muqsit* to experience fairness and equitability in their life. The SMY usage of *muqsit* lets us accept non-favorable situations with equanimity or a sense of impartiality.

## *Letting Go of the Problem with MUQÎT*

The sound pattern for MUQSI**T** and MUQÎT vary only slightly but these differences dictate the contrasting situations for which these Names apply. While the /s/ in MUQSI**T** indicates thinking about the failure to reach a goal for which you see no physical control possible, the /î/ in MUQÎT denotes feeling under outside control. In other words MUQÎT applies in times where your response to the worrying, /mu/, situation does not include mental effort, but instead after giving up physical control you accept, or even one might say petition, outside control. Facing a health problem might provide an example of such a scenario where MUQÎT makes sense. Certainly everyone holds the pleasant feeling of good health as a goal which people often take for granted when they have it. When an illness arises it can create a nagging /mu/ feeling. If you have everything deemed feasible in seeking the best treatment possible, you can still often have a continuing struggle with a /mu/ feeling. In using MUQÎT in these situations you acknowledge, with the /q/, you do not have any more means to control the physical body and the illness that pervades it, and thus let an outside force, through the /î/, take control. This finally permits a letting go of any attempt for mental control, or mental effort, devoted to the situation, as signified by the /t/.

Besides the difference of /s/ versus /î/, the target feelings, /t̲/ in MUQSI̲T̲ versus /t/ in MUQÎT, also diverge, but only slightly, since both have the effect of giving up mental control. In effect the /t/ and /t̲/ both wash away the emotional turmoil, or disturbance brought on by the annoying situation denoted by the /mu/ with the elimination of the issue in case of the /t̲/ happening with reluctance. This subtle effect on the final impact of these two words occurs, in large part, due to the previous difference. In MUQSI̲T̲ the lingering effect of the mental effort /s/ shades the removal of the problem with slight regret. For MUQÎT the acceptance of outside control means that the release involves no regret. Use MUQÎT whenever you face instances where you have done what you can for a problem and have turned it over to an outside force.

## Traditional Use of MUQÎT

*Muqît* translates into English as *nourish* or *sustain*. Muslims traditionally use *muqît* to sustain or nourish the experience of a spiritual feeling. The SMY usage of *muqît* can engender a feeling that an outside force directs or sustains you in a time of need.

## *Taking Matters into Your Hands with MUQTADIR*

MUQÎT, MUQSI̲T̲, and MUQADDIM all deal with situations in which you cede physical control and do not take any steps to personally change the situation. You either let an outside force take control, with MUQÎT, or drop the matter, with MUQSI̲T̲, or retreat to find inner strength, with MUQADDIM. MUQTADIR offers a non-passive alternative that opts for action, as indicated by the target /r/ feeling. The initial /muq/

still corresponds to falling short of a goal and not being in control of the physical situation. The intermediate sounds/feelings that get you to action include a /t/ and /d/. The /t/ expresses a release of mental control; in this instance the /t/ relinquishes the control that the /muq/ situation has on your mind. Once free from the feeling of not being able to achieve a physical goal you secure a fresh mental start with the /d/. Then, having grabbed on to the feeling of being in mental control you can take advantage of the arousing /r/ in order to take action, or to put it another way, to "have the courage to change what you can."

MUQTADIR can help give you resolve in those situations where at first you might feel helpless, but do not want to acquiesce to the powers in control. Obviously the use of this word comes with a caveat. One should not tackle a challenge with the help of MUQTADIR without first taking into account the possible ramifications of your actions. Thus using MUQTADIR on the spur of the moment runs the risk of too little preparation or forethought. It seems best to prepare for the use of MUQTADIR through times of reflection, after you have thoroughly considered the implications of what you plan to attempt. With such caution in place MUQTADIR can help you overcome your feeling of not being in control and let you endeavor to change or adjust matters as you deem appropriate.

## Traditional Use of MUQTADIR

*Muqtadir* translates into English as *the powerful*. Muslims traditionally use *muqtadir* to develop confidence in their ability to control their own fate. This understanding of *muqtadir* fits the SMY interpretation quite well.

## *Increasing Determination with MUGHNÎ*

If you find yourself short of a physical goal, you can decide to persevere. Practicing the Name MUGHNÎ can help in such efforts. When faced with such a /mu/ scenario, the immediate response of /gh/ signifies a strong desire to hold on to physical control, an indication that you have not given up on obtaining your objective. Along with the desire for physical control comes firm mental control denoted by the /n/. Paradoxically this leads to feeling under external control, and the presence once again of the combination of internal and external control—this time as a /nî/ combination. In other words, by staying in command you have chosen to follow the path of a higher power, Allah to the Sufi. Put another way, by not giving up and remaining firm you align with the powerful force of universal consciousness prevalent in the universe. A familiar adage might frame this: "God helps those who help themselves."

MUGHNÎ represents a Name for which the best practice entails using the Name during times of reflection on instances when you have fallen short of a goal and anticipate a similar situation in the future when you would like to dig in and not give up, but instead push on with determination. You may also want to use this Name during the actual circumstance when such a scenario plays out. However, it seems advisable that in these cases you would have thought this action through prior to engaging in it.

## Traditional Use of MUGHNÎ

The English translation of *mughnî* is *the enricher*. Muslins traditionally use *mughnî* in order to bestow or petition for a blessing. The SMY usage gives this interpretation a slight twist. It suggests using *mughnî* in order to persevere toward a goal. If you look at the goal as a blessing then the SMY usage matches the traditional.

## *Chapter Summary*

This first group of /mu/ Names includes seven that apply various approaches to physical control to address situations in which you fall short of a goal. One Name, MUGHNÎ, simply tightens resolve to persevere in an effort to dispel your disappointment. In contrast MUHAYMIN allows you to gently dismiss a problem and gather energy for control, while MUḤYÎ brings a more enthusiastic approach to gathering physical energy. Both of these latter two Names can provide a needed energy boost during meditation.

Some of these Names have rather subtle differences, particularly the sub-group of four Names that follow the /mu/ with a /q/, a combination that indicates giving up physical control while failing to reach a goal. The several responses to such futile feelings yield different paths. You can: step back from the issue and gather mental control with MUQADDIM; exorcise the mental control the problem has on you with MUQSIT; withdraw from the problem and reach for outside assistance with MUQÎT; or regroup and start anew with a fresh perspective with MUQTADIR.

# CHAPTER 15
## USING MENTAL EFFORT TO CONFRONT PROBLEMS

The six Names beginning with /mu/ covered in this chapter take a mental control-oriented approach to a worrisome situation by employing either /s/, /t/, /n/, or /z/ as the follow-up feeling to the frustrated /mu/. Sometimes a failure to reach a goal evokes a mental response based on the way the problem arises and/or the personality of the individual in the trying situation. The use of some facet of mental control to address predicaments comes quite naturally, with many options available for the variety of situations one faces.

## *Moving On with MUHSÎ*

MUHYÎ and MUHSÎ differ by only a single element, the most important element of each sequence. As you recall from the previous chapter, MUHYÎ brings in energy needed for rejuvenation with the /y/. Instead with the /s/ MUHSÎ represents mental energy in the form of a stream of consciousness, an effort to establish internal control. The final sound/feeling in MUHSÎ, /î/, brings in the feeling of outside control—another juxtaposition of internal and external control. The goal of MUHSÎ, the /î/, indicates a need for a form of autopilot, an outside force to take command and free us from the lament of the /mu/. The /s/ simply provides the means to this end.

This difference between MUHYÎ and MUHSÎ further helps to clarify the usage of the latter. MUHYÎ can help bring in energy. For situations where MUHSÎ applies, the intake of energy would not prove beneficial. The problem prompting the /mu/ feeling in a MUHSÎ scenario stems from a lack of understanding. The presence of the /s/ represents a need to bring clarity to the situation. Whenever confusion rules over a situation, whenever you cannot find your way forward and seem mired in the blues of a /mu/ state, you can flush those blahs out with the /h/ and then as the /s/ searches for a way through the impasse, the solution appears—an /î/. You finally admit your lack of direction and cede control over to the outside force, Allah to the Sufi.

## Traditional Use of MUḤSÎ

*Muḥsî* translates into English as *the one who knows, appraisal* or *reckoning*. Muslims traditionally use *muḥsî* to promote one's ability to pay attention to detail as an accountant would. The SMY interpretation seems to stand in contrast to the traditional one. However, you can draw a parallel between the two. In the common usage a person employs *muḥsî* to promote the ability to appraise a situation. The SMY analysis calls for using *muḥsî* whenever you cannot fathom how to proceed, in other words whenever you lack the ability to appraise a situation. So the traditional and SMY viewpoints agree about the times for which *muḥsî* applies. The difference between the two approaches lies in where the perception of control lands. For the traditional approach the supplicant asks to be given the ability to appraise the situation. The SMY user forsakes this ability and lets the outside force assume control.

## *Taking Action with MUSAWWIR*

The Name MUSAWWIR applies whenever you encounter mental roadblocks to accomplishing an objective. It seems that many people often get stuck on certain negative thoughts about aspects of a job and therefore hesitate to move forward. You might think, "Oh, this task takes more energy (or smarts, or something else) than I have. How will I even be able to get it done?" even though you still could accomplish many preliminary steps, which could likely unblock the obstacles that have caused the anguish, the /mu/ feeling. The /s/ in this instance represents the mental chatter, stream of consciousness that keeps you going over and over the issue that generated the /mu/ feeling.

The intermediate sound employs a double /ww/ to eliminate the negativity that has paralyzed your efforts and kept you from doing anything. Once you have cleared the negative portion of the /mu/ feelings you can apply energy, /r/, to the situation and get yourself moving forward, no longer at an impasse. If during times of reflection you think about projects that you have put off or avoided because of nagging doubts, it may prove wise to practice the way out offered by MUSAWWIR.

The situations for which MUSAWWIR applies differ from those times when you should use SALÂM. Both of these Names work with situations where you think about problems. SALÂM helps to still mental chatter, clear your mind, and relax. The /mu/ feeling indicates an emotional response to a problem. With MUSAWWIR you clear away the negative emotion and act.

## Traditional Use of MUSAWWIR

*Musawwir* translates into English as *the fashioner*. Muslims traditionally use *musawwir* to generate motivation to get working on an objective. The SMY usage duplicates this.

## *Feeling Hopeful with MUTA'ÂLÎ*

Two of the Names dealing with a /mu/ feeling have an initial response of /t/. The /t/ in this context has the effect of releasing the control that the /mu/ has on the mind. In other words, in the face of a disturbing or anxious /mu/ moment the /t/ takes your mind off of the problem. The situations where it makes sense to ignore the unsettling /mu/ feeling would typically be ones you have faced previously. Such times occur often for most people. Perhaps you feel an upsetting /mu/ when thinking about a familiar situation at work. Or maybe a relationship with a friend has prompted such feelings. In these instances perhaps you sense something missing, something falling short of what could be a pleasant interaction. When these chronic anguish-producing encounters put you into a bad /mu/ mood, you can take preemptive action with the /t/ response. The two Names with the /mut/ beginning take separate tracks after the /t/, in effect sweeping away the problem. One Name, MUTA'ÂLÎ, turns hopeful and looks to an outside force, while the other, MUTAKABBIR, bristles with confidence.

Sometimes when you experience apprehension or anxiety about a familiar problem you can decide that ignoring it, as happens with

/mut/, would serve as the best approach. Perhaps you consider the issue simply a trifling that should not matter, maybe it's a recurring problem that you feel comfortable dismissing, or perhaps you feel that getting riled up only compounds the predicament. Once you decide to pay no attention to unsettling feelings, it can cause an emotional moment of questioning due to uncertainty or lack of confidence. A cathartic /'/ can clear that emotion. Once you have overcome the emotional questioning about the dismissal of the nagging feelings you can afford to relax. The /â/ provides this relaxation. From that relaxed state it becomes easy to let the matters that instigated the negativity ebb away. The /l/ provides this smooth flowing vibe. Finally, then in a relaxed, easy going manner you can accept the feeling of outside control, /î/, as though you put your faith in the powers of universal consciousness, God, or Allah, to see you through the problem.

Using MUTA'ÂLÎ during day to day events can help you as it gives pause to minor troubles and lets you feel more hopeful, rather than mulling things over. Practicing MUTA'ÂLÎ during times of reflection can facilitate the automatic engagement of the Name at an appropriate later time. Finally, MUTA'ÂLÎ often has a useful role in meditation. If you have a practice of watching the breath and expecting to feel a pleasant /ma/ in anticipation of MALIK or MATÎN but instead a bothersome /mu/ emotion comes to your awareness for some reason, you can learn to adapt to this scenario by dismissing the /mu/ with /t/ and following through with the remainder of MUTA'ÂLÎ. This sequence can smooth over minor interruptions to a meditation session.

## Traditional Use of MUTA'ÂLÎ

*Muta'âlî* translates into English as *exalted* or *most high*. Muslims traditionally use *muta'âlî* to promote a feeling of worthiness or being lifted up in spirit. The SMY usage of *muta'âlî* takes you out of a funk and lets you feel comfortably under the auspices of an outside force.

# Feeling Confident in the Face of Adversity with MUTAKABBIR

While MUTA'ÂLÎ finds use whenever you might harbor doubts about dismissing an issue, MUTAKABBIR works for instances when you have confidence and relish jettisoning your unsettling mood. For times whenever you fail to obtain a goal, a /mu/ situation, you can use the Name MUTAKABBIR in order to cultivate feelings of confidence and optimism and not let the disappointment that triggered the /mu/ feeling linger.

The target of MUTAKABBIR consists of not just the alert and energized /r/, but an /r/ that comes on the heels of a strong feeling of holding on to something pleasant, a double /b/, a very optimistic combination, the /bbir/. To reach this desired state MUTAKABBIR uses two intermediate sounds/feelings, a /t/ and a /k/. The /t/ releases any mental control that the /mu/ might have exerted upon you. Again as with MUTA'ÂLÎ you let go of the /mu/ feeling, but with MUTAKABBIR you do not have reservations. You release the control the /mu/ feeling has on your mind with confidence. The next step in the progression of MUTAKABBIR brings us to a /k/ and the release of any physical control. You can understand the /k/ in this context as letting go of control to keep you from expending effort to effect a change to the initial physical conditions that precipitated the /mu/ feeling. Once you have cleared out any lingering mental effects initiated by the /mu/ via the /t/ and have freed yourself from any desire to get further embroiled in the state of affairs with the /k/, you can now embrace the strong feeling of pleasantness, the /bb/. It feels good to rid the mental and physical control associated with what precipitated the /mu/ discomfort. This positive /bb/ feeling then bleeds over into the energetic /r/. In other words you can go about your business with positive energy ignoring the problem. You move on, refreshed.

## Traditional Use of MUTAKABBIR

*Mutakabbir* translates into English as *the majestic* or *the supreme.* Muslims traditionally use *mutakabbir* to promote a feeling of self-confidence. The SMY interpretation does lend itself to a majestic sense of carrying oneself. With *mutakabbir* you can go on with your life without letting yourself get bogged down by minor emotional baggage.

## *Dealing with a Desire for Revenge Using MUNTAQIM*

Whenever another person or thing causes you to miss an objective or lose a pleasant goal you experience a /mu/ feeling. Often a craving for control, an /n/ feeling, occurs as the natural initial reaction to such circumstances. Humankind's innate survival instinct dictates a need to be in control. Most people, especially those accustomed to having their way, have this instinctual /n/ reaction to unfavorable outside manipulation. In such circumstances many have the tendency to act without thinking in a purely reactive mode. This can lead to incidents that prove embarrassing at the least and often more problematic. The Name MUNTAQIM helps modulate this /n/ reaction to externally instigated /mu/ moments in a manner that keeps you from hastily engaging in behavior that you might later regret.

MUNTAQIM has a target feeling of pleasantness. You should not want to follow up on a desire for revenge, but rather seek justice in a socially acceptable manner and avoid regretting an impulsive knee-jerk reaction. The intermediate sounds that dissolve the initial revengeful /mun/ urge back to a goal of a simple /m/ include the intermediate steps achieved through /t/ and /q/. The /t/ abolishes the control that the /mun/ has on the mind. However, getting the revenge just out of the mind does not go far enough. The instinctual physical urge also needs swept away via the /q/. Once you have quelled the /mun/ moment's influence on your mind and body a simple pleasant /m/ can return.

### Traditional Use of MUNTAQIM

*Muntaqim* translates into English as *revenge*. Muslims traditionally use *muntaqim* when seeking revenge for a perceived wrong they endured. While it may seem that this traditional usage of *muntaqim* directly contradicts the SMY usage, a closer inspection shows how these two viewpoints converge. A traditional interpretation indicates that a person seeking revenge for a wrong should use this name. The SMY guidance suggests the same, i.e, if you harbor feelings of revenge, you should use this name. Now with the traditional usage one expects that Allah will serve justice against those who committed a wrong. This should be all well and good, as long as the supplicant does not take the act of revenge upon themselves. With the SMY analysis it is understood that any desire to act out against a person who has wronged you will be nullified with *muntaqim*. So ideally in either case wantonly acting on the feelings of revenge gets prevented.

## *Letting a Disappointment Hang On with MUZILL*

Sometimes it makes sense not to fight against a disappointing feeling but instead let it stew or fester. You may understand this through the expression, "No pain. No gain," although in this case it does not refer to physical pain of a workout leading to bulkier muscles as a result. Instead /mu/ indicates emotional pain. If you run from a negative emotional experience without absorbing the lesson that it has, you may have to relive it again and again until you have soaked in its meaning. MUZILL can let you take in the low /mu/ state and lead you to its acceptance, which comes in the form of the target /l/. To get to this accepting, flowing /l/ state requires the intermediate sound/feeling of /z/. The /z/ turns down your stream of consciousness so that the /mu/ doesn't occupy you in a pressing manner, but rather lets you accept the /mu/ and leads into the flowing state, emphasized by a double /ll/.

Not all /mu/ feelings should get addressed with MUZILL. Exercise caution when using or exploring this sequence. Develop an understanding of the various Names that can address the common /mu/ feelings before embarking on the path of MUZILL. However, letting a disappointment sink in can allow you to see yourself as someone vulnerable and as somebody who does not know all the answers. This understanding of the self can balance an overly optimistic or egotistical person. MUZILL can also help people with low esteem by letting them feel the acceptance of this natural state. Some Sufis use MUZILL in order to evoke a feeling of low esteem, along with the claim that until you have felt the divine quality of low esteem you cannot dissolve the false self.[48]

## Traditional Use of MUZILL

*Muzill* translates into English as *the dishonorer*. Some Muslims use *muzill* to debase or bring someone down. SMY takes the viewpoint that the Names should be used for personal growth and self-knowledge, not as an attempt to thwart or challenge another person. The SMY interpretation of *muzill* hits rather close to the Sufi viewpoint of needing to experience the divine quality of low esteem.

## *Chapter Summary*

The Names in this group take a mental approach to solving problems stemming from feeling that a goal eludes you. Only one of these finds use during meditation. MUTA'ÂLÎ can help get your meditation session back on track by releasing feelings of doubt and bringing you back to a mindful state. MUTA'ÂLÎ also serves to dispel negative feelings experienced during daily living and lets you connect to a divine presence.

The others Names of the chapter work on particular problematic situations. MUHSÎ gives solace whenever you lack insight on how to proceed. You can overcome negative emotional blocks and get back on a positive track through the use of MUSAWWIR. MUTAKABBIR generates confidence to proceed. If you need to quell a desire for acting against someone that wronged you, MUNTAQIM can help quiet those revengeful instincts. Finally, MUZILL facilitates acceptance of disappointment.

# CHAPTER 16
## PLEASURE SEEKING TO WORRISOME MOMENTS

The Names in this chapter help find the silver lining in a situation where a goal cannot be obtained. Two Names take the unorthodox approach to anxious moments by initially responding with a sound indicating pleasure, one with an /m/ and the other with a /b/. A third Name in this chapter uses a /j/ response to the /mu/. This gets included even though the sound immediately following the /mu/ does not directly engage the pleasure dimension of emotion, i.e., involve the lips for articulation. The control expressed by the /j/ lies between mental and physical, due to the point of articulation, and thus does not fit the criteria for inclusion with either of the previous chapters. Additionally, the goal for this Name—/b/— gives further reason to place the Name in this chapter.

## *Finding Pleasure in Challenges with MUBDÎ'*

When faced with challenging situations where you must solve some sort of problem, whether logistical, stylistic, artistic, human resource based, or some other issue, you have a better chance at attaining a successful solution by accepting the challenge with a positive attitude. MUBDÎ' can help you achieve this type of approach to demanding tasks. The /mu/ feeling comes from the problem. A pleasant, positive, /m/ goal exists but at first it remains unrealized, empty as the /u/ indicates. By grasping this circumstance as a positive opportunity you, in effect, respond to the /mu/ with a /b/ feeling. The subsequent /d/ indicates that this optimistic acceptance expressed by /mub/ has led to a feeling that you mentally have the situation under control. At this point comes the paradoxical feeling of being under an outside influence, the /î/. This might be thought of as a natural consequence of the leap of faith you have taken to attack a problem as an opportunity—as though you have left your fate to the unknown. The

159

hamza, /'/, at the end of the Name dismisses the feeling of outside control, enabling you to deal with the issue at hand.

An example of where MUBDÎ' would apply might help you understand how it works. Consider an artist who faces a blank canvas. This person has a positive, pleasant goal in mind, a finished painting. However, because the painter has not yet accomplished that goal the /m/ comes with a /u/ attached. Accepting this challenge in a positive manner and keeping that mindset expresses the /mubd/ portion of MUBDÎ'. The artist still needs to emotionally let go of control of the outcome and accept external control, as indicated by the /î/, before releasing the sequence and getting on with their work. The hamza, /'/, allows this release. Some artists will characterize the external control as a muse, a feeling that their artwork comes through some outside force or conduit.

Of course MUBDÎ' can apply to non-artistic situations which call for solving novel tasks. Challenging undertakings share some characteristics with creating art. In tackling problems you have to take the initiative and combine elements that you work with in a fresh or original way. And although you might not feel or believe in the presence of a muse, you will find it necessary to let go if you want to get started on a problem. Otherwise your inability to control the outcome at the starting part can keep you paralyzed. One needs to let go and have faith to accomplish goals. MUBDÎ' helps us do this.

## Traditional Use of MUBDÎ'

*Mubdî'* translates into English as *the originator*. Muslims traditionally use *mubdî'* to generate originality, to take the initiative in getting things done. The SMY interpretation of *mubdî'* fits well with the traditional one.

## *Dealing with Thoughts of Death with MUMÎT*

Every person eventually faces death. Our human condition ensures that outcome. Many people face death with fear. However, such irrational fear does not gain us anything. In fact it only increases a person's anxiety and studies show that elevated levels of anxiety have negative health effects. So, one should not face thoughts about death with fear but with equanimity. The Name MUMÎT can help you quell your fear of death, yours or another person's who you hold close to you, and let you face it with calmness.

Death does not constitute a positive experience, but one should see life as a positive /m/ experience. However, life eventually leads to death, so the /m/ associated with life turns into /mu/ when looking at the bigger picture. The goal of MUMÎT consists of the /ît/ combination, that is to say, you should let your inevitable death into the hands of a greater, outside power, /î/, and let go of any control these thoughts have with the /t/. An /m/ works as the intermediate sound/feeling necessary for reaching this goal. Why see thoughts about death as pleasant? No other options make sense. Using a sound associated with control in an effort to make death go away obviously fails. Fighting death with the physical arousal of /r/ doesn't work. Relax about thoughts of death with an /â/ and in effect dwell on the thoughts. Unpleasant /û/ emotions about death have negative impact on health. So accept death as part of life—part of a pleasant existence.

It helps to understand the pleasant /m/ as the transition in this Name if you see it connected to the subsequent /î/. If you can see the creation of your life, and all life for that matter, as something beyond your control, you should be able to sense and feel the presence of an outside force, the /î/, in the issue of death. With this sanguine /m/ acceptance of /mu/ thoughts and feelings about death, you can move through these fears and trepidations, see your existence as beyond your control (with /î/), and then let go of efforts to control death (with /t/).

## Traditional Use of MUMÎT

*Mumît* translates into English as *the creator of death*. Some militant Muslims use *mumît* against a perceived enemy in hope of destroying it. Sufis and SMY have a different interpretation of its use. They recommend using *mumît* in order to soothe the fear of death.

## *Tackling a Concern with MUJÎB*

Some problems exist that could get done by any of several or possibly a large number of people. For example, take a volunteer organization where details of the next meeting need to be addressed. Maybe a speaker needs to be contacted, or arrangements made for accommodations of a guest. If no one has specific duties to cover these jobs then someone must volunteer. MUJÎB can help you assert yourself and take on such tasks while feeling good about it. The /m/ represents the good feeling that the finished task would generate, and the /u/ reflects the job's unfulfilled status. You can get to the target, /b/, of feeling good about the circumstances via the two intermediate steps. First, the /j/ lets you feel emotionally in control of the situation. Then in direct contrast the /î/ lets you feel under control by an outside force. You can understand this paradox of being in control and being controlled when you consider the relative influences. You feel in control because you have taken action to solve a problem. However, because your actions do not help you as an individual but work for something which holds sway over you, you feel the presence of an outside force—the commitment that you made.

MUJÎB can work in daily circumstances especially if you have practiced or contemplated the Name in anticipation of times where it would apply. As with most of the Names, once you have practiced and meditated on them during times of reflection, over time you will find that they will come to the surface as needed in everyday situations.

MUJÎB can even prove useful during meditation. It can help you overcome a flagging commitment to keep up a practice to which you have dedicated yourself. In this instance the /mu/ problem concerns your dwindling commitment and the outside force which you seek union with in meditation, Allah for the Sufi. One needs to use MUJÎB with caution. While this sequence can get you focused on a chore or extend meditation sessions, your use of MUJÎB may cause you to ignore more pressing concerns. Do not underestimate the power of the mind to block out pain that should get your attention. Ignored pain during meditation that leads to serious physical problems, e.g., lack of circulation from sitting on a foot causing permanent damage, will happen only over an extended period of time, usually more than an hour. Most meditation sessions, especially for beginners, fall short of this criterion. However, meditation practices do often grow and habits adopted along the way generally tag along. I would not make a habit of continual use of MUJÎB in meditation for these reasons.

## Traditional Use of MUJÎB

*Mujîb* translates into English as *responsive*. Muslims traditionally use *mujîb* when they need encouragement to take action and accomplish tasks from which they may have shied away. The SMY usage also reflects this notion of encouraging action.

## *Chapter Summary*

Our third collection of Names with an initial /mu/ takes the paradoxical approach of finding something pleasurable in the failure to reach a desirable goal. These Names do not have a masochistic essence, but rather a practical one. MUBDÎ' allows you to take on a problem with enthusiasm, while MUMÎT helps you deal with feelings concerning death and dying. Finally, MUJÎB lets you feel good about striving for a resolution to an existing problem.

# CHAPTER 17
## GLOBAL RESPONSES TO FRUSTRATED MOMENTS

This chapter includes four Names that don't fit into the physical, pleasurable, and mental response to /mu/ situations. Two Names in this chapter have the cathartic ayin, /'/, as the initial response to unsettling /mu/ emotion. Whenever falling short of your goal invokes an emotional pent-up feeling—sometimes characterized as a lump in the throat—you may be able to relieve the tension with an ayin, /'/. The other two Names presented here use the hamza to disconnect from the disappointment expressed by the /mu/ and allow you to move past the obstacle onto something new.

### Getting Relief with MU'ÎD

Most people find themselves in situations in which they strive for an ideal or goal but face obstacles or challenges that thwart efforts to secure it. Such struggles can create disturbing distress. When you stew on such emotional turmoil the ayin can provide the first step in resolving this dilemma. The follow-up to the /'/ consists of some form of control. What kind of control depends upon the source of the precipitating conditions. If some kind of physical malady has generated your distress MU'ÎD will best suit your needs. Some examples of this include illness, muscle strains, and other intrusions on an otherwise healthy existence. Everyone seeks the ideal hale hardiness that at some point they have experienced or at least witnessed in others. However, in times of sickness or whenever injuries limit activity you can experience a troubling /mu/ feeling because a return to healthiness seems unobtainable. The ayin releases the anguish, the pent-up emotion built by frustrated efforts to achieve the desired physical state. Once the cathartic /'/ has cleared the emotional palate the solution appears—the /îd/ combination that allows you to feel you have a grip on the problem because an outside force has control. MU'ÎD can help you cope with these troubling feelings by providing hope that you can get assistance for your maladies by surrendering to an outside, powerful force.

Although using MU'ÎD to help cope with an illness or injury can provide emotional succor, using a Name does not substitute for sound medical care. Certain Names, when used judiciously, can augment therapeutic treatment from a reliable physician or therapist. The proper application of Names can foster emotional equanimity which has been shown to boost the immune system and promote better healing.

## Traditional Use of MU'ÎD

*Mu'îd* translates into English as *restorer* or *renewal*. Muslims traditionally use *mu'îd* to renew energy and restore health when afflicted with ailments. This traditional usage fits the SMY guidelines.

## *Accepting Praise with MU'IZZ*

MU'ÎD finds use for emotional reactions to physical shortcomings, especially health infirmities. You can also experience a swirling of feelings associated with a /mu/ that merit a /'/ response from social embarrassment. In these instances the use of MU'IZZ can prove beneficial. For example, if you do a particular task in an awkward manner or express an idea that others find objectionable it can cause humiliation which MU'IZZ can address. The /mu'/ corresponds to the failure to be seen as competent. The /zz/ lets your stream of consciousness shift to the background in order to avoid dwelling on the discomfort.

The use of MU'IZZ doesn't only apply to gaffes. Whenever you receive accolades for an accomplishment or notable deed that you have rendered, it usually induces a sense of pleasure, /m/. For a modest or shy person, praise can produce an uncomfortable /mu'/ feeling. Others for whom praise comes on a regular or routine basis might have no difficulty savoring the pleasantness that accompanies praise. In other words these folks can easily find themselves in an /ma/ or /mâ/ state that may or may not take them to a suitable target emotional state. MU'IZZ allows a humble person to accept the commendations of others in a modest, natural, easygoing manner.

The response to those unwanted /mu'/ moments in the spotlight consists simply of letting a low-key stream of consciousness take over, i.e., adopting a /zz/ state of mind. By just letting thoughts go without trying to figure anything out or attributing any value to them you can accept a situation without letting it deflate or swell your ego. If you find that your ego gets deflated or inflated whenever you perceive yourself being judged by others, remember MU'IZZ and contemplate this Name to keep your ego on an even keel.

## Traditional Use of MU'IZZ

*Mu'izz* translates into English as *the honorer*. Muslims traditionally use *mu'izz* to express honor or praise. The SMY usage of *mu'izz* has a connection with this traditional one, since SMY recommends using *mu'izz* when you receive honors or when your honor runs the risk of being smeared.

## *Waiting in an Alert State with MU'AKHKHIR*

Everybody has experienced times when they can't have what they want, but just need to step back and not worry about it. MU'AKHKHIR has a bit of the flavor of the adage "good things come to those who wait." MU'AKHKHIR applies to times where it makes sense to dismiss the /mu/ feeling because you do not need to or should not act at the moment but can wait in a prepared alert state, signified by the /r/.

A hamza, /'/, forms the initial response to our thwarted desire. This creates a break from the disappointing /mu/. The hamza allows a fresh outlook on the situation which the double /kh/ provides. The /kh/ indicates an emphatic need to refrain from trying to control the situation, and its dual appearance further stresses this sentiment. In other words quit being a control freak: "You can't always get what you want." The final sound, /r/, indicates, you still need to stay alert. Stay in the game, but you don't have the driver's seat at the moment.

## Traditional Use of MU'AKHKHIR

*Mu'akhkhir* translates into English as *the delayer*. Muslims traditionally use *mu'akhkhir* in an effort to postpone an occurrence until a more propitious time, or to simply avert a negative outcome. This interpretation parallels the SMY one.

## *Remaining Steady with MU'MIN*

MU'MIN can prove useful in everyday living whenever distracted by something that does not fit your established value system, for example, somebody promoting a rule or custom that you find objectionable, or some Facebook post that expresses a viewpoint counter to your ideals. If you recognize a distressing /mu/ from such interactions, you can return to feeling in control, the target /n/ of MU'MIN, with two intermediate steps. First, you break free from the /mu/ with a /'/. The hamza allows the pleasant /m/ to appear—it feels good to get past the disagreeable interruption. Once a pleasant sensation has replaced the distracting /mu/ a feeling of taking control follows.

MU'MIN can also serve to keep minor disturbances from getting you off track during meditation. Your unconscious mind can play tricks on you by getting you to think that you need to stop meditating to attend to a physical discomfort, when in fact the distress comes from a psychosomatic source. The tension may feel physical but your mind can control it. When the pleasantness of meditation practice gets interrupted by unwanted and unexpected unpleasant sensations, you can easily lose focus. Such loss can be remedied by the Name MU'MIN, as the hamza disrupts the distraction and allows pleasant control to return.

The repetition of MU'MIN to allow the continuation of a meditation session does not pose the same risk as repeating MUJÎB. The breath (/'/) in MU'MIN releases tension, but the /j/ of MUJÎB holds on to control. If you find the break provided by the breath in MU'MIN effective in dissolving the /mu/ then you have a handle on the source of the problem. MUJÎB ignores the problems and pushes through. MU'MIN addresses the issue.

## Traditional Use of MU'MIN

*Mu'min* translates into English as *source of faith* or *remover of fear*. Muslims traditionally use *mu'min* to develop a feeling of security in their faith and in their life's situation. Sufis believe that *mu'min* can free you from doubt. The SMY usage of *mu'min* lets you remove the unwarranted unpleasant distractions that occur during daily life and/or during meditation.

## *Chapter Summary*

The Names in this chapter follow the /mu/ with either the emotional ayin, /'/, or the distant hamza, /'/. In two Names the ayin indicates that the failure to reach the pleasant objective has created an emotional reaction or blockage. MU'ÎD can improve your attitude toward an illness or physical problem, while MU'IZZ helps deal with uncomfortable feelings from being in the spotlight. The hamza in two other Names creates a break from the disappointing /mu/ and allows you to move past the incident. MU'AKHKHIR allows you to wait expectantly, while MU'MIN lets you return to feeling in control as you dismiss disconcerting intrusions.

# CHAPTER 18
## DEALING WITH EMPTY FEELINGS
## AND FEELINGS OF AWE

The Names discussed in this chapter all begin with /w/. The common substrate of the emotional state for which these Names apply presents as an "empty" feeling. Emptiness in an emotional context typically infers a negative condition. Depressed persons often use the word *empty* when asked how they feel, but other persons not considered depressed can endure such states, for example, someone simply having a blah day, or someone missing seeing a friend or relative. In terms of the three dimensions of emotional, such an empty state succinctly describes the one pole of the pleasure dimension, the empty pole, unpleasantness. Certainly an objective description of a depressed person's empty feeling would ascribe unpleasantness to that state.

Using a Name beginning with /w/ for a prevailing emotional valence of unpleasantness appears to violate the SMY rule that a Name must begin with a sound that matches the current emotional state. In a strict sense it does break this rule. However, SMY allows the /w/ to begin sequences in instances of unpleasant (or empty pleasure) valence because the initial position of the lips for the /w/ matches the position of the lips for the unpleasant/empty /û/. When a vowel other than /û/ follows the /w/, the emotional effect of releasing unpleasantness occurs because the lips move away from the position for /û/ into a new emotional mood that differs from unpleasantness. Thus a Name beginning with /w/ starts with the releasing or discharging the unpleasant/empty /û/ mood, and therefore does match the current mood. Simply by employing SMY principles and using such a Name you have taken a step toward freeing yourself from this /û/ mood. During times of emotional emptiness using a Name beginning with /w/ can help bring relief.

Although some Names beginning with /w/ work with negative empty states typical of some depressed moods, other Names with an initial /w/ apply to states one would not necessarily consider negative, or perhaps only subtly negative. Sometimes a /w/ works to dispel an emptiness of something yearned for, a positive thing. If you feel a lack of somebody's trust or a person's affection, it can present a concern best addressed with a /w/.

The /w/ has still another manner in which it can operate. If your emotional state exists at a neutral pleasure level, then a /w/ comes across as uplifting. In scenarios harboring potential for a positive emotion, using a /w/ can convey a feeling of awe. Such times include witnessing natural beauty and great works of art where the /w/ expresses that "wow" feeling. A religious person can use certain Names beginning with /w/ when they feel that they have temporarily strayed from the positive presence of God and wish to regain a feeling of closeness to their object of worship.

The nine Names beginning with /w/ in this chapter can apply to either the negative empty conditions or more or less neutral empty states. In addition to distinguishing between the type of valence for the /w/ in the Names in this chapter, the Names also fall into two general categories, five that begin with /wâ/ and four that begin with /wa/. Some of the Names beginning with /wâ/ will work with unpleasant moods that feel lethargic or maybe just lack energy. One commonly finds such unpleasant and lethargic moods in depressed persons, although these /wâ/ Names can help persons not considered clinically depressed, but rather simply in a funk or the throes of a bad day or rotten afternoon. Other Names beginning with /wâ/ can help to fill emptiness with moments of awe and wonder. The four Names beginning with /wa/ will apply to situations where you do have an appreciable amount of energy, when the negative or empty feeling has not zapped your energy.

## *Stepping Back with WÂLÎ*
People of faith often deal with troubling, unenergetic, empty feelings by turning to an outside force, God or Allah to most. Putting one's faith in God's hand or asking God for comfort can provide solace to a

believer. The Name WÂLÎ can help make it feel that such solicitation has value. The /wâ/ corresponds to the lethargic emptiness. The target, /î/, of feeling under the control of an outside power comes simply by allowing things to proceed without interference, as denoted by the /l/.

An alternative way to look at WÂLÎ takes the point of view that the /lî/ combination indicates letting go of control, but leaving the outside force as an unknown, and therefore not part of a faith system. Still a third option for understanding WÂLÎ would recognize the outside force as a known entity in the world for which you have little choice but to submit. For example, a government policy that requires something of you, perhaps taxes. When you experience an unsettling emptiness, whether from an unknown cause or from the seemingly oppressive nature of the society in which you live, repeating WÂLÎ can fill the void and allow you to continue functioning or meditating.

## Traditional Use of WÂLÎ

*Wâlî* translates into English as *governor*. Muslims traditionally use wâlî to reach out to a higher power for restraint or self-control. The SMY usage of wâlî shares some of this understanding. Instead of looking for restraint from a higher power the SMY interpretation simply recognizes that force as being in control.

## *Washing Away Emptiness with WÂ͟HID*

Sometimes you might feel empty, devoid of feelings and energy, and lacking a purpose or direction. This kind of glumness can trigger a serious depressed state of mind, if left unchecked. The Name WÂ͟HID can help keep the mood from shifting into a dire feeling of hopelessness and move it back to a purposeful awareness in which you feel in control. While the /w/ works by clearing out emptiness and unpleasant feelings, the /h̲/ clears the lethargy expressed by the /â/. The target of /d/ (the short /i/ has no significant impact) leaves you feeling in control, simply by being proactive and instigating the flushing of the emptiness away. Using WÂ͟HID amounts to giving yourself a slap and saying, "Snap out of it." This approach can prove quite effective for dealing with amorphous bouts of the "blahs" where you catch yourself in a down state for no apparent reason. The Name has less success with more chronic periods of the blues.

## Traditional Use of WÂHID

*Wâhid* translates into English as *the unique*. Muslims traditionally use *wâhid* when they want to stand out and just be themselves. The SMY interpretation of *wâhid* does not agree or disagree with this general traditional definition and usage. Using *wâhid* with SMY guidelines can take you out of a funk and let you feel in control. One might characterize this as awakening from a sluggish, bewildered state and letting you see yourself as a unique individual.

## *Picking Yourself Up with WÂRITH*

WÂRITH provides an approach to an empty, languid feeling by directing energy, in the form of /r/, into the mood in order to disperse lethargy and allow a feeling of light control, /ith/ to take over. The type of empty mood appropriate for WÂRITH often involves a situation where you need to move past a poor choice or result. Dwelling on past mistakes, those "might have been" feelings or those "I should have" thoughts, can put you in a downward spiral that ends up in a depressed mood. To escape such doldrums you need to lift yourself up and take action, move past the regrets, and face the future with possibilities of better times. WÂRITH can help you achieve this outlook. The /w/ rids you of the negative affect, while the /r/ provides the energy to perk you up and overcome the /â/. Finally the /th/ generates gentle control. The subtle control afforded by the /th/ works better in this situation than other sounds associated with control, such as /n/, /s/, or /d/ because of the tentative nature of the new start and follow-up to the funky mood.

WÂRITH can also apply to times of wonder whenever something beautiful or magnificent captures your attention in a moment of awe. In these instances the /r/ helps you embrace the release of emptiness and inspires you to an energetic state by exchanging the /â/ for an /r/. The /ith/ insures gentle control of the newly infused energy. Whenever something strikes you as amazing WÂRITH can remove aloofness or hesitancy to connect or show emotion and let you register the moment with some gusto.

## Traditional Use of WÂRITH

*Wârith* translates into English as *the supreme inheritor*. Muslims traditionally use *wârith* when they wish to inherit blessings from their God. The SMY usage suggestion for *wârith* does help you feel blessed by lifting you up from a bad mood or by helping you embrace an experience.

## *Responding to Wonder with WÂSI'*

The Name WÂSI' can prove useful whenever you just want to take a break from responsibilities of everyday existence. The world contains many wonders. Too often people rush through the world and don't stop to contemplate or appreciate any of them. However, meditating on the Name WÂSI' can help you establish a connection and embrace the awesome nature of the universe. The /wâ/ combination allows you to replace a neutral feeling with one of awe, that sense of wonder and amazement that you get when you try to fathom some of the exquisite phenomena that abound on our planet. If you make an attempt to categorize or rationalize an object of astonishment, it involves a stream of consciousness, an /s/ emotional quality. However, the verbal effort leaves you in realization that words cannot do the experience justice. This recognition triggers an emotional buildup, which gets cleared by the /'/.

## Traditional Use of WÂSI'

*Wâsi'* translates into English as *the all-embracing*. Muslims traditionally use *wâsi'* when they want to develop the ability to accept conditions they find difficult to process. The SMY interpretation does not recommend usage for dark times, as the target feeling of the name, the release of emotional swelling through an ayin, will not lead you away from darkness, but rather put your emotions on your sleeve. However, the SMY usage can help you whenever you do feel empty. It can rid you of the emptiness and fill you with emotional appreciation for things of value and beauty. *Wâsi'* can be thought of as all embracing, in the sense that it helps you embrace the world and see beauty in "every grain of sand."

## Embracing the Void with WÂJID

Periodically clearing the mind of distracting, nagging issues that you face on a regular basis can help you stay mentally balanced. In these instances the /w/ comes gladly as a sought-after elixir, a desirable flush of the woes currently plaguing you that allows you to experience some peace, a relaxing /â/ moment. The subsequent /j/ allows you to hold on to the fresh feeling of global control provided by the relaxing and cleansing /wâ/. This in turn sets you up to feel in mental control via the /d/.

WÂJID also works with moments that make you stop and take in a particular scene, feeling, or idea with amazement, a /wâ/ moment. The /j/ grabs on to this emotional treasure and the /d/ keeps the whole process firmly under control, allowing you to savor the time.

### Traditional Use of WÂJID

*Wâjid* translates into English as *the finder*. Muslims traditionally use *wâjid* when they wish to find something that has been lost or misplaced. Although the application of the SMY interpretation of *wâjid* does not lend itself to finding a specific item, the usage of *wâjid* can generate an emotion akin to finding something special.

## Letting Things Flow with WALÎ

The Name WALÎ works in a similar manner to the Name WÂLÎ. The target for both Names, the /lî/ combination, involves letting things flow and come under control of an outside force. The obvious difference between these two Names, the /â/ in WÂLÎ versus the /a/ in WALÎ, indicates that WALÎ does not address the same lethargic initial state that WÂLÎ does. Instead WALÎ works for situations with neutral energy levels. The difference means that WALÎ addresses less dire unpleasant times, times during which the lost feeling has not dragged you down into a quagmire that has zapped your energy, but rather times in which you perhaps feel alone or a bit lost. The solution for these insecure moments requires you to let go of control and have faith that things will work out.

WALÎ, also like WÂLÎ, can work with times of wonder whenever you feel like leaving your fate in the control of an outside force, God. With WALÎ the experience does not carry an overwhelming relaxing feeling as it lacks an /â/.

## Traditional Use of WALÎ

*Walî* translates into English as *protecting friend* or *guardian*. Muslims traditionally use *walî* to promote a feeling that a higher power (i.e., Allah) watches over them. The SMY usage overlaps with this traditional one.

## *Trusting the Moment with WAKÎL*

If repeated attempts to achieve minor goals fail it may induce a negative empty feeling, a feeling of failure. Rather than beating yourself up over little things you need to learn to "not sweat the small stuff." WAKÎL allows you to step back and trust that things will work out even though you do not have everything you might wish for. The /k/ releases physical control. It lets you disengage. The /î/ hands over control to an outside force. Of course you need to trust this force to have faith in it. The final /l/, the target, puts you on autopilot and gives you respite from your self-flagellation.

WAKÎL also finds use in situations where you experience emptiness because you sense another person does not trust you. If you want to let someone feel that you are not trying to control or manipulate them, the /k/ of WAKÎL will release any control on your part, while the /î/ lets you feel as if an outside force, in this case the other person, has control. The final /l/ lets matters proceed smoothly.

Meditation presents another scenario for which WAKÎL may find use. Disinterest in and detachment from meditation signifies a yearning to engage in something else, a desire to do something different with your time. You can free yourself from such wishes, from the feeling that meditation has nothing for you, by using the /w/ to expel the negative, empty feeling, and then revoking control over your physical situation via /k/, and letting an external force take control. At times one can lose sight of the purpose and benefits of meditation and see the process as pointless, a folly. WAKÎL provides a refresh that can wash that malaise away and provide a new faith in the act of meditating.

## Traditional Use of WAKÎL

*Wakîl* translates into English as *trustee* or *advocate*. Muslims traditionally use wa*kîl* to develop trust in a higher power, usually thought of or referred to as God or Allah. The one SMY interpretation of wa*kîl* lends itself to this developing trust in a higher power. A second interpretation has the Name helping others trust you.

## *Repairing a Relationship with WADÛD*

One can often experience a bond with another person that generates a sense of awe, or feeling of love. This happens most often with a spouse but can occur with others, too. Most such relationships experience ups and downs. Periods when the connection seems to waver can engender a yearning for the better times. In such empty moments you can use the Name WADÛD to get your partnership back on track.

The main source of friction in a relationship usually stems from stubborn resistance to another person's viewpoint that manifests in the form of a disagreement over some issue. The emotional state that you find yourself in after an argument can vary. You might fall into a /mu/ feeling of missing a goal of wanting to convince your partner to change their mind. Perhaps you hang on to a strong /gh/ feeling of trying to control the situation or you just get angry and feel the associated emotional /r/. A very common mood that settles in after the echoes of the recriminations dissipate is a /û/—an empty feeling, lack of a loving connection.

Although one might wish for the return of the pleasant /m/ emotion of love, this would put you right back into the /mu/ cycle of failure to obtain a goal. Perhaps the best one could hope for in the aftermath of a quarrel with a loved one is to regain composure, best exemplified by a /d/. So if you start by releasing the /û/ via a /w/ it puts you on track to settling the mental anguish which arguments foment and a /d/

feeling can emerge. However, WADÛD doesn't end there. The empty /û/ reappears. This time it reflects the emptiness gained through your mental control (as denoted by the /dû/). You need to let your partner sense that your control has no personal goal. By emptying yourself of motives you disarm the other person and let them see you in a cogent state of mind without an ulterior motive. It takes away the adversary they just faced in an argument and lets a reboot of the relationship take place. The final /d/ reemphasizes the mental control needed for both sides to find reconciliation.

Another way to look at the /û/ in WADÛD and the overall message of WADÛD concerns an important aspect of healthy relationships. One must nurture the giving of the self to the relationship. Giving implies foregoing your own pleasure, the /û/ feeling, in order to provide for another. This does not imply that you should never find any pleasure in a relationship, only that at times one needs to abstain from pleasure in order to ensure a strong relationship. The key to understanding how WADÛD works lies in knowing that love cannot be all taking but must have a generous dose of giving. Someone who has developed a mature sense of self-awareness knows not to leave his or her ego unchecked in loving relationships. In order to stay humble, yet still drink fully of the sweetness of love, one can practice the Name WADÛD.

## Traditional Use of WADÛD

*Wadûd* translates into English as *the loving*. Muslims traditionally use *wadûd* to express or develop a loving manner. The SMY interpretation of *wadûd* concurs with this.

## *Embracing Good with WAHHÂB*

WAHHÂB can help you get over little bumps that seem to happen to everyone on a somewhat regular basis. When a small setback leaves you feeling down, empty, you can use WAHHÂB to help you remember the good things in your life. The /w/ helps wash away the current blue feeling due to some minor setback. The /hh/ flushes away the entire context of emptiness and its dismissal, i.e., it clears out the remnants left behind by the /w/. Finally, the /âb/ lets you relax and feel good in your renewed state.

You can also use WAHHÂB for empty times, where a positive outcome looms as a goal but not a reality. If you feel empty and lack any feeling of awe, but instead yearn for a release from your emptiness, your current mood corresponds to a /û/ state, for which a Name beginning with /w/ can apply. If you set your target state as one of pleasant relaxation, then WAHHÂB can help you reach that objective.

Sometimes good fortune can leave you feeling amazed and wondering how or why your fate led you to such a positive outcome. WAHHÂB can help you digest those times and savor them and help you get past the speechless incredulity. The goal for this situation consists of the /âb/ combination, a relaxed, feel-good state. To achieve this end the /hh/ gently pushes the wonder away before the /â/ affords you relaxation. Finally, the /b/ lets you hold and enjoy the moment.

## Traditional Use of WAHHÂB

*Wahhâb* translates into English as *the bestower*. Muslims traditionally use *wahhâb* to encourage good fortune to get bestowed upon themselves or another. The SMY usage of *wahhâb* corresponds to this traditional one in the sense that using *wahhâb* can help you feel blessed, that a blessing has been bestowed upon you.

## *Chapter Summary*

Some of the Names with initial sounds of /wâ/ help you deal with empty, lethargic moods. WÂLÎ finds use whenever you struggle with lack of direction and energy. WÂHID helps you develop confidence when self-doubt leads to empty feelings. You can use WÂRITH to move past a bad choice or experience that has gripped you. Other Names beginning with /wâ/ afford a way to embrace positive experiences. WÂSI' facilitates a feeling of awe for amazing things in the universe, while WÂJID lets you relax, chill, and embrace a quiet moment.

Some Names beginning with /wa/ address times of emptiness or yearning devoid of lethargy. If you feel lonely, you can work with WALÎ to overcome the problem. WAKÎL allows you to move past small nagging issues and feelings of failure. You can cultivate special relationships with loved ones through the practice of WADÛD. WAHHÂB replaces distracted emptiness with relaxation and sustained pleasantness.

# CHAPTER 19
## RESPONDING TO BLOCKAGE WITH AYIN

The ayin, /'/, represents a wild card in the sphere of human speech. Because the point of constriction for this stop consonant occurs right on the vocal cords, the ayin connects to the act of speaking in a way that no other speech sound does. As a result the ayin has a global effect on one's emotional makeup. Because of its unvoiced nature, it acts as a release from emotional blockages and emotional buildups. As you practice mindfulness of your emotional states you can encounter moments of perplexity and opaqueness when you can't categorize your emotional status into a simple breakdown of normal emotion dimensions, when you cannot register a distinctive feeling other than confusion or perhaps blockage. If such a swelling from lack of identifiable emotional valence occurs, then a Name starting with ayin can move you past this blockage and put you in a more stable mood. The ayin can remove such obstacles because of its cathartic nature. It releases the constriction that happens at the source of emotion expression, your vocal cords.

This chapter presents six Names beginning with /'/ that offer different options for proceeding past your blockage depending on the nature of the situation that led to the emotional buildup and the goal one might have to resolve the blockage. Of these six Names three utilize the /l/ sound/feeling, a feeling that lets things flow, perhaps the most logical approach to blockages. Two other Names contain the /z/ sound/feeling. Because the /z/ lets your ever present stream of consciousness mellow, it can ease the mind away from the source of the emotional blockage. Two of the three Names that contain an /l/ and both of the Names with a /z/ also contain an /î/. This admission of outside control into the mix can assuage the personal emotional drive behind many emotional blockages by letting you lean on or seek refuge in a higher power (or perhaps to a non-theist let the right-brain take over).

Note the distinction between using a Name beginning with /'/ in response to not reaching a goal and using a Name beginning with /mu/, which also expresses falling short of a goal. Names that begin with an ayin apply whenever the failure to reach a goal has created an emotional blockage, essentially a more intense feeling than what the /mu/ expresses. Additionally, with times appropriate for a Name beginning with /mu/ the lack of attaining the goal has the focus, whereas with Names using an initial ayin the awareness centers on the emotional buildup.

## Developing Understanding with 'ALÎM

Many things in the world challenge our understanding. We attempt to increase our knowledge through various means of study, through books, through following a teacher, through self-study. Sometimes efforts to comprehend a particular matter fall short and cause emotional distress, as though blocked from gaining realization of something—a failure to obtain insight. 'ALÎM can help you get past these emotional blockages and develop a sense of satisfaction. Even though the issue may not be comprehended intellectually, understanding comes on a deeper level.

The /'/ provides the release from the frustration of not being able to make a breakthrough on a topic of investigation. The /l/ lets the mind ease off of its emotional quest and take an easy going approach to the matter at hand. The /îm/ combination then follows letting you feel under the pleasant control of an outside force. With the taking over of an outside power and the resulting pleasant sensation, the urge for understanding morphs into a realization that transcends the original quest.

## Traditional Use of 'ALÎM

'Alîm translates into English as *all-knowing* or *omniscient*. Muslims traditionally use *'alîm* to develop their intellectual acuity or understanding of the world. The SMY usage parallels this traditional one.

## *Recapturing the Meditative State with 'ALÎ*

The Name 'ALÎ differs from 'ALÎM by omitting the final /m/. This difference permits 'ALÎ to work in situations that do not have a specific goal looming behind the emotional blockage. The pursuit of a goal establishes a feeling of satisfaction as our target; the /m/ represents this in 'ALÎM. For blockages that occur due to unspecified or unknown reasons, simply releasing the blockage and allowing outside control to prevail can provide a solution. A feeling of being lost without any direction serves as an example that fits the profile for using 'ALÎ. However, the lost feeling referred to in this case doesn't imply emptiness, but instead an emotional wrenching kind of lost. The /'/ takes away trepidation about feeling lost. Then the /l/ turns off the innate drive that searches for answers. Once you bypass this urge and let things flow with the /l/, the feeling associated with the /î/ can enter your consciousness. For a religious person it lets them feel guided by a higher power. For a non-religious person, the /î/ feeling here could represent the letting go of left-brain effort. This of course would have to go beyond just letting things flow. That gets accomplished via the /l/. The /î/ feeling should take things further and engender an awareness of a presence seemingly outside of what you normally identify as the self.

The Name 'ALÎ can prove useful for meditation whenever you reach a point of emotional confusion about the purpose of your meditation efforts. 'ALÎ also can help whenever you feel lost. This use of 'ALÎ differs from that of RASHÎD, another Name used when feeling lost. RASHÎD works when the lost feeling manifests with an urgent energy. In contrast, 'ALÎ's usage corresponds to emotional times of reflection when you have a goal of simply dispelling the lost feeling. RASHÎD can help give you a direction via the /sh/, but 'ALÎ just lets things move along via the /l/.

## Traditional Use of 'ALÎ

*'Alî* translates into English as *highest* or *exalted*. Muslims traditionally use *'alî* to develop a spiritual connection to a higher power. The SMY interpretation of *'alî* essentially matches the traditional, in the sense that using *'alî* can generate a feeling of spiritual connection to such a power. However, the SMY guidelines suggest an appropriate reason for employing the name. That is, just desiring a connection for a higher power does not by itself constitute an SMY reason for using *'alî*. The basic rule of SMY still applies with *'alî*. Match your mood to the initial letter. To use *'alî* your mood should correspond to an emotional buildup that needs to be addressed via an /'/.

## *Removing Blockage Created by Another with 'AFÛW*

Sometimes the source of the emotional blockage comes from within, from a lack of confidence or a lack of understanding. However, some blockages occur due to an identifiable outside source, as for example, a person causing you discomfort or interfering with you in a manner that disrupts your activity or inconveniences you. Without an acceptable way to respond to such disturbances an emotional buildup can ensue. This situation can find relief through 'AFÛW. The /'/ releases the emotional buildup. The content feeling associated with the /f/ will smooth out any lingering disturbance. The subsequent /û/ acknowledges the lack of any pleasant feeling, or even the presence of an unpleasant feeling, perhaps. Without this recognition the work of the /w/ would not have the same effect. Once you express the /û/, the unpleasantness at the core of the scene, i.e., the discomfort you feel, the /w/ serves as an efficient scrubber of the negative vibes.

You can also find use for 'AFÛW in a meditation setting. Although the ideal conditions for meditation consist of an environment devoid of outside stimuli, one does not usually meditate in an idyllic, silent, retreat-like atmosphere. Cars may pass by. A person could make a noise in another room. Electronic equipment, a motor, or an engine might turn on and intrude on your peace. Such interferences pose difficult challenges to maintaining a productive meditation session. Many base the location and time for meditation on the optimal odds of avoiding these intrusions. However, no matter how much you might try to avoid all outside interruptions during meditation they can still happen.

If you experience a sensory intrusion from someone or something in your environment during your meditation session it doesn't always cause an emotional blockage. Using SHAHÎD to remedy these irritations can often work. However, if a distraction leads to a buildup of emotion then 'AFÛW can relieve this swelling of negativity and help you forget about the momentary disruption and get you back into productive meditation.

## Traditional Use of 'AFÛW

*'Afûw* translates into English as *pardoner*. Muslims traditionally use *'afûw* to either ask for forgiveness for something that they have done or to develop their ability to forgive others. SMY recommends using *'afûw* to smooth over interruptions or infringements created by another person or object and forgive those persons or things that precipitated the disturbance.

## *Accepting Good Fortune with 'AZÎM*

The Name 'AZÎM can help you accept emotional scenes which may at first provoke an emotional blockage. In situations where someone receives accolades or undesirable recognition a person might feel uncomfortable, perhaps get "choked up." Of course not everyone reacts this way whenever others show gratitude for a job well done or potential condemnation in some other way. However, for those who experience such anguish, if your efforts deserve acclaim then going with those compliments in a graceful manner will put you in a more mindful state than embarrassment, diffidence, or false modesty. Likewise by accepting your foibles without letting your emotions cloud your thoughts 'AZÎM can help you overcome painful public moments and allow yourself to feel normal. 'AZÎM works by first releasing the emotional blockage with the /'/. Then the /z/ dulls the stream of consciousness that naturally occurs before letting an outside force take control via the /î/. The outside force in this situation could consist of the folks who caused the emotional reaction. Of course from a Sufi perspective the outside force to which one surrenders would always be Allah. In either case the intention is to feel controlled by an outside force and let it result in a pleasant sensation, /m/.

Both 'AZÎM and MU'IZZ work to help deal with embarrassment. Which one you apply in a given situation depends on how the situation initially causes you pause. Use MU'IZZ whenever the first response comes as a smile, but shyness or an introverted nature adds a /u/ and then delivers emotional blockage necessitating the 'izz continuation. If instead the emotional reaction hits you without registering a fleeting smile, then 'AZÎM should be your choice.

Although embarrassing moments call for using 'AZÎM, the Name can also prove useful in other settings. You can use 'AZÎM whenever you get emotionally tied up in something good that you don't fully understand. 'AZÎM allows you to let go of trying to analyze and control the moment and just enjoy it.

## Traditional Use of 'AZÎM

'Azîm translates into English as *the great one*. Muslims traditionally use 'azîm whenever they feel down and want to feel some of the greatness they associate with Allah. The SMY interpretation of 'azîm does also have this flavor, that is, you can use 'azîm to overcome feeling not worthy or inadequate—a way to augment your self-image and perhaps feel great.

## *Moving Past Emotional Blockages using 'AZÎZ*

'AZÎM and 'AZÎZ differ only in the target emotion. Both Names apply to times of emotional stress. 'AZÎM applies to feelings of embarrassment and has a goal of ridding that for a positive image. For 'AZÎZ, the initial conditions correspond to generic emotional turmoil. Once this emotional confusion gets released via the ayin the goal becomes subduing mental chatter in order to keep the confusion from coming back. 'AZÎZ can prove useful whenever you need to move past an emotional blockage and not get stuck analyzing the situation, but rather trusting the forces in control. Again, as before, with the Sufis this means trusting Allah. Examples of emotional states for which 'AZÎZ can help include shyness, uncertainty, and fear.

The initial /'/ removes the emotional blockage. Then the first /z/ helps to keep the chatter of stream of consciousness from prevailing or distracting. The /î/ recognizes your lack of control and recognizes the presence of an outside force. The Name concludes with a second /z/ that reinforces the effort to dampen the chatter of the mind. Use 'AZÎZ to conquer fears of the unknown. Whenever you have no choice but to forge into uncharted territory, whether that consists of an actual physical trek or into a new social or business situation, you can use 'AZÎZ to dispel the trepidation and quiet the jitters of a uneasy mind.

## Traditional Use of 'AZÎZ

'Azîz translates into English as *the mighty*. Muslims traditionally use 'azîz when they want to develop a feeling of power. This interpretation fits with the SMY idea of when to use 'azîz. When you face the unknown, the use of 'azîz can help you feel less fearful, which if not powerful is at least a step in that direction.

## *Easing the Way with 'ADL*

Sometimes when you face responsibilities you can feel tentative and unsure. You may possess an adequate skill set or knowledge base, but nerves get in the way of executing in a satisfactory manner. This lack of confidence can gnaw at you and lead to an emotional buildup, a crisis in confidence. In these types of instances you need to learn to just let things flow and rely on your abilities to complete your task. The Name 'ADL provides a way to approach this type of emotional blockage and gives you the capability of working unimpeded. The /'/ provides the cathartic thrust that releases the blockage. The /d/ steps in and brings mental control. It holds on to the control that comes from the release afforded by the /'/ and helps to keep your mind from going into mental gymnastics trying to analyze why you have encountered such a blockage and why you couldn't engage in what you know you can do. The /l/ follows and lets you proceed without trying too hard. It puts you into a natural flow.

## Traditional Use of 'ADL

*'Adl* translates into English as *just* or *equitable*. Muslims traditionally use *'adl* to facilitate their ability to deal with others in a fair and equitable manner. The SMY usage of *'adl* fits with this traditional one in the sense that the use of *'adl* can help you feel at ease with decisions as a leader or someone in charge of a particular task.

## *Chapter Summary*

Names beginning with the ayin apply to situations where your emotions get stirred up and you experience intense feelings, as if you might burst. The standard emotional analysis of breaking down your emotional state in the three dimensions of emotions doesn't apply at these times because of physiological overload. The ayin remedies this acute state by momentarily flushing out the system. This cathartic release can lead to various solutions depending upon the initiating conditions. 'ALÎM allows you to overcome blockages concerning a search for knowledge. When you experience emotional reactions due to another's actions' infringement on some aspect of your territory then 'AFÛW can ease the situation. Emotional buildups caused by shyness and irrational fear can use 'AZÎZ for relief. 'AZÎM promotes acceptance of recognition for accolades and foibles, while 'ADL helps build confidence when you doubt your leadership ability. Finally, 'ALÎ provides a way to deal with generic pent-up emotion.

# CHAPTER 20
## EMBRACING THE WORLD

This chapter includes three Names that begin with /j/, a stop consonant with the point of articulation at the middle of the tongue. As a stop consonant this sound invokes a feeling of holding to a sentiment. The nature of this sentiment gets dictated via the manner of articulation. Since the middle of the tongue stops the flow of air, the emotional quality of /j/ equates to a global embracing of control. This embrace appears global in the sense that it includes both physical and mental aspects of control. That is, the control that gets held, or embraced, goes further than just controlling the physical surroundings. The mind comes into play, too, in the sense that an idea worth retaining looms as motivation or justification of the physical control. This contrasts to the feeling generated by the /g/ which looks simply for physical control without regard to any mental concept that could or may have driven this physical control. The /j/ also differs from the /d/, since the /d/ embraces an idea or abstract concept without a specific physical context. The feelings generated by the /j/ imply embracing the world, or at least the particular segment of the world that has your present attention. With the /j/ things seem right, the scenario, the context, your thoughts, all just work.

## Finding the Flow with JALÎL

Sometimes when the just right feeling of /j/ spontaneously appears you want to take a laissez-faire approach. JALÎL encourages and enhances this penchant. The sound most conducive to letting things flow, /l/, appears twice in this Name. These flowing laid back sounds bracket an /î/, a feeling of outside control. Thus the Name JALÎL can take moments of feeling in overall control and enhance our mindfulness by letting things flow and allowing a feeling that something outside of us has control. Of course the outside force for

Sufis is Allah, but from a non-religious viewpoint JALÎL can still prove useful. It can allow you to let go of your ego-driven self and luxuriate in a feeling of embracing the world. From a traditional mindfulness perspective the flow of outside control of the /lîl/ really is the same as mindful awareness of the moment, in which you have stopped the inner dialogue.

If you practice a daily routine of meditation, you might find that the habit of meditating engenders a /j/ feeling when sitting down to begin meditating. If so, you might find that repeating JALÎL a number of times helps you to have a more productive session. However, remember to engage in JALÎL because you feel the embrace of emotional control not because you think that you should feel it.

## Traditional Use of JALÎL

*Jalîl* translates into English as *sublime*. Muslims traditionally use *jalîl* to feel a connection to a divine presence. This usage fits well with the SMY practice of using *jalîl.*

## *Acting with Authority with JABBÂR*

While JALÎL takes a laid back approach to the embracing /j/, JABBÂR takes the opposite track. Instead of wanting to sit back and enjoy a sublime moment, if you would rather embrace the sensation of everything feeling just right by taking control of proceedings, then JABBÂR would be the Name to use. The /bb/ follow-up to the /ja/ in JABBÂR acknowledges and holds on to the good feeling that the /j/ generated. The subsequent /âr/ combination removes any relaxed attitude, any indulgent /â/, and replaces this passivity with an arousing /r/. Thus, JABBÂR generates an aroused state of feeling in global control of a very positive situation.

## Traditional Use of JABBÂR

*Jabbâr* translates into English as *the compeller*. Muslims traditionally use *jabbâr* when they wish to develop a forceful personality or attitude toward an issue or a relationship. Indeed, this interpretation goes well with the SMY recommendation for using *jabbâr*. Use *jabbâr* whenever you feel in control of things and want to act.

## Finding the Right Thing with JÂME'

The Name JÂME' takes a different approach to feeling in control. Instead of just letting things flow along with JALÎL or having a target of action as with JABBÂR, JÂME' opts for relaxation and enjoyment of the feeling. The /'/ at the end of the Name, the target, indicates that this enjoyment leads to an overwhelming emotion that the ayin cathartically releases. JÂME' applies in situations when the feeling of having everything under control engenders a calming response. You feel no need to act and the idea of letting things flow seems foreign because you would rather embrace your good fortune. The /âm/ combination lets you relax and enjoy yourself, to celebrate the occasion. Finally, the ayin cathartically releases the engulfing emotion engendered by the /jâm/ combination.

Another usage for JÂME' occurs at times of meal preparation whenever you have an abundance of nourishing food. Having the pleasure of ample desirable nutrition should make at least part of you feel in control, relaxed, and pleasant—the /jâm/ combination. This easily generates an emotional response ripe for expression via the /'/.

### Traditional Use of JÂME'

*Jâme'* translates into English as *the gatherer*. Muslims traditionally use *jâme'* when they wish to enhance their ability to gather things that they need. The SMY interpretation indicates using *jâme'* for times when things are working out, perhaps a time when all things you need have been gathered together.

## Chapter Summary

The emotion associated with the /j/ makes you feel in global control. Thus Names beginning with /j/ work whenever you have a poised presence, a demeanor of assurance. JALÎL lets you luxuriate in your self-assurance without being egotistic. In contrast, JABBÂR allows you to follow through and act with confidence. Finally, JÂME' allows relaxation and enjoyment of the situation.

# CHAPTER 21
## ODDS AND ENDS

This final chapter on the list of the ninety-nine practices includes five Names grouped together into a single chapter in order to avoid several much shorter chapters. The initial letters in these five names include /a/, /â/, /dh/, and /f/. There are three Names beginning with a vowel—one with the relaxed /â/ and two with /a/ which has some unpleasantness or emptiness factored into the relaxed state, since the /a/ sits between the relaxed /â/ and the empty /û/. One should note that in a minority of the lists of the Ninety-nine Names of Allah that I have encountered, the three Names in this section get written with an initial hamza or /'/. This pseudo-letter does not carry any vocalization but consists merely of a brief exhale or breath stoppage. I suspect the presence of the hamza in these has something to do with the fact that the Names otherwise begin with a vowel. In any case the presence of the hamza has the emotional impact of taking pause. I do not believe that such a pause at the beginning of a Name has a significant effect on the Name's usage.

The sound /dh/ appears as the initial sound in only one Name. Although the letter usually gets translated from Arabic as /dh/, some sources list it as /z/. It also comes close to the English voiced /th/, but it often is heard by English speakers as the English /z/. However, the point of articulation is dental, not alveolar (which explains the use of "d" in the representation of the sound). The continuous /dh/ shares some qualities with the /z/, the sound it closely resembles. However, the dental point of articulation takes the /dh/ away from a pure mental stream of consciousness and adds an element of gentle control of physical awareness.

The final Name in this section, and the list of practices, begins with /f/. Of the ninety-nine Names, this one stands alone in terms of the classification system that I have employed for the other Names due to its unique initial sound. No other Name begins with this sound. There are other sounds that have only a single Name with that particular sound, including one Name beginning with /t/ (TAWWÂB) and one with an initial /z/ (ZÂHIR). However, these latter two Names belong in the category dealing with mental control. The /f/ does not belong in any of the previously cited categories. The articulation of the /f/ involves both the teeth and lips. The lips engage the pleasure dimension of emotion and since the teeth connect to the jaw they bring the arousal dimension into play. This allows the /f/ to modulate emotions in a distinct manner.

## *Relaxing in a Mindful Way with ÂKHIR*

Generally speaking, given our hectic and often frantic lifestyles a relaxed state often looms as a goal, and once found then all bodes well. True, a relaxed state would not necessarily call for any guidance or SMY Name to help you maintain a mindful state. However, one can be too relaxed at times, especially if you need to be paying attention to a situation. A relaxed state should not equate to a vegetative one. At times you need to keep aware and stay mindful of your surroundings to some extent during relaxation. ÂKHIR can help if you find yourself in a situation where you don't have to act but still want to be aware. You should note that ÂKHIR does not work when you actually feel empty. For any empty feelings you should call on a Name beginning with /w/. Also don't use ÂKHIR for tired feelings. Such feelings get addressed with Names beginning with /ḥ/. ÂKHIR goes with states where the relaxation sits comfortably with you, where you don't want to wallow in it, but wish to temper it with just the right amount of arousal to stay in the moment. That explains the target here, the /r/. It's not an /r/ of action, but just enough arousal to take the edge off of lethargy. To get from the /â/ to the /r/ you use the intermediate sound/feeling of /kh/. This generates an emphatic release of physical control. If you don't include this release of physical control you can't comfortably go from relaxed /â/ to aroused /r/ without the urge to act. The /kh/ keeps the /r/ from looking for an action to perform.

With physical control released the /r/ merely keeps the energy at the proper level to feel present.

## Traditional Use of ÂKHIR

*Âkhir* translates into English as *the last*. Muslims traditionally use *âkhir* when they wish to delay an event or to put off an occurrence of something in order to be last with it or make it last. The SMY interpretation gives this traditional one some clarity. You can think of the benefit of using *âkhir* as allowing you to partake of relaxation in a manner that lets it last while staying focused. You can use *âkhir* if you wish to just chill, or be the last to move on to something.

## *Taking on Something New with AWWAL*

The /a/ feeling doesn't correspond to a distinct emotional quality. It lies between the relaxed /â/ and the empty /û/. One might characterize this as an aloof state, perhaps sort of empty or remote. The Name AWWAL takes this state of remoteness and emphatically dispels the emptiness with the /ww/ and puts you in a groove with the /l/. AWWAL takes you from indifference to feeling that everything seems in harmony. Situations where AWWAL can apply might include times when you need motivation to shake off a somewhat listless attitude and get into some endeavor that for some reason you have been procrastinating about beginning.

## Traditional Use of AWWAL

*Awwal* translates into English as *the first*. Muslims traditionally use *awwal* when they want to feel as though they are at the head or front of something. The SMY usage of *awwal* can promote the feeling of belonging or working in synchronization. Does this equate to a feeling of being the first? The SMY interpretation appears less dramatic. However, because going from apathy to connectedness does create a significant turnaround, one might easily consider that they have arrived at the beginning of something new.

## *Feeling in Tune with AHAD*

With AWWAL the aloof /a/ feeling gets swept away and allows you to better function in your environment. AHAD has a different target, one of mental control, as denoted by the /d/. This difference illuminates the proper usage and effect of each of these Names. With AWWAL you address the milieu in which you find yourself. AWWAL facilitates engagement with your surroundings after you have given up caring. In contrast AHAD gives you mental control in place of not caring. This effect, in contrast to that of AWWAL, takes places internally.

AHAD achieves this mental control over your apathetic /a/ state via the intermediate /h/. The /h/ gently flushes away the languid /a/. Once freed from this uncaring condition the mental control offered by /d/ can percolate into your consciousness. While AWWAL addresses your attitude toward external reality, AHAD deals with your self-awareness. If you feel indifferent toward your surroundings, use AWWAL to remedy the situation. Whenever your lack of concern centers about your inner world, use AHAD.

## Traditional Use of AHAD

*Ahad* translates into English as *the one*. Muslims traditionally use *ahad* whenever they wish to experience a feeling of being united or connected to all. The SMY interpretation of *ahad* does lend itself to this traditional usage in the sense that the SMY application takes you from not caring about your mental processes to feeling in control. While this might not correlate to feeling connected to everything, if you think about how feeling apathy makes you feel isolated, then flushing away that sentiment and replacing it with one of assurance could easily make you feel part of something bigger.

## *Stepping Back with* DHÛL-JALÂL-WAL-IKRÂM

The single Name beginning with /dh/, DHÛL-JALÂL-WAL-IKRÂM, holds the distinction of also being the longest of the ninety-nine Names. The appropriate times for using this Name occur when you apply measured mental efforts to control the physical world indicated by the /dh/. That is, whenever you engage in careful thinking about how to do things with the resources at your hand. Of course this concept paints with a broad brush, as most people employ such thinking many times and on many scales, from small projects to gigantic undertakings. Furthermore, the /û/ that follows the /dh/ indicates that the mental efforts start empty or unpleasant. Thus if you already have ideas that generate a pleasing response, you do not need to use this Name. The target of this Name consists of a relaxed, pleasant, fulfilled state, expressed in this Name via the /âm/. You want to have good positive ideas about controlling your world. Getting to this goal involves a rather lengthy, but still quite cogent, process.

The bulk of the work to achieve the objective gets done by the /l/ sound. The /l/ appears four times in the Name. A somewhat lengthy narrative of how this Name works goes like this. When you search for an answer of how to deal with a situation, first let the mind stay loose. The first /l/ takes on this job. Then make sure you have emotional control. Here the /j/ goes to work. Don't forget to let this flow (the second /l/) and relax (the /â/). The relaxing will really help to let things move along smoothly (the third /l/). Then release any troubling feeling that the task in front of you has generated (accomplished by the /w/). After this liberation you need to reestablish the groove (the last /l/). Finally, now that you have found the harmony with the repeated /l/s, release physical control (the /ik/) and convert any agitation or frustration that your efforts have generated, that physical tension (the /r/), into the desired relaxed, pleasant state (the /âm/).

To reiterate the above analysis in plainer English, the process that the Name DHÛL-JALÂL-WAL-IKRÂM takes you through might be stated as: if you wish to wrap your mind about controlling your life's environment, try to just let things go mentally, grab on to the emotional core of your being, flush out negativity, let go, and relax.

## Traditional Use of DHÛL-JALÂL-WAL-IKRÂM

*Dhûl-jalâl-wal-ikrâm* translates into English as *Lord of majesty and bounty.* Muslims traditionally use *dhûl-jalâl-wal-ikrâm* when they wish to address Allah and the good fortune they experience through his blessings. The SMY usage of *dhûl-jalâl-wal-ikrâm* does seem compatible with the translation. We want our efforts in this world to beget something of beauty that can generate pleasant, comfortable surroundings.

## *Being Open to New Experiences with FATTÂH*

We have arrived at the last of the ninety-nine Names, FATTÂH. I don't have any special reason for leaving this last other than it stands by itself. I could well have put it first or any place in the list, as the order of the list does not matter. When or which of the Names you learn or practice, should be based exclusively on the emotional needs or goals that you have.

The times for using FATTÂH occur when you feel at ease, when you feel content with your place in the universe and you see or feel a need to begin a new journey. With FATTÂH you can take these easy-going moments as opportunities to strip away lethargy and face the world in an open, unbiased manner. The /f/ corresponds to the contentment that indicates that this Name will apply. The /tt/ portion of the Name clears away any mental control that the contented state might have on you. This strips you of whatever lackadaisical habits you might harbor. The /âh/ combination has the goal of eliminating the relaxed feeling that naturally accompanies contentment, since as you will recall the strong /h/ will exhaust or sweep out the emotion connected with the preceding sound. By purging contentment and relaxation FATTÂH puts you in a natural inquisitive state. By nature we human creatures have an innate tendency to explore and learn about new things. With FATTÂH you can allow this beautiful predisposition to flourish.

### Traditional Use of FATTÂH

*Fattâh* translates into English as *the opener*. Muslims traditionally use *fattâh* when they wish to be open to new beginnings or new opportunities. They often will use *fattâh* whenever they feel stuck in something undesirable and wish to start anew, open a new chapter. The SMY interpretation of *fattâh* opens you to new opportunities of discovery. This usage holds close to the traditional one. By SMY standard practices you should hold a mental state of contentment whenever you use this Name. Thus, if you wish to use *fattâh* in order to escape a less than ideal situation, you need to first allow yourself to obtain contentment. This, of course, is much easier said than done, but nonetheless quite essential in order for *fattâh* to prove effective.

## *Chapter Summary*

The Names in this chapter were grouped together to avoid having several chapters with one or two Names. Three of the five begin with a vowel sound—the only three Names that begin with vowels. One Name begins with the relaxing /â/. Often you wish to feel relaxed but if you get too relaxed you could use ÂKHIR to stay prepared on a "wait-and-see" situation. Two Names begin with the simple /a/, a sound associated with a somewhat relaxed yet somewhat empty feeling. AWWAL drains away emptiness and leaves you ready to contribute, while AHAD erases apathy and generates mental involvement.

A beginning sound for a single Name in this chapter, a /dh/, has characteristics of stream of consciousness and mental control. You can use DHÛL-JALÂL-WAL-IKRÂM to bring harmony to thoughts and meditations on your mental control and how it affects your existence in the world. However, since the tip of the tongue touches the back of the teeth for this sound the control has a physical aspect. It denotes mental control in the "real world."

An /f/, a sound that indicates contentment, appears as the initial sound for the final Name in the chapter. Although being in a content state might seem ideal, that doesn't mean that we cannot make optimum use of our contentment. FATTÂH presents a way to utilize a content mood to our advantage—when you are ready it can help begin a new journey.

# CHAPTER 22

## THE ONE

You have reached the end of the ninety-nine Names—the exercises of SMY. Sufis state that Allah has an infinite number of Names, or attributes. Yet, the tradition has always been to list ninety-nine. In the context of SMY principles the list provides a robust repertoire to address myriad psychological situations, some problematic others fortuitous, a person might encounter in any lifetime, whether in the seventh century or the twenty-first. That does not imply that the ninety-nine Names exhaust all possible words that could prove beneficial using SMY. I would expect that one could generate other lists. Years ago I tried, but only briefly and without success. I returned to the existing list because I found the Names in it helpful. It took me years to approach mastery of the entire list. Notice I said "approach" mastery. There is more than a lifetime of learning awaiting you with the ninety-nine Names. So, should the list be shorter? Is ninety-nine too many? What Name could we leave off? I really have not entertained these questions. I have simply studied the list and found my efforts rewarding.

One Name that the Sufis work with more than any other is not on the list of ninety-nine. I refer to the Name Allah. Most people translate Allah as the Arabic word for God. Sufis also translate Allah to mean "the one." Simple repetition of Allah remains a staple in most Sufi organizations, along with the phrase shown phonetically as la-î-la-ha-il-la-lah, and translated as "there is no god but the one." With both Allah and the longer phrase, /l/ comprises the key sound. By forming or saying the /l/ sound you use your mental control to put yourself into the flow of the universe, into the gravitational pull of consciousness.

From the viewpoint of SMY the Name ALLAH can prove useful at any time you wish to dip your rudder in the waters of your conscious stream and guide yourself into the flow. A quiet soft breath of ALLAH can bring you back from little slips out of self-awareness and back to the moment. This gentle prod affords a way to keep your emotional keel aligned without investing energy in taking stock of your current emotional profile. A feeling of wanting to get back in the groove, or back to letting go should precipitate its usage. The justification of the repetition of ALLAH, from an SMY viewpoint, comes easier than any of the other Names. If you desire to step back from whatever you had been attending to and let things flow without any particular goal you have matched the criteria for using ALLAH. The /a/ corresponds to the stepping back, while the /ll/ lets thing flow, and the /h/ just takes you to the end of the flow of that moment.

You may wish to use ALLAH at the beginning of a meditation session, or at some point in the middle, or whenever. The number of times does not matter. Your desire to step back and let things go does matter. The expression of ALLAH, the stepping back and letting things flow, can be interpreted as a form of surrender—considered a key to the Islamic faith. The word *Islâm* translates as surrender to the will of Allah. A quick SMY analysis adds insight to this meaning. You can see that *Islâm* and SALÂM share most of their sounds. However, the initial vowel of *Islâm* indicates that meaning doesn't start with stream of consciousness, but rather from a feeling of austere outside control, the /i/. One interpretation of this might be a relationship with a higher power. The /s/ of course represents stream of consciousness. The /is/ combination gives us thoughts about our relationship to this higher power. The /l/ lets you replace the chatter with unobstructed flow. The concluding /âm/ brings pleasant relaxation as your reward. Together the SMY interpretation of *Islâm* might read: our relationship with the higher power should not be one of questioning but instead one of stepping back and letting things flow, surrendering. If we accomplish this we shall be justly rewarded.

# CHAPTER 23
## ESTABLISHING AN SMY PROGRAM

With ninety-nine individual Names to choose from, each a separate practice in its own right, it can seem overwhelming to someone new to SMY to know where to start. Although one can approach the Names from any number of valid ways, I will present several plans that can help ease the formidable task of choosing which Name or group of Names to focus on and the order to proceed. First, comes a strategy for someone pursuing a more or less traditional meditation practice, in which they sit quietly with the purpose of just being present and stilling all mental and emotional chatter. This provides the most straightforward method of applying SMY and allows the user a structured program that can begin slowly and build through experience. The guidelines in this path work closely with the various elements of the *Yoga Sutras*.

A second approach to using SMY involves what one could call devotional practices, although the flavor of the devotion deviates from the traditional way of understanding such term. To take advantage of this lane of SMY one need not be of a religious bent. The devotion felt toward a deity as defined by a religious path such as Christianity or Islam can work with this set of practices; however, the only element essential to devotional SMY is a strong belief that some perceived positive force of consciousness or panpsychism exists, and that you feel a fervent positive connection to that force.

A third strategy will suit someone who wishes to utilize the Names to provide benefits for daily living. The primary tactic here involves self-reflection and self-study aimed at understanding psychological and emotional weakness and strengths and how to mobilize the strengths and shore up the weaknesses so that a more robust and mindful existence can be realized. This route will suit someone with a sense of independence and desire for personal exploration and understanding.

In addition to having a daily time for reviewing and contemplating personal situations in which Names might prove beneficial, a person using SMY in this fashion should also have a goal of applying the Names in real-time to the very situations one has contemplated.

In order for any of the above approaches to yield positive results one should set aside time each day to engage in serious effort toward the desired goals inherent in the chosen path. These three delineated options are not mutually exclusive. One can certainly practice Names geared toward devotion during a meditation session; or one can contemplate daily situations for SMY usage before or after meditation. However, it would perhaps be wise to take on one path at a time and gain some progress before tackling a second track.

Each of the following suggested programs for SMY presents specific Names; however, the details of how these Names work have not been included in this section, since this information has already been presented in previous chapters. Please refer back to the individual explanations of Names to shore up your understanding, when taking on the task of using a new Name. Knowing how the Names work can often prove beneficial and facilitate the process of solidifying them in memory. You should aim for the feeling that the essence of the Name lives within you.

## *SMY and Meditation*

Some of the suggestions for a traditional meditation practice hold true for meditation using SMY; use a quiet place with as few distractions as possible; develop a daily habit of time and place—early in the morning seems best for most folks. The most crucial step—that of clearing the mind—is where SMY diverges from other practices. Instead of ignoring all thoughts and feelings you need to monitor them in a way that allows you to gradually gain control of them so that you can sustain deep meditation.

The ultimate goal of SMY used for meditative purposes would be a blissful state of feeling one with the universe. This coincides with Patanjali's goal of yoga and I would surmise the goal of satori in Zen and other Buddhist meditation systems. As previously noted the Name MAJÎD most closely approximates this lofty aim. But to sit as a beginning and attempt to realize the emotional pattern of this Name makes no sense. However, we can set this as a goal and then work backward from it to arrive at a suitable beginning point.

The Name with the best approach to MAJÎD is MATÎN, but one cannot begin at this Name either. A good segue to MATÎN is MALIK, and this one is approachable from the start of a program with a caveat. You can practice the emotional pattern of MALIK as long as you have control over the three dimensions of emotion, i.e., neutral on arousal, pleasure, and control. Essentially this means that you are sitting comfortably, relaxed but alert. You have no emotional disturbance or negativity of any kind and are not feeling overjoyed for some reason—and your mind is free from internal dialogue. With these conditions satisfied MALIK is as easy as watching the breath. As you inhale be aware of a pleasant /m/ sensation. Let this feeling mellow and flow unimpeded (feeling /l/) until you begin to exhale and then feel the release of air as a /k/. Repeat. This can morph into MATÎN by going from an external focus to an internal one. This can only happen in a non-forced manner. How will you know it has happened? With MALIK your attention dwells on the physical surroundings. The /m/ feels good physically—particularly in the chest as the air fills the lungs. The release felt on the exhale is physical—you notice the discharge of air as it happens without your volition. As you repeat the MALIK sequence pay attention to the feelings and don't think about the Name. If you can remain neutral on arousal and control (no fidgeting and no inner dialogue) eventually the awareness shifts. As you inhale and feel the sensation you will recognize the pleasantness in the mind instead of the physical self. When this occurs, release the mental registration that occurred—this occurs as a /t/. This in turn engenders the paradoxical /în/—something outside of your volition has taken over and in thus doing a larger *you* now feels totally in control. This happens due to the merging of the outside force with the inside self. With practice this MATÎN pattern can be repeated until it becomes very strong, but it will take time. At first a switch back to MALIK will often occur or other interference (mentioned later) will infringe on the moment. Keep working at sustaining MATÎN and you should eventually arrive at MAJÎD. Getting there from MATÎN has no roadmap. Perhaps the most succinct description of this final progression might be described as taking the merging of the outside force with the inside self to its ultimate conclusion. No words of advice on this matter will help you accomplish it—just perseverance and dedication.

This seems quite simple—just three Names for a meditation practice using SMY? Not so fast. There are many pitfalls and side trips one often encounters while attempting to navigate the MALIK to MATÎN to MAJÎD hierarchy. You can lose your equilibrium on any of the three emotion dimensions. You might grow tired or antsy and generate an /h/ or /r/ sensation that interrupts any attempt to maintain a proper MALIK countenance. Your pleasure level could fluctuate and a /mu/ or /mâ/ or even a /b/ could appear. Mental control can easily slip away into a /s/ or /z/ stream of consciousness. And a confusing emotional state might arise that could require release through an ayin.

## Changes in Pleasure Perception

Two subtle and one stark change in the level of pleasant sensation may occur while practicing the MALIK and MATÎN breathing awareness. One common occurrence happens whenever the /ma/ slips gently into /mâ/. Technically this marks a change in the arousal dimension, but it comes in response to the pleasantness felt. This happens whenever the process of following your breathing becomes too routine and you enter into a relaxed state that will not allow a proper continuation. Once you become aware of the relaxation, you can adjust via either MÂLIK-UL-MULK, for simple physical relaxation, or MÂNI', for a relaxed /â/ due to a mental concept or idea. MÂLIK resolves the relaxation while the remainder of the Name adjusts your disappointment (/mu/) for getting off track. With MÂNI' the /ni'/ brings the internal awareness that led to mental relaxation under control and releases the emotional reaction to the change. With the successful application of either of these remedies a continuation with MALIK should be within grasp, although the return to MALIK will not occur without difficulty for a beginner.

A second subtle change that may occur during monitoring MALIK or MATÎN occurs whenever the inhalation fails to engender a pleasant /ma/, but instead leaves you falling short of that goal and falling into a muted /mu/. The appearance of the /u/ can happen due to a variety of reasons, but one that seems common is impatience. As you watch the MALIK or MATÎN breathing there may come a subtle tiring of the game—perhaps brought on from frustration of not reaching "nirvana" or maybe it happens just from boredom or tiredness. Whenever you fall short of the goal of pursuing MALIK or MATÎN in this fashion you have several quick remedial options. You can add some mental control with MUHAYMIN, or bring in physical energy with MUḤYÎ, or flush away a negative thought with MUTA'ÂLÎ in order to get back on your MALIK track. Other options would include MU'ÎD to counter an emotional reaction to /mu/, and perhaps the simplest approach, MU'MIN to push aside the interference from /mu/. Refer to the chapter on these Names for further details on their appropriate usage.

One robust pleasure alteration to a /ma/ remains—the holding on to the good feeling that starts out as /ma/ but morphs into a /b/. If you experience this clasping on to the pleasure of the moment during meditation you can engage in a time of devotional practice. See the following section on devotional practices for hints on how to proceed in this manner. If you would rather stick to traditional meditation, then you can use either BASÎR or BADÎ' to let the /b/ feeling pass. The former of these two works to bring you back to the present if you feel your attention wavering. The latter one will provide a relief valve if your emotions have swelled and need a release.

## Changes in Mental Control

Whenever you begin a meditation practice with SMY the ever present mental chatter will likely come along to disrupt your attempts to quiet the mind. Most of what you need to understand about using SMY for addressing these issues of stream of consciousness was presented in the chapter on Names beginning with /s/ and /z/. This section adds information on how to incorporate the single Names into a practice to develop a seamless sequence of Names that keeps you on track to a successful experience.

If you use SALÂM to combat thoughts engaged in trying to figure something out or solve a problem (identified as Wrong Thinking in a previous chapter), the final /m/ in the Name can lead you to MALIK. Before attempting to engage with MALIK make sure that SALÂM has subdued the chatter. After SALÂM has smoothed the agitation brought on through worrying, it proves easy to move back to MALIK. However, if you need to use SABÛR or ZÂHIR to dissipate daydreams and imaginative thought, the goal state of /r/ makes such a transition to MALIK more difficult. Once SABÛR or ZÂHIR has rooted out mental meanderings and you have become suitably situated in the present with a somewhat aroused /r/, it may take an application of RAQÎB to enable a return of MALIK. This works because the final /b/ of RAQÎB should easily drop into the opening /m/ of MALIK. For both SAMAD and SAMÎʻ the transition to MALIK can take place without an intermediate Name. With SAMAD the final mental control should allow an /m/ to appear on a subsequent inhalation. The cathartic release at the end of SAMÎʻ puts you in a clear state which should prove conducive to an /m/ also.

The transitions mentioned in the preceding paragraph work on a theoretical level and for a person experienced with SMY they can be readily realized. However, a beginner should expect to have to work on the various processes before becoming adept at them. Just remember that SALÂM can quell the mind when looking for answers on how to proceed, and the use of MALIK needs no justification whatsoever—just a quieted mind.

## Changes in Physical Comfort

The act of sitting for a prolonged period pushes the limits of many folks' physical capacity. It is only a matter of time before you feel tired or get fidgety. If you tire then a Name beginning with /ḥ/ could provide a benefit with the best candidate being ḤAYY. Getting from ḤAYY back to MALIK requires only knowing when you feel energized to return. Sometimes it only takes one slow deep breath of ḤAYY before you can slip back to MALIK. Other times require a sequence of the energy infusing process. Additional Names with an initial /ḥ/ may also prove useful. See the chapter on these Names for more on them.

From the perspective of the *Yoga Sutras* physical interruptions to meditation stem from incorrect posture. When your posture fails to be "steady and comfortable," as prescribed by Patanjali, you will likely experience attacks from the pairs of opposites. Whenever you cannot stay steady and have a restless urge to shift or adjust posture that often comes after sitting for long stretches, a Name beginning with /r/ can resolve this bothersome contradictory impulse to both relax and move. The trio RAHMÂN, RAHÎM, and RA'ÛF all have a place in reviving sagging energy reserves that manifest as a desire to move and adjust posture. When you give in to the urge to adjust your posture, feel the energy, the /r/, of the movement. Realize that you need the energy only temporarily and will drain it away with either an /h/ or a /'/. Use RAHMÂN when you feel that you can regain control and a pleasant equanimity through the /h/ that purges the restlessness. Turn to RAHÎM whenever you don't feel you have enough control to reach a satisfying, relaxed state, but need to submit to an outside force, or perhaps just feel that you lack control to regain a pleasant state. Finally, resort to RA'ÛF when the physical issue nags you in a manner in which you simply need to move past the arousal since pleasantness seems unlikely to work based on your experience, for example an issue due to an ongoing strain or ache. The chapter on Names beginning with /r/ provides more on the subtle difference in the usage of these three Names. For each of them the transition back to MALIK requires no intermediate Name, as the final sound of each lends itself to easily moving into the pleasant /m/ provided the annoying arousing interference has subsided.

If your posture feels uncomfortable and an attempt to inhale the /ma/ of MALIK results in a feeling of /mu/, you've encountered the pleasant/unpleasant pair—a more subtle affront than the /ra/ opposites. You can rid yourself of the discomfort through one of the Names beginning with /mu/. MUHAYMIN, MUHYÎ, MU'ÎD, and MUTA'ÂLÎ provide different approaches to regaining control in these circumstances. MUHAYMIN and MUHYÎ provide a physically oriented response to the discomfort. MUTA'ÂLÎ uses a mental strategy of ignoring the distress. Turn to MU'ÎD whenever the issue builds an emotional swelling that seeks release. Learning which one works in a particular situation takes time and experience. The key in getting any one of these to work cannot happen through stubborn persistence, but only through letting things flow in an organic and holistic fashion. A review of how these Names work can be found in previous chapters. Self-study—a key observance required by Patanjali—will be the key to success in this and indeed all efforts to learn and apply SMY.

You may also find other Names than those listed in the previous paragraphs beginning with /r/ and /mu/ to have value in addressing bodily issues encountered during meditation. Names beginning with /q/ also belong in the discussion of physical comfort. To sit for a long time you reluctantly give up physical control—the essence of the /q/. Some of the Names discussed previously could provide benefits in this regard. Don't hesitate to explore the nature and possible value to yourself of each of the Names beyond what you read from this or any source.

## Emotional Catharsis and Mediation

At times emotions arise during meditation that are difficult to assess or categorize. Instead they may just bubble up generating a feeling of almost bursting. These instances can take advantage of a Name beginning with the cathartic /'/. The most appropriate candidates for such emotional times encountered during mediation include 'ALÎ, 'ALÎM, and 'ADL as discussed in a previous chapter. For each of these three the transition back to MALIK should flow easily—just make sure that you have let the emotions settle sufficiently before returning.

The above discussion concerning various potential intrusions on a practice of MALIK or MATÎN cover most common situations one might encounter. They don't exhaust all possibilities, but should prove more than sufficient for beginning an SMY program on meditation.

## *Using SMY as a Devotional Platform*

Our existence in this world offers a vast array of often wondrous, sometimes frightening circumstances. The difference between what thrills us and what confounds us can be simply a matter of perspective. Many times we have to decide whether our cup is half empty or half full. The optimist will choose the half-full option. If you feel blessed with good fortune, it can generate a strong positive emotion to savor—a /bâ/ moment. For some people this feeling arises within when they sit quietly and contemplate the mystery of consciousness and its place in the universe. If this holds true for you, then you can enhance such affirmative moments with devotional SMY.

Four Names provide a means for taking advantage of a devotional proclivity and lead the practitioner to a glorious feeling—the same one attained through MAJÎD—of being connected to Divine Consciousness or a universal panpsychic force. Sufis speak of the ninety-nine names of Allah as "the healing Names of the one love.[49]" For Sufis devotion to God or Allah always equates to love. The single sound most attuned to love is /b/—that feeling of holding on to an exquisite goodness. The addition of /â/ indicates the relaxing of effort and thus giving in to this feeling, the surrender. BÂSIT, BÂQÎ, BÂ'ITH, BÂRI' provide means to achieve this goal.

The simplest of these four, and thus the entry point to SMY devotion, is BÂSIT. Practice of this Name will allow you to focus on a strong emotional connection to your object of devotion and let any stream of consciousness fade into the background. As your practice continues one of several scenarios typically develops. You may feel something akin to a physical surge which generates a spontaneous urge to lift up your palms. If this occurs bring the Name BÂQÎ into focus, and allow the hands to change positions on their own—a /q/ movement that enhances the experience into what may be characterized as something divine. BÂQÎ also comes into play even if the physical reaction to /bâ/ amounts to a sense of release of control, a submission, but without any movement.

If the /bâ/ feeling associated with BÂSIT or BÂQÎ begins to fade you can respond in one of two ways to maintain your devotional fervor. First, if the faltering /bâ/ creates a bit of swirling emotion or emotional confusion you can release this buildup with BÂ'ITH. Alternatively, if you counter the weakening passion with desire to inject energy to sustain the process, you should switch to BÂRI'. This will push the energy away and allow a reverent continuation of your devotion.

As you practice one of these Names it may prove helpful to monitor the breath. As you inhale feel that pleasantness associated with your feelings of devotion and relax into that feeling. This intake of air corresponds to the /bâ/ portion of the Name. At this point you need not have any inclination or plan as to which Name will proceed. That choice should occur in an organic fashion as you stay mindful of your emotional parameters. If you notice an involuntary physical urge to express your feelings perhaps via hand movement, then make the motion in an austere way as you exhale—the /qî/ finish to BÂQÎ. If you detect an emotional buildup, perhaps due to the apprehension of losing the /bâ/ feeling, feel the release of this through an ayin as you breathe out and let this engender some confidence—the /'ith/ of BÂ'ITH. If nothing physical or emotional pervades your awareness, exhale away any stream of consciousness using /sit/—the completion of BÂSIT. Whenever you detect a physical push aimed at continuing your mood, release the energy with the /ri'/ in BÂRI'.

Don't expect to get to a blissful state every time you sit down to a devotional session. On first embarking on such a path, you might wonder how much time it will take. Nobody can say whether you need to engage in these practices ten minutes a day or two hours a day, or that it will take a month or years. The *Yoga Sutras* say that samadhi is closest to those who desire it the most. Although ardent desire can work as an assent, one needs to realize when that desire has crossed a boundary from beneficial to detrimental. The point where pushing too hard will most likely manifest occurs during practice of BÂQÎ. The spontaneous lifting of the hands can feel intoxicating, and the desire to maintain that feeling can be overwhelming. This may result in your continuation past the true feeling represented by BÂQÎ. The signal that indicates this has transpired consists of a switch from a feeling that an outside force has control over the position of the hands to the use of personal force to keep them in place. In other words a change from a /q/ to an /r/. At this point one should cease using BÂQÎ and switch to BÂRI'. The /r/ essentially acknowledges the return of control, while the hamza moves you past the /r/, and thus engenders the release of physical arousal. At this point sustaining BÂRI' or a resumption of BÂQÎ, BÂSIT, or BÂʿITH can ensue, as long as you can maintain a true /bâ/ feeling. Otherwise you should terminate your session.

## *Tackling Emotional Issues with SMY*

Usage of the Names of Allah based on the guidelines of SMY can generate benefits outside of a traditional meditation setting. One such rewarding practice involves devoting some time each day to reflect on various events of the day and noting the emotional lows that occurred with the goal of seeing where a different approach—one using SMY— might have led to a better outcome. Placing this set-aside time at the end of a day seems most beneficial, although for some a different schedule might work best. Self-reflection of this nature requires at least these two things: honest evaluation and the ability to discern the underlying emotional valences and emotion sequences that took place. If you can honestly and correctly evaluate the rough spots of the day in this fashion you will be able to determine which Name will prove beneficial in a future similar situation.

Applying the Names of Allah in this manner provides useful guidance for daily living. The *Yoga Sutras* also offer principles for how to live in the list of five self-restraints and five observances. No Name works as a remedy to a prohibited act, although we can point to instances where Names might prove useful in turning us away from violating one of these yamas. For example, MUNTAQIM can help you avoid a violent response to a perceived affront and BÂṬIN could assist in avoiding sexual promiscuity. We can also see where some Names lend themselves toward fulfilling a niyama. QUDDÛS seems well suited for engendering self-study. More than one Name can facilitate contentment, including MUQADDIM, QAYYÛM, and others.

The SMY rules do not lend themselves to the application of the Names to the lists of restraints and observances like it does with the modifications of the mind. The five mental variations all exist as stream of consciousness, and as such, can be addressed with Names beginning with the phoneme corresponding to this quality. If you have a problem with conforming to a yama or niyama, such as contentment or possessiveness, the issue may appear in more than one situation.

With SMY you always need to look at the emotional and psychological qualities of the moment and not specific physical circumstances or goals. However, it does seem clear that many of the Names can help you achieve contentment or self-study or help you refrain from violence or work toward many of the other ten goals, but don't try to mold SMY to a particular objective other than efforts toward emotional equanimity and mindful awareness.

Certainly the list of yoga's "ten commandments" has value by providing broad stokes that paint a picture of upright and moral living so that you know what actions to avoid and what behaviors in which to engage. But as we go through daily life we don't always live up to these standards. So it behooves us to ponder events that took us to an undesirable psychological state or perhaps led us to stray from the path we know to be correct. Establishing the initial emotion or emotional sequence that triggered such episodes will be important for selecting the correct Name to work on the issue. This might seem like an abstract, vague instruction. Fortunately, the proper initial sound can be achieved by looking at a list of scenarios that avoids talking about emotion dimension, but instead uses common terms to establish the mood and what exercises to pursue. Here is a representative, although not exhaustive, list of situations often faced and the initial sound(s) of Names that apply to them:

1. A failure to reach a goal indicates a /mu/ mood.

2. A high degree of agitation signals an /r/ would be the starting point.

3. Flagging energy or waning attention means a /h/ or /h̠/ held sway.

4. An urgent feeling for physical control points to a /gh/ mood prevailing.

5. A situation in which you reluctantly did not have control signifies a /q/ feeling.

6. Emptiness, numbness, or sadness requires a Name starting with /w/.

7. Emotions feeling like they could burst or like a lump in the throat calls for a Name beginning with an /'/

8. Illicit attraction to pleasure has a /b/ at work.

Of course many incidents could involve more than one of the above situations. At times you may feel tired and sad and also regret for not achieving an objective. You must decide which of these qualities stands out as the most salient. Ultimately there is no one correct answer. The important thing is to pick a reasonable approach, apply effort, and note the results. If the same type of scenario keeps reappearing and your first choice doesn't seem to have yielded significant results then reevaluate and begin again.

Once you have established the specific emotion to work with you can begin to sift through all the Names that begin with that specific sound, or the sound used to clear that mood, as in the case of /w/ and / '/. In all likelihood someone new to SMY will need to refer to the text or notes to bring an inventory of appropriate Names to mind. It could take quite a while before you can recall every Name that starts with a given sound. As each Name has a specific usage you need to not only be able to come up with a list of candidate Names based on initial sound, but be able to select the one Name that best fits the situation. A review of the chapter on those Names may be necessary for a beginner but eventually you should be able to recall specifics of each Name through merely seeing the list or by just thinking the list. At some point you will develop the ability to know the correct Name to use by just reviewing your past memories, but until then you can revisit the previous chapters, or your notes to arrive at a Name. I recommend devoting a notebook to keep your responses and usage of the various Names as you contemplate them. SMY should be above everything a personal practice. Use what you have found in this tome as a starting point but everyone has their own personal relationship with the Names. It will help you solidify yours if you take notes.

Once you have chosen a Name, make an effort to fit the emotional valences indicated by the Name into the situation that you are reviewing. For example, if the problem of lack of energy caused you to not reach a goal then practice MUḤYÎ. That is, recall the feeling of not reaching the goal and then purge it with a strong exhale (a /h̲/) then inhale physical energy (/y/) and let a feeling of outside control take over. Practice this a few times until it feels solid. Then when faced with the same type of situation in the future you can perhaps recall the process as you attempt to overcome the problem. By reflecting with SMY on troubling issues you will develop psychological habits that will enable you to eventually control or avoid similar concerns whenever they arise in the future.

## Using SMY to Enhance General Mindfulness and Express Gratitude

While you may use SMY in a contemplative setting to address potential and very real psychological difficulties, you can also utilize your time of reflection to apply SMY to positive experiences in order to express appreciation and promote mental clarity and mindfulness. Many religions tout the concept of gratitude as part of daily prayers alongside the supplications for things desired. SMY models this two-fold approach to times of reflection, which are essentially a form of prayer. The difference between SMY and traditional prayer lies in the focus of the practice. With traditional prayer one aims their pleas to a higher power, while with SMY the purpose centers on personal emotional equanimity. Some SMY Names refer to external control, which can be interpreted as a higher power, but SMY also recognizes the ability to feel an outside force as part of our intrinsic psychological makeup.

We often take the enjoyable things of everyday living for granted—the comfortable home, the ample nutritious food, our steady nurturing relationships and pleasurable interactions. By taking time to reflect on these it can enhance your daily experiences. If you make it a habit of remembering these positive occurrences and associate them with an SMY Name that engenders mental clarity, then instead of your mind trailing off in some stream of consciousness about an unrelated activity or incident the next time you prepare food or tidy up the premises, you may be able to recall an appropriate SMY Name. Doing so while actively engaging in the activity allows you to become more mindful of your existence and in tune with your existence as an awake and aware being in a wondrous world.

The process for selecting an SMY Name for joyous times parallels that used for dealing with psychological problems. First, identify the most salient emotion. For upbeat happenings the corresponding sound will likely be: /ma/ for mellow times of enjoyment; /mâ/ for very mellow goings on; /b/ for robust pleasure; /w/ for feelings of awe; /k/ when involving willful giving; /j/ whenever mental and physical delights combine; /sh/ whenever something in your environment triggers mental recognition; /'/ when bursting with a powerful unspecified surge of emotion. Once you have the initial sound, review the possible Names through the text or notes, unless or until you have the Names committed to memory. Pick what you see as the best Name for the setting, then work through the individual feelings associated with the sounds in the Name. Tie each phoneme to a real emotional response to the particulars of the occasion. For example, while recalling an instance of joyous giving using KARÎM first, feel the relinquishing of your volition to the cause (/k/). Then just concentrate on the energy you expended for another entity, one outside yourself (/rî/). Finally, feel how this resulted in a personal reward of pleasantness (/m/). If you practice this during reflective times then you will eventually be able to apply the process as it unfolds in a real situation.

# CONCLUSION

Sufis consider "God to be the only object of contemplation" and say that "when the Truth seizes upon the object of your pointing and annihilates it, then there is no longer an indicating person nor an object indicated."[50] This flavor of philosophy parallels the objective of the *Yoga Sutras*—union with divine consciousness. Furthermore Sufis and Patanjali approach this goal in a similar fashion. Sufis wish to control the *nafs*, psyche or mental energy—an excellent translation of the goal stated in Patanjali's second sutra.

Although we note these parallels between Patanjali's work and Sufi philosophy, we cannot confirm direct influence of the *Yoga Sutras* on Sufi practices, or vice versa.[51] Peter Ouspensky writes in his book *In Search of the Miraculous* that his one-time mentor, the Russian philosopher G. I. Gurdjieff, claimed that esoteric schools such as Sufism and classical yoga had a common single origin in the past, and at some point this unified school split. One faction settled in India and focused on philosophy from which the *Yoga Sutras* emerged. Another sect migrated to the Middle East where this division apparently developed practices that we now associate with the Sufis.[52] But this assertion came without any verifiable source. Certainly the *Yoga Sutras* present a coherent detailed philosophy but lack concrete corresponding practices, while the Sufis, on whole, have myriad practices but no succinct philosophy that puts the practices into a framework. Andrey Safronov, a current Russian philosopher, suggests that the similarity in psychological techniques between the *Yoga Sutras* and Sufism "should be explained either by some earlier borrowings or—and this is more probable—by the fact they both had the same object of research—the human psyche."[53] This second explanation seems more plausible when just considering the overall approach of the two schools, which is what Safronov did. However, the matching of explicit Sufi practices to individual impedances to the goal of yoga specified by Patanjali, as I have shown in this work, gives some credence to the first idea. However, it seems unlikely that we will ever find conclusive proof that the Names of Allah and the *Yoga Sutras* share a common heritage even if such a link at one time existed.

Whether you find a teacher to help you understand the use of SMY or you simply read about SMY and apply the principles on your own, what you derive from engaging with the exercises that comprise SMY depends on how much personal effort you expend. To gain benefits from SMY requires work. It requires studying the materials that comprise SMY, specifically: the relationships between sounds and emotions; how physiology and psychology intertwine in a very real sense; and the basic units of SMY—the Names of Allah. More importantly SMY necessitates self-study. You need to learn how to recognize your moods and feelings, how to develop mindfulness of your emotional and mental landscape, and how to mindfully modulate your moods using knowledge of the emotional values of sounds. Most of all SMY requires patience. You need to realize that it takes time before SMY can begin to generate positive results. You need to keep at it to reap benefits.

Mentally learning about SMY will not prove beneficial if you do not grasp the concepts in a non-verbal, emotionally integrated manner. In order to fully recognize moods and feelings you must experience them in an intuitive fashion. If you just think about the emotional sequences you will not benefit from the practices. SMY is not an intellectual pursuit. You will not become proficient in SMY simply by memorizing the emotional valence labels applied to each sound and recalling the order in which a particular practice uses these. It requires a holistic process of recognition and experience.

Some people will read about the practices or hear something from another source about them and criticize SMY as cluttering the mind with cognitive processes that defeat the purpose of meditation. A summary of such assessment might sound like: "We meditate to clear the mind, but doesn't SMY just do the opposite?" In response to this challenge I say consider that in the standard approach to meditation the mental distractions experienced by beginners have no purpose, and thus the standard advice to ignore them makes sense. But SMY does not clog the mind with useless information. The ideas and constructs of SMY comprise tools that can help you experience more satisfying meditation. Yes, at first your mind may feel overburdened with the concepts from SMY, but you can minimize this problem by focusing only on a small amount of new material as you learn, and not adding new practices until you have solidified the ones with which you have already engaged and understood fully on an emotional level. Psychologists have pointed out that achieving proficiency in a skill comes in three stages. For the first stage you have to verbally repeat or even read the instructions of each step as you do it. As you progress to the second stage you don't have to repeat or read each step, but still have to recall the steps perhaps in an abbreviated manner as you apply them. Finally, when you achieve mastery you can perform the skill without thinking about the steps involved and simply do them. This same process holds for learning SMY. If you persist you will find that it does not take long before you will feel comfortable with an SMY pattern without having to consider the cognitive aspects of the practice. What seemed at first like mental chatter turns into simple awareness of a process as it unfolds. In the end using SMY does not defeat the purpose of meditation, but instead augments the chances of realizing your meditation objective. Whenever an intrusion of any kind appears you simply recognize it for what it is and adjust your emotional awareness through the proper SMY subtle response to maintain equanimity.

Although SMY can enhance meditation or devotional practices, applying SMY principles to the Names of Allah has perhaps an even greater potential for providing benefits by helping us face daily situations in a manner that promotes emotional equanimity and spiritual growth. The emotion formulas that the Names represent comprise a viable philosophy, a very real and accessible code of how to live, that uses the natural universal language of human emotions, instead of the Greek of Plato and Aristotle or the French of Descartes or the English of Hume and Locke. The use of the Names under SMY guidelines can help you make better choices for how you take care of your mental health, how you interact with other persons and your environment, and how you understand your place in the world. I argue that it accomplishes this in a more efficient and effective manner than being written in a human language in which philosophers pontificate.

Sufis consider the Ninety-nine Names of Allah attributes of the divine and through remembrance practices with the Names everyone has the potential of sensing or merging with divine presence. A more liberal interpretation regards the exercises utilizing the Names a vehicle for tuning into universal consciousness. Certainly the Names provide ample opportunity to experience the powerful feeling of outside control, Allah, universal consciousness, or however you wish to identify such force, but SMY really takes you further than that. SMY allows you to stay in the moment and keep you from getting hung up on daily distractions whether they be simple trials or full-blown ordeals. Yes, you can feel divine/universal presence, but you can also feel your own internal control and your other emotional qualities and potentials thus allowing you to achieve emotional balance and equanimity. In order to learn how to execute the practices described in this work you will necessarily have to learn about yourself, and how your emotions lie at the core of your being. Without gaining this ability to exercise emotional control you are at the whims of a very fickle world. Only by making an effort can you determine whether SMY can provide you with the means to attain this self-realization. I hope that SMY allows you to enjoy a more mindful and meaningful life.

# ACKNOWLEDGMENTS

The inspiration that initiated the journey that led to this work first came at Kripalu ashram. A weekend of yoga and chanting captivated me. I was hooked. To the initiates and leaders of that wonderful facility I can't thank you enough for providing a welcoming venue that opens horizons and facilitates spiritual growth to so many.

I owe sincere thanks for the acquisition of my research skills to my Ph.D. advisor at Tufts University, Dr. Philip Holcomb. In the many research projects that I have conducted along the path leading to my discoveries I have had the assistance of too many to name, including fellow graduate students and students in research classes that I have taught.

Writing always needs a second, or third set of eyes to keep the narrative within the lines of reason. In this regard I am grateful for feedback from the review of this manuscript to Dr. Margaret Mangus, a linguist whose specialty is sound symbolism—the study of the meanings of individual sounds. Additionally, I need to thank my editor Demi Stevens for her diligence in pouring over the pages of this tome. Her careful guidance has made this work much more readable.

Finally, I need to thank my wife. For more than five decades she has been my mate as we have navigated this wondrous thing called life. She has kept me grounded throughout that time and I can't imagine life without her.

# BIBLIOGRAPHY

Al-Jamal, Muhammad Sa'id. (2001). *The Meaning of the Names of Our Lord.* Petaluma, CA: Sidi Muhammad Press.

Al-Jamal, Muhammad Sa'id. (1994). *Music of the Soul.* Petaluma, CA: Sidi Muhammad Press.

Al-Rawi, Rosina-Fawzia. (2015). *Divine Names: The 99 Healing Names of the One Love.* Northhampton, MA: Olive Branch Press.

Armstrong, Karen. (2011). *Twelve Steps to a Compassionate Life.* New York, NY: Random House.

Dass, Ram. (1971). *Be Here Now.* San Cristobal, NM: Lama Foundation.

Douglas-Klotz, Neil. (2005). *The Sufi Book of Life: 99 Pathways of the Heart for the Modern Dervish.* New York, NY: Penguin Group.

Chodron, P. (2013). *How to Meditate.* Boulder, CO: Sounds True.

Ernst, Carl W. (1996). "Sufism and Yoga According to Muhammad Ghawth," *Sufi, 29*(1):9–13.

Friedlander, Shems. (1978). *Ninety-nine Names of Allah.* New York, NY: Harper & Row.

Hanson, R., & Mendius, R. (2009). *Buddha's Brain.* Oakland, CA: New Harbor Publications.

Harris, S. (2014). *Waking Up.* New York, NY: Simon & Schuster.

Kabat-Zinn, J. (1994). *Wherever You Go There You Are.* New York, NY: Hyperion.

Kabat-Zinn, J. (2012). *Mindfulness for Beginners.* Boulder, CO: Sounds True.

Khan, Vilayat Inayat. (1974). *Toward the One.* San Francisco, CA: Harper & Row.

Jakobson, Roman, & Waugh, Linda. (1990). *On Language.* Cambridge, MA: Harvard University Press.

Mangus, Margaret. (1999). *Gods of the Word.* Kirksville, MO: Thomas Jefferson University Press.

Mangus, Margaret. (2013). "A History of Sound Symbolism," in *The Oxford Handbook of the History of Linguistics*, Keith Allen, ed. Oxford, UK: Oxford University Press.

Meyer, Wali Ali; Hyde, Bilal; Muqaddam, Faisal; & Kahn, Shabda. (2011). *Physicians of the Heart: A Sufi view of the Ninety-nine Names of Allah.* San Francisco, CA: Sufi Ruhaniat International.

Nurbakhsh, Java. (1992). *Psychology of Sufism (Del wa Nafs).* London, UK: Khaniqahi-Nimatullahi Publications.

Ouspensky, Peter. (1949). *In Search of the Miraculous.* New York, NY: Harcourt Brace Jovanovich.

Pei, Mario. (1949). *The Story of Language.* Philadelphia, PA: J.B. Lippincott.

Shah, Idries. (1970). *The Sufis.* Garden City, NY: Doubleday and Co.

Stade, Robert. (1970). *Ninety-nine Names of God.* Ibadan, Nigeria: Oluseyi Press Ltd.

Suchy, Yana. (2011). *Clinical Neuropsychology of Emotion.* Guilford Press, ebook.

Taimni, I K. (1961). *The Science of Yoga.* Madras, India: The Theosophical Publishing House.

# END NOTES

---

Mindfulness Practices

1   Ram Dass. (1971). *Be Here Now.* San Cristobal, NM: Lama Foundation.

2   Vilayat Inayat Khan, quoted from sufiway.org/about-us/the-origins-of-sufism, as found February 20, 2016.

3   See *The Revival of Religious Sciences, by* Al-Ghazali, as discussed online at www.ghazali.org/site/ihya.htm for example, as found on February 20, 2016.

4   For example, see https://ia801603.us.archive.org/21/items/Yogaorder.org/YogaAndSufism.htm as found on Feb 11, 2021.

5   However, over the past decade or so the number of Sufi in western countries has continued to grow.

6   Idries Shah. (1964). *The Sufis.* Garden City, NY: Doubleday and Co. found in the Introduction by Robert Graves.

7   Inayat Khan. (1974). *Toward the One.* San Francisco, CA: Harper & Row.

8   Vilayat Inayat Khan quoted from a lecture given in 1981 at Omega Institute in Bennington, VT.

9   Karen Armstrong. (2011). *Twelve Steps to a Compassionate Life.* New York, NY: Random House.

10  Research on the relationship between sounds and meanings will be discussed in a later chapter.

11  Hanson, R, & Mendius, R. (2009). *Buddha's Brain.* Oakland, CA: New Harbor Publications.

12  Harris, S. (2014). *Waking Up.* New York, NY: Simon & Schuster.

13  For example: Kabat-Zinn, J. (1994). *Wherever You Go There You Are.* New York, NY: Hyperion; and Kabat-Zinn, J. (2012). *Mindfulness for Beginners.* Boulder, CO: Sounds True.

14  For example: Kabat-Zinn, J. (1994) *Wherever You Go There You Are.* New York, NY: Hyperion, p18.

[15] See Hanson, R, & Mendius, R. (2009). *Buddha's Brain.* Oakland, CA: New Harbor Publications, for example.

[16] See *The Science of Yoga,* (1961), by I K Taimni, Madras, India: Theosophical Publishing House.

[17] See *Psychology of Sufism (Del wa Nafs),* (1992), by Dr, Java Nurbakhsh, London, UK: Khaniqahi-Nimatullahi Publications

[18] Information concerning Al-Biruni's translation of the *Yoga Sutras* comes from http://yoga-sutra-comment-eng.blogspot.com/2014/02/the-arabic-translation-of-patanjalis.html found February 29, 2016. Shlomo Pines and Tuvia Gelblum took approximately two decades to translate the work from Arabic into English. They published the translation a chapter at a time in the *Bulletin of the School of Oriental and African Studies*, University of London; Vols. 29.2, 40.3, 46.2, & 52.2, 1966, 1977, 1983, 1989.

[19] For a comprehensive look at the physiology of emotions see Yana Suchy's 2011 book *Clinical Neuropsychology of Emotion*, Guilford Press, ebook.

[20] Peter Lang, a professor at the University of Florida, first proposed the idea of using three dimensions of emotions in the 1980s. Later he dropped the dimension for control because he saw a high correlation between emotional pleasure and the emotion feeling of being in control and a correlation between emotional unpleasantness and not being in control. I feel discarding the dimension of control is a mistake. His work did not consider situations that would engender pleasant external control, such as a feeling that you are being guided by a higher power.

[21] Mangus, Margaret. (2013). "A History of Sound Symbolism," in *The Oxford Handbook of the History of Linguistics*, Keith Allen, ed. Oxford, UK: Oxford University Press.

[22] Many linguists have written about the three vowels in all languages. See *The Story of Language*, by Mario Pei, Lippincott, Philadelphia, PA, 1965, for an example. Also, note that the IPA lists two different /â/ sounds, one created with slightly rounded lips. In most languages these sounds are not perceived to be different. A speaker who uses one might consider someone who speaks the other to have an accent, but still recognize it as representing the same sound.

[23] I will use /â/ /û/ and /î/ to represent the three primary vowels (found in father, moon, and see) throughout the book instead of the representations used by the international phonetic alphabet (IPA). I believe that the general reader would find the IPA confusing.

[24] I conducted the studies referred to in labs where I held teaching and research positions.

25  Robert Zajonc published this research.

26  I conducted this study at Dickinson College where I held a teaching position.

27  Vilayat Inayat Khan, *Toward the One,* p. 235.

28  The /r/ consonant used in this work does not use the tongue. The trilled /r/ which involves vibrating the tongue occurs in some languages, but not in English.

29  I conducted this study at Dickinson College where I held a teaching position.

30  Ker Than published a study in the July 2006 issue of *Evolution and Human Behavior* showing that lower pitch in men is perceived as more dominant.

31  See Roman Jakobson and Linda Waugh's book, *On Language,* Harvard University Press, Cambridge, MA, 1995, for example.

32  This result is from an unpublished study I did at Tufts University as a graduate student.

33  The consonants /ch/ and /j/ have both stop and fricative attributes. For this work I only consider the stop characteristic, since impact of this feature overpowers the fricative property.

34  In some languages there is a third sub-class based on the voicing distinction called pre-voiced. Since English and most other Indo-European languages have no such sounds, perceiving them as speech sounds introduces a difficult to near-impossible task for most native English speakers. Research has shown that the brain apparently loses most of its ability to recognize novel speech sounds after the first two years of life. Although these sounds may provide those who use them a valuable means of expression of emotion and thus theoretically could be used in SMY, this current version of SMY makes no use of them. I have not studied the psychological significance of pre-voicing. Just for the record though, the technique used to express a pre-voiced stop consonant involves vibrating the vocal cords before any air is released. The sound originates in the throat before the mouth is open and the vibration actually stops before the air is released.

35  The list of ninety-nine names of Allah varies slightly depending on the source that you use. Some lists vary by one or two Names. Other lists have a wider variation. The list used in this work corresponds to the lists in three separate sources: *The Sufi Book of Life* by Douglas-Klotz, *Divine Names* by Al-Rawi, and *Ninety-nine Names of Allah* by Friedlander. Two of the ninety-nine names of Allah used do not consist of single words, but rather simple Arabic phrases. These are Dhûl-jalâl-wal-ikrâm and Mâlik-ul-mulk.

[36] The idea that a SMY word works by taking you from an initial emotional state (that corresponds to the emotional valence of the first sound of the word) to a target emotion (that corresponds to the final sound(s)) has not been, to my knowledge, tested in a scientific setting. I have provided considerable evidence for the relationships between phonemes (individual speech sounds) and emotional qualities, but I have not been able to take the next step and show in a controlled setting that you can modulate emotional sentiments through a sequence of sounds that in effect make up a word. I leave this task to a future investigator.

[37] Al-Rawi, Rosina-Fawzia. *Divine Names: The 99 Healing Names of the One Love,* p.17.

[38] Jon Kabat-Zinn. (2012). *Mindfulness for Beginners.* Boulder, CO: Sounds True, p. 38.

[39] Rick Hanson. (2009). *Buddha's Brain.* Oakland, CA: New Harbinger Publications, p. 187.

[40] Pema Chodron. (2013). *How to Meditate.* Boulder, CO: Sounds True, p. 73.

[41] ibid., p. 85.

[42] When I say "traditional" usage I'm painting with a broad stroke. Many, many books have been written about the Names. I will glean from the several that I have read and present impressions garnered from these. Understand that other sources may have different ideas about what is traditional.

[43] Having an open mind to beliefs does not mean you have an open mind to actions, if actions violate another person's freedoms.

[44] Shaykh Muhammad Sa'id al-Jamal ar-Rifa1`I as-Shadhuli. (1994). *Music of the Soul.* Petaluma, CA: Sidi Muhammad Press, p. 72.

[45] Sam Harris. *Waking Up.* New York, NY: Simon & Schuster, p. 127.

[46] Bob Dylan, winner of the Nobel prize for literature in 2017, wrote the song "In Every Grain of Sand."

[47] The practice of yoga often gets divided into several sub-types. "Hatha yoga" refers to practice of postures, or asanas to use the popular Sanskrit term. "Bhakti yoga" involves the practice of devotion to a deity. The yoga of knowledge, of understanding your true nature through study, gets dubbed "jnana yoga." Although "raja yoga" once meant something else it now most often gets connected to the study of the *Yoga Sutras.* This study also gets called "astanga yoga," "royal yoga" or "classical yoga." Finally, the term "karma yoga" describes yoga of action, of doing all things in a pure spiritual, selfless way.

[48] Douglas-Klotz, Neil. *The Sufi Book of Life: 99 Pathways of the Heart for the Modern Dervish,* p.68. The author uses *mudhil,* a common alternative spelling to *muzill.*

[49] "The 99 Healing Names of the One Love" is the subtitle of Al-Rawi's book, *Divine Names.*

[50] Safronov, Andrey, http://yoga-sutra-comment-eng.blogspot.com/2014/02/the-arabic-translation-of-patanjalis.html found December 3, 2020.

[51] But see Ernst, Carl W. Ernst's 1996 "Sufism and Yoga According to Muhammad Ghawth," *Sufi, 29*(1):9–13.

[52] Ouspensky, Peter. (1949). *In Search of the Miraculous.* New York, NY: Harcourt Brace Jovanovich, p. 15.

[53] Safronov, Andrey, http://yoga-sutra-comment-eng.blogspot.com/2014/02/the-arabic-translation-of-patanjalis.html found December 3, 2020.

Made in the USA
Middletown, DE
18 November 2021

52114298R00146